Etiquettes *of* Companionship

Imām ʻAbdulwahhāb ash-Shaʻrānī

Translated by

Muḥammad Ṭāhir Maḥmood Kiānī

Crowned & Renowned

بسم الله الرحمن الرحيم

Had it not been for the company of good people... I would have disliked to remain in this world.

- Imām ash-Shāfi'ī

Dedication

This translation is dedicated to the righteous
who are an amalgamation of spiritual tranquillity and activity
who preach love, cordiality, peace, fellowship and harmony
whose company is a source of knowledge and wisdom
- of divine blessings, favours, mercy and bliss -
and to those who aspire to be like them.
We ask Allāh ﷻ to make us like them.
Āmīn.

Etiquettes

of

Companionship

an English Translation of

رسالة الأنوار

في آداب الصحبة عند الأخيار

Risālat al-Anwār

fī Ādāb aṣ-Ṣuḥbah 'inda'l-Akhyār

The Epistle of Lights

on the Etiquettes of Companionship according to the Elite

Imām 'Abdulwahhāb ash-Sha'rānī

(898AH/1493CE – 973AH/1565CE)

Translated by

Muḥammad Ṭāhir Maḥmood Kiānī

COPYRIGHT

Title of book: Etiquettes of Companionship

Author of book: Imām ‘Abdulwahhāb ash-Sha‘rānī

Translator of book: Muḥammad Ṭāhir Maḥmood Kīānī

First published: April 2016

tmkiani@hotmail.com

Cover, design, typesetting and layout by: Crowned and Renowned Publications (Crenowned);

with support from S, Z, Q and M Kiani

ISBN: 1532751958

ISBN-13: 978-1532751950

بسم الله الرحمن الرحيم

In the Name of Allāh سبحانه وتعالى, the Divinely-Compassionate, the Ever-Merciful

Contents

About the Author

IMĀM 'ABDULWAHHĀB IBN AḤMAD ASH-SHA'RĀNĪ was born on 27th Ramaḍān 898AH/1493CE in his maternal grandparents' house in the village of Qalqashandah, near Cairo, and then, when he was 40 days old, he was brought to his parents' home in the village known as Sāqiyat Abū Sha'rah where his ancestors, who were the descendants of Muḥammad ibn al-Ḥanafiyyah ﷺ, the son of Leader of the Believers 'Alī ibn Abū Ṭālib ﷺ, had settled in the 6th century AH. He spent his youth in Sāqiyat Abū Sha'rah, to which we refer the ascriptions 'ash-Sha'rāwī' and 'ash-Sha'rānī'.

Imām ash-Sha'rāni's father, Shihābuddīn Aḥmad, died in the year 907AH/1501CE when the Imām was only 9 years of age, and so his elder brother, 'Abdulqādir (d.956AH/1549CE), took the young Imām into his care and arranged for his studies.

His Studies

In the year 911AH/1505CE, when he was 12, the Imām moved to Cairo, where he studied at al-Azhar and stayed at the Ghamrī Masjid for 17 years. He had already committed the Holy Qur'ān to memory by the age of 7 years, with help from his brother, but it is said that here he studied and memorised *al-Minhāj* of an-Nawawī (d.676AH/1277CE), the *Alifiyyah* of Ibn Mālik (d.672AH/1274CE), *at-Tawḍīḥ* of Ibn Hishām (d.761AH/1360CE), and many others.

The Imām studied all the sciences that were required of an Islāmic scholar, including all the Qur'ānic sciences, all the Ḥadīth sciences, jurisprudence, scholasticism (*kalām*), grammar, biographies, *taṣawwuf* (Islāmic spiritual behaviourism), etc. In jurisprudence, he studied books on all four legal schools, and in *taṣawwuf*, works of a whole galaxy of scholars, such as al-Ghazālī (d.505AH/1111CE), Ibn al-'Arabī (d.638AH/1240CE), al-Yāfi'ī (d.768AH/1366CE), as-Suhrawardī (587AH/1191CE), al-Qushayrī (d.465AH/1072CE), etc.

His Family

Imām ash-Sha'rānī's father had died when the Imām was of a tender age, and thereafter taken under the guardianship of his brother. The Imām was first married at the age of 30 years, to Zaynab, and thereafter 3 more times successively to Ḥalīmah, Fāṭimah – who bore him his only son, named 'Abdurraḥmān (d.1011AH/1602CE) – and Umm Ḥasan, who was a *sharīfah*, respectively.

His Ḥajj

Imām ash-Sha'rānī performed Ḥajj thrice in his lifetime – the first with his brother 'Abdulqādir in 947AH/1540CE, and thereafter in 953AH/1546CE and then again in 963AH/1555CE.

His Teachers

During his study years, Imām ash-Sha'rānī had frequented many scholars and teachers in all the relevant fields of study, but the most prominent among those who trained him in spirituality are 'Alī al-Marṣafī (d.930AH/1523CE), 'Alī al-Khawwāṣ (d.939AH/1532CE), Afḍaluddīn (d.942AH/1535CE), Nūruddīn ash-Shūnī (d.944AH/1537CE) – who is said to have introduced special gatherings for invoking salutations and blessings on the Prophet Muḥammad ﷺ, and Amīnuddīn ad-Dimyāṭī. He also studied under Imām Jalāluddīn as-Suyūṭī (911AH/1505CE) in his earlier age until he was 13, but as-Suyūṭī passed away before the Imām could gain further benefit from his knowledge and wisdom. His teachers also include Shamsuddīn ad-Dīrūṭī (d.921AH/1515CE), Shihābuddīn al-Qasṭalānī (d.923AH/1517CE) and Shaykh Zakariyyā' al-Anṣārī (d.926AH/1520CE), etc.

His Works

His total writings are said to be over 70, of which most are on *taṣawwuf*, but he focussed on almost all of the essential and popular sciences of the time, including jurisprudence, Qur'ānic sciences, creedal sciences, poetry and medicine. Some of his popular works include:

- *al-Mīzān al-Kubrā*
- *Minhāj al-Wuṣūl ilā 'Ilm al-Uṣūl*

- *al-Yawāqīt wa'l-Jawāhir fī 'Aqā'id al-Akābir*
- *Laṭā'if al-Minan*
- *al-Anwār al-Qudsiyyah fī Ma'rifat Qawā'id aṣ-Ṣūfiyyah*
- *al-Muqaddimat an-Naḥwiyyah fī 'Ilm al-'Arabiyyah*
- *al-Ajwibat al-Marḍiyyah 'an A'immat al-Fuqahā' wa'ṣ-Ṣūfiyyah*
- *Risālat al-Anwār fī Ādāb aṣ-Ṣuḥbah 'inda'l-Akhyār*
- *etc.*

His *Zāwiyah*

After leaving the Ghamrī Masjid, the Imām established himself at Madrasah Umm Khond where he sought spiritual accomplishment and where the people would visit him for studies and gatherings of *dhikr* of Allāh تعالى.

Later, the Imām moved to a much larger masjid that was built by Qāḍī Muḥiyyuddīn 'Abdulqādir al-Uzbekī and annexed with a large portion of land that he endowed on this masjid, which later became a religious school and upon which was built the *zāwiyah* (spiritual and academic retreat) for our Imām. The endowment was such that it provided economic independence to Imām ash-Sha'rānī and his descendants, as well as to those who resided at the seminary. Continuous *dhikr*, studying and prayers were organised at the *zāwiyah* and with food aplenty it was frequented by many visitors who were offered to take some of it away with them. Boasting over 200 residents and over 70 guests on a daily basis, the *zāwiyah* grew in popularity, as did that of the Imām. The number of his students and disciples grew very quickly and into their thousands, and the Imām provided for them all. He would even arrange to send groups of his students to Ḥajj and also for their marriage, at his own expense, as well as providing financial assistance to his contemporary scholars and jurists – all to the credit of the *zāwiyah*.

His Spiritual and Legal Affiliations

Imām ash-Sha'rānī followed the Shāfi'ī school of law and legal methodology and the Shādhilī spiritual path. However, he was open to opinions, thoughts and discussions, regardless of legal or spiritual attachment.

His Ascetism

Having led early life in poverty and endowed with riches later on, Imām ash-Sha'rānī had experienced both ends of the economic divide and most of the in-between. However, whether small his means of livelihood or plenty, he refused aid from the government or any of the elite. He would return anything the state officials would give him as gift or financial assistance. His level of ascetism and love for devotional worship was such that he would spend most of his time in study and prayer, and he would soak his clothes in cold water to stop himself from falling asleep.

His Death

Imām 'Abdulwahhāb ibn Aḥmad ash-Sha'rānī breathed his last on 12th Jumādā al-Ūlā 973AH/1565CE and was buried inside his *zāwiyah*.

His *zāwiyah* was succeeded by is son, 'Abdurraḥmān, who was unable to run it as successfully as his eminent late father had done.

This Book

Commonly known as *Ādāb aṣ-Ṣuḥbah* – Etiquettes of Companionship, the full title of this work is *Risālat al-Anwār fī Ādāb aṣ-Ṣuḥbah 'inda'l-Akhyār* – The Epistle of Lights on the Etiquettes of Companionship according to the Elite. It is one of Imām ash-Sha'rānī's most popular works and his finest examples of authorship, with eloquence and subtleties to assist in guiding the reader to the teachings of the Holy Qur'ān and the Noble Sunnah of the Messenger Muḥammad ﷺ in a manner that is a uniquely distinctive of the Ṣūfīs.

It is full of counsel and advice from some of the most prominent scholars and shaykhs (spiritual masters) of the 10th century AH and before, especially those with whom the Imām was more acquainted or had sought company with, which he compiled and authored out of dire necessity to fill the void where knowledge had come to miss the fruits of action. His prime focus were his contemporaries, but it goes without saying that it is still relevant today as it was many centuries ago – a universal and timeless masterpiece. It encourages practical discipline and training to individuals as well as to groups – the latter especially because the human is a social being who cannot live a proper life on his own.

Social cohesion; mutual tolerance; ethics; love; cordiality; brotherhood; morality; discipline; refraining from anything that may even remotely cause offence to others; abstaining from leaning towards the unnecessary; encouraging *dhikr* (remembering Allāh ﷻ), supplications and prayer, etc., are some of the counsels that this epistle encourages, all of which cannot truly be gained and nor practised without associating with others. It is thus a motivation to associate with other people, especially those who are spiritually accomplished and have reached the higher degrees of moral standing. It is often said, 'learn or teach' and this epistle teaches us to learn the codes and etiquettes of accompanying others – how we ought to sit, stand, walk, eat, drink and talk, etc. when in the company of various kinds of people. It also trains us to teach the higher moral values through deed and not merely by word.

The Holy Qur'ān conveys to us the instruction of Allāh ﷻ telling us to 'be with those who are truthful,'[1] as it is only they who deserve to be accompanied and from whom we must take our learning and training. It is these honest and morally upright people who can connect us to our Creator ﷻ and to His Beloved ﷺ, and from whom we may acquire the knowledge, wisdom, secrets and subtleties to help us lead a noble life so as to be successful in this mortal world and in the Hereafter. It is only they who can help us purify our inner selves and free us of our egos and of our mundane desires that have held us back from achieving much more than we truly can. Moreover, it is they who transmit to us the practical message of the Qur'ān and the Sunnah, with guidance from the Noble Prophetic Companions ﵃ and the Successors ﵏, and from the righteous who came after them, generation after generation, until we see those teachings manifested in the elite who have come to be known as 'the People of Verity' – they include our contemporary scholars, shaykhs and teachers.

This epistle may be used as a groundwork for those who seek the higher stations of disciplining the soul, strengthening the heart and freeing the mind. It is essential to study it with love and passion and and an eagerness to achieve what ought to be achieved in the degrees of the spiritual realm that follow. However influential it may be, its noble impact is more effective when studied under the guidance and according to the explanation of an accomplished trainer, teacher and shaykh.

This Translation

It gives us much joy that, by the grace of His Beloved Messenger Muḥammad ﷺ, Allāh ﷻ has allowed us to offer the very first English translation of this epistle to the world. We consider it an honour and a privilege, and we cannot possibly express in words the emotions of elation and spiritual bliss we experience. We fail to find the words by which we may express our humble gratitude and praise to Allāh ﷻ for giving us the opportunity that He ﷻ has bestowed upon us. *al-ḥamdu li'Llāh, thumma al-ḥamdu li'Llāh.*

[1] Holy Qur'ān, Sūrat at-Tawbah (9), Verse 119.

As for our work on this translation, the original Arabic text of this epistle does not appear with headings, and so, for ease and benefit to the reader, numbered headings have been added to all the distinct rights of people and the etiquettes of the veracious among them that are mentioned herein. Any essential and additional text has been placed in square brackets, especially where the natural flow of the English translation might otherwise have been compromised, or where the meaning was vague and the reader might have struggled to understand it. Prayers for the shaykhs and scholars have only been inserted (in round brackets) at the first mention of their name if they were not found in the original text, and every time if the prayers appear within the original text – though it is obvious that our prayers for them are incessant.

As with every translation, it is not always possible to convey the truest form of its original intended meaning; 'lost in translation' is very real. However, attempts have been made to translate and to transmit to the reader the best possible meaning according to the intention of the author. Any weakness, misunderstanding, mistranslation or any other mistake is our own and we would be glad if the reader makes us aware of it so that we may rectify it.

Gratitude

We are thankful to our family, teachers, trainers, shaykhs, imāms, scholars, students, friends, acquaintances and strangers alike, who make our life 'a life of companionship' for without the company of good people we would find ourselves lost and susceptible to the gloom of despair and unwanted solitude and loneliness. We offer our gratitude to those who provided us with helpful advice and suggestions in the translation, design and editing of this book. Our special thanks go to my beloved student Imam Wasim Khan for providing the Arabic text – may Allāh ﷻ bless him, his family and his loved ones with the best of all good in this life and in the Hereafter for the wonderful continuous charity he has provided us. *Āmīn.*

Prayers

We ask Allāh ﷻ to help us learn and understand the rights of others and also the etiquettes of companionship, and to implement them in our daily lives. *Āmīn.*

We ask Allāh ﷻ to forgive us of any mistakes, errors, flaws, shortcomings, etc., in this translation and otherwise; bless my parents a lofty abode in the Hereafter and grant them, and all of us in our current as well as the Next Life, the company of good people who honour the etiquettes of companionship. *Āmīn.*

We ask Allāh ﷻ to bless Imām 'Abdulwahhāb ibn Aḥmad ash-Sha'rānī, his parents, his teachers, his shaykhs, his students, his followers and his admirers the best Hereafter that He ﷻ bestows. *Āmīn.*

Our most humble praise and gratitude is to our Creator and Master – Allāh ﷻ, who has enabled us to offer what we could never have achieved without His ﷻ blessings.

May salutations and blessings incessantly shower upon our Beloved Messenger Muḥammad ﷺ, his Household ﷺ, his Companions ﷺ, his descendants and his followers, for ever and ever.

Āmīn, yā Rabb al-'ālamīn.

Muḥammad Ṭāhir Maḥmood Kiānī

12th Rabī' al-Awwal 1437AH/24th December 2015CE

Author's Introduction

ALL PRAISE IS TO ALLĀH ﷻ – the Lord of all the worlds. I invoke blessings and salutations on our Master Muḥammad ﷺ - the Explicating Light, upon all the Prophets ﷷ and Messengers ﷷ, and upon all of their Descendants ؓ and Companions ؓ.

Need for this Epistle

This is an epistle that has been undertaken because of the need for bringing knowledge into action.

It consists of three chapters and a conclusion.

I ask Allāh ﷻ that He ﷻ gives benefit by it to the ignorant as well as the knowledgeable person of this age.

[Āmīn]

CHAPTER 1

The Merits of Companionship for the Sake of Allāh ﷻ

1.1 Association versus Reclusion

You should know – may Allāh ﷻ enable me and you that which He ﷻ loves – that companionship for the sake of Allāh ﷻ is certainly from among the strongest links of Islām, from among the greatest doorways to goodness and to which the earlier and the latter scholars have inclined. As for those who warned against it and said: "Reclusion from it is closer to being safe from calamities, further from bearing the rights of when associating with others and more prudent for preoccupying oneself in devotional worship," this [advice] is for the disciple when he is unaccomplished. However, when he has reached the end of his [spiritual] quest and accomplished his [inner] state, such that he begins to observe Allāh ﷻ together with His ﷻ creation, it is better for him to associate with others. In fact, and as some have said, it is obligatory for those like him to associate with others. Nevertheless, the gnostic (*'ārif*) craves being on his own towards the end of his life just like [he did in] the beginning; he does not find [enough] time with which he may reach out to the people, just like it happened with the Messenger of Allāh ﷺ when Sūrat an-Naṣr[2] was revealed to him ﷺ. Thus, it is notable not to be said that 'reclusion is unreservedly more excellent' and nor that 'association (*khalṭah*) is unreservedly more excellent'.

1.2 Real Companionship

It is clear that the companionship of the inferior with the superior is not really companionship; it is merely educating and serving since

[2] Holy Qur'ān, Sūrat an-Naṣr (110).

the companion of a person is 'he who drinks from the same ocean and embraces the same station' [i.e. he is of equal status].

Thus, to apply [the word] '*ṣuḥbah* - companionship' [for the relationship] between the disciple (*murīd*) and the *shaykh* (master), and between the Prophetic Companion ﷺ and the Messenger ﷺ is a figurative application and not a real one.

1.3 Traditions on the Merits of Loving One Another for the Sake of Allāh ﷻ

Now that you know this, we shall mention to you something from the traditions that have been transmitted on the merits of those who love one another for the sake of Allāh ﷻ, because the mind becomes strong when it is made aware of the proof.

The Two Shaykhs [Imāms al-Bukhārī and Muslim] have reported in their two [collections of] Ṣaḥīḥs:

> *There are seven whom Allāh ﷻ will shade in His ﷻ shade on the Day when there will be no shade but His ﷻ shade: i. a just ruler, ii. a youth who is preoccupied in the worship of Allāh ﷻ, iii. a man whose heart is attached to the masjids, iv. two men who love one another for the sake of Allāh ﷻ – they come together for His ﷻ sake and they separate for His ﷻ sake, v. a man whom a woman of high status and beauty invites (for indecency) and he says, 'Verily, I fear Allāh ﷻ,' vi. a person who gives in charity and he keeps it so discrete that his left (hand) does not know what his right has given, and vii. a person who when he makes dhikr (remembrance) of Allāh ﷻ in solitude, his eyes overflow with tears.*[3]

Muslim reported:

> *[I swear] by the One ﷻ in Whose ﷻ Divine Hand is my life! You will never enter Paradise until you believe, and you will never believe until you love one another. Shall I not tell you something that if you do it you will love one another? Spread peace among yourselves.*[4]

He also reported:

---

[3] al-Bukhārī, *al-Jāmi' aṣ-Ṣaḥīḥ*.

[4] Muslim, *al-Musnad aṣ-Ṣaḥīḥ*.

> *A man visited his brother for the sake of Allāh ﷾, so Allāh ﷾ sent an angel to his path who asked, 'Where are you headed?' He replied, 'I am going to (visit) a brother of mine in this village.' (The angel) asked, 'Does he owe you a favour that you wish to profit from?' He replied, 'No. It is only that I love him for the sake of Allāh ﷾.' (The angel) said, 'Rejoice, for I am sent to you by Allāh ﷾ - verily, Allāh ﷾ loves you as you love Him ﷾.'*[5]

Ibn 'Asākir and others have reported:

> *There are seven who will be in the shade of the Divine Throne ('Arsh) on the Day when there will be no shade but its shade: i. a person who makes dhikr of Allāh ﷾ and his eyes overflow with tears, ii. a man who loves a servant (of Allāh ﷾) purely for the sake of Allāh ﷾, iii. a man whose heart is attached to the masjids out of his intense love for them, iv. a person who gives in charity with his right (hand) and he tries to conceal it from his left (hand), v. a ruler who is just with his subjects, vi. a man to whom a woman presents herself (for indecency) and he avoids her out of the awe of Allāh ﷾, and vii. a man who goes on an expedition with a group and they encounter the enemy and are overcome, he protects their lives until he and they are safe or he is martyred.*[6]

In *al-Asmā'*, al-Bayhaqī reported:

> *There are seven whom Allāh ﷾ will shade in the shade of His ﷾ Divine Throne on the Day when there will be no shade but its shade: i. a man whose heart is attached to the masjids, ii. a man whom a woman of high status and beauty invites (for indecency) and he says, 'Verily, I fear Allāh ﷾', iii. two men who love one another for the sake of Allāh ﷾, iv. a man who lowers his gaze away from the prohibitions of Allāh ﷾, v. the eye that guards in the way of Allāh ﷾, and vii. the eye that cries out of the fear of Allāh ﷾.*[7]

He also reported in *Shu'ab al-Īmān*:

> *After belief (īmān) in Allāh ﷾, prime intelligence is being cordial with people. The people of cordiality in this world have*

---

[5] Muslim, *al-Musnad aṣ-Ṣaḥīḥ*.
[6] Ibn 'Asākir, *at-Ta'rīkh*.
[7] al-Bayhaqī, *al-Asmā' wa'ṣ-Ṣifāt*.

a degree in Paradise, and whoever has a degree in Paradise will be in Paradise.[8]

He also reported:

After belief, prime intelligence is to be loving towards people, and to commit goodness to all good and bad (people).[9]

Ad-Dāraquṭnī reported:

The Believer shows kindness (to others) and he is (also) shown kindness to. There is no goodness in someone who does not show kindness and (he is) is not shown kindness to. The best of people is the one who is the most beneficient to them.[10]

Abū Dāwūd reported:

Someone who loves for the sake of Allāh تعالى and hates for the sake of Allāh تعالى, gives for the sake of Allāh تعالى and witholds for the sake of Allāh تعالى – his faith (īmān) is complete.[11]

He also reported:

The best of actions is loving for the sake of Allāh تعالى and hating for the sake of Allāh تعالى.[12]

He also reported:

The best (aspect of) faith is that you love for the sake of Allāh تعالى, hate for the sake of Allāh تعالى, employ your tongue in the dhikr of Allāh تعالى; that you like for the people what you like for yourself and you dislike for them what you dislike for yourself; and that you speak good or remain silent.[13]

Imām Aḥmad reported that:

On the Day of Judgement, Allāh تعالى will say: 'Where are those who love one another for the sake of My majesty? Today I will shade them in My shade'.[14]

He also reported:

---

[8] al-Bayhaqī, *Shu'ab al-Īmān.*
[9] al-Bayhaqī, *Shu'ab al-Īmān.*
[10] ad-Dāraquṭnī, *al-Afrād.*
[11] Abū Dāwūd, *as-Sunan.*
[12] Abū Dāwūd, *as-Sunan.*
[13] Aḥmad, *al-Musnad.*
[14] Muslim, *al-Musnad aṣ-Ṣaḥīḥ.*

The Believer who associates with the people and tolerates their grievances is superior to the Believer who does not associate with the people and does not tolerate their grievances.[15]

He also reported:

The strongest link of Islām is that you love for the sake of Allāh ﷻ *and that you hate for the sake of Allāh* ﷻ*.*[16]

With a sound chain [of narration], he also reported:

Those who love one another for the sake of Allāh ﷻ*, their apartments in Paradise will be seen like the eastern or western rising star. It will be asked, 'Who are they?' It will be said, 'They are those who love one another for the sake of Allāh* ﷻ*.'*[17]

He also reported:

The most beloved of actions to Allāh ﷻ *is loving for the sake of Allāh* ﷻ *and hating for the sake of Allāh* ﷻ*.*[18]

He also reported:

One who is pleased that he experiences the sweetness of faith should love another but only for the sake of Allāh ﷻ*.*[19]

Aṭ-Ṭabarānī reported:

After belief, prime intelligence is to be loving towards people.[20]

He also reported:

Verily, those who love one another for the sake of Allāh ﷻ *will be in the shade of the Divine Throne.*[21]

He also reported:

There are three who will be in the shade of the Divine Throne on the Day of Judgement – the Day when there will be no shade but its shade: i. a person who knows that Allāh ﷻ *is with him wherever he turns his attention, ii. a man whom a woman invites to herself (for indecency) and he avoids her out*

---

[15] Aḥmad, *al-Musnad*.
[16] Aḥmad, *al-Musnad*.
[17] Aḥmad, *al-Musnad*.
[18] Aḥmad, *al-Musnad*.
[19] Aḥmad, *al-Musnad*.
[20] aṭ-Ṭabarānī, *al-Awsaṭ*.
[21] aṭ-Ṭabarānī, *al-Kabīr*.

> *of the fear of Allāh تعالى, and iii. a person who loves for the sake of the awe of Allāh تعالى.*[22]

He also reported:

> *Those who love one another for the sake of Allāh تعالى will be upon chairs (made) of corundum (placed) around the Divine Throne.*[23]

He also reported:

> *Allāh تعالى said: 'My love is incumbent for those who love one another for My sake, those who sit together for My sake, those who strive (to help) one another for My sake and those who visit one another for My sake.'*[24]

He also reported:

> *If there were two servants (of Allāh تعالى) who loved one another for the sake of Allāh تعالى – one in the east and the other in the west, Allāh تعالى will bring them together on the Day of Judgement saying: 'He is the one whom you used to love for My sake.'*[25]

He also reported:

> *No two people love one another for the sake of Allāh تعالى except that Allāh تعالى will place a chair for them and have them seated thereupon until He تعالى completes the Reckoning (on the Day of Judgement).*[26]

He also reported:

> *He who loves a people will be raised among their group (on the Day of Judgement).*[27]

He also reported:

> *Those who love one another for the sake of Allāh تعالى will be in the shade of Allāh تعالى on the Day when there will be no shade but His تعالى shade – upon pulpits of light; (other) people will be terrified but they will not be terrified.*[28]

He also reported:

---

[22] aṭ-Ṭabarānī, *al-Kabīr*.
[23] aṭ-Ṭabarānī, *al-Kabīr*.
[24] aṭ-Ṭabarānī, *al-Kabīr*.
[25] al-Bayhaqī, *Shu'ab al-Īmān*.
[26] aṭ-Ṭabarānī, *al-Kabīr*.
[27] aṭ-Ṭabarānī, *al-Kabīr*.
[28] aṭ-Ṭabarānī, *al-Kabīr*.

> *There are some servants of Allāh ﷻ who are neither Prophets ﷺ and nor martyrs (but) the Prophets ﷺ and the martyrs will envy them due to their (lofty) stations and their proximity to Allāh ﷻ. It was asked, 'O Messenger of Allāh ﷺ, who are they?' He ﷺ replied, 'People from various places who had no close kinship between them, who loved one another for the sake of Allāh ﷻ and greeted one another. On the day of Judgement, Allāh ﷻ will place pulpits of light for them in front of the Divinely-Compassionate (Allāh) ﷻ and have them seated upon them. (Other) people will be terrified but they will not be terrified.'*[29]

He also reported:

> *On the Day of Judgement, Allāh ﷻ will raise may groups (of people) in whose faces there will be light - (they will be) upon pulpits of pearl. The people will envy them yet they are neither Prophets ﷺ and nor martyrs. It was asked, 'Who are they?' He ﷺ replied, 'Those who love one another for the sake of Allāh ﷻ, (hailing) from various tribes and various places, congregating upon the dhikr of Allāh ﷻ - making remembrance of Him ﷻ.'*[30]

He also reported:

> *There are apartments in Paradise whose exteriors can be seen from their interiors and their interiors from their exteriors. Allāh ﷻ has prepared them for those who love one another for His ﷻ sake, those who visit one another for His ﷻ sake and those who strive (to help) one another for His ﷻ sake.*[31]

Al-Bazzār and Abu'sh-Shaykh reported on the authority of Abū Hurayrah ﷺ:

> *There are pillars of corundum in Paradise upon which there are apartments of chrysolite whose doors remain open. They glisten like the glistening of the brightly-sparkling star. We asked, 'O Messenger of Allāh ﷺ, who will reside in them?' He ﷺ replied, 'Those who love one another for the sake of Allāh ﷻ, those who strive (to help) one another for the sake of Allāh ﷻ and those who meet one another for the sake of Allāh ﷻ.'*[32]

---

[29] aṭ-Ṭabarānī, *al-Kabīr*.
[30] aṭ-Ṭabarānī, *al-Kabīr*.
[31] aṭ-Ṭabarānī, *al-Awsaṭ*.
[32] al-Bazzār, *Kashf al-Astār*; al-Bayhaqī, *Shu'ab al-Īmān*.

At-Tirmidhī reported:

Allāh ﷻ has said: 'Those who love one another for the sake of My Majesty shall have pulpits of light. The Prophets ﷺ and martyrs will envy them.'[33] *(at-Tirmidhī) said: "It is a ḥasan ṣaḥīḥ (fair, sound) ḥadīth."*

He also reported:

A person will be with whom he loves and he will have what he earned.[34]

He also reported:

There are three things that if they are in anyone he will experience the sweetness of faith: i. that Allāh ﷻ and His Messenger ﷺ are more beloved to him than anything other than them, ii. that he loves a person but he does not love him except for the sake of Allāh ﷻ, iii. that he hates returning to disbelief after Allāh ﷻ has saved him from it just as he hates being cast into fire.[35]

He also reported:

A Believer is like a (brick) structure for the Believer; each part of it strengthens another.[36]

Ibn an-Najjār reported:

You should have lots of fellows (in faith) because every Believer will have (the right of) intercession on the Day of Judgement.

Al-Ḥakīm reported:

A person's looking at his fellow with yearning is better than seclusion (i'tikāf) in this Masjid of mine.

Ibn Abū ad-Dunyā reported:

Allāh ﷻ said: 'My love is true for those who love one another for My sake. Today, the Day of Judgement, I will shade them in the shade of the Divine Throne – the Day when there is no shade but My shade.'[37]

He also reported:

---

[33] at-Tirmidhī, *al-Jāmi'*.
[34] at-Tirmidhī, *al-Jāmi'*.
[35] at-Tirmidhī, *al-Jāmi'*.
[36] at-Tirmidhī, *al-Jāmi'*.
[37] Ibn Abū ad-Dunyā, *al-Ikhwān*.

No person initiates fellowship for the sake of Allāh ﷻ except that Allāh ﷻ initiates for him a degree in Paradise.[38]

He also reported:

Offer your food to whom you love for the sake of Allāh ﷻ.[39]

Al-Ḥākim and others have reported:

Allāh ﷻ said: 'Those who love one another for My sake will be upon pulpits of light. The Prophets ﷺ, the Utmost Honest and the martyrs will envy them due to their (lofty) stations.'[40]

Al-Bayhaqī reported:

One who wants to experience the taste of faith should love another person and not love him except for the sake of Allāh ﷻ.[41]

He also reported:

Certainly, Allāh ﷻ says: 'Verily, I (sometimes) desire to punish the inhabitants of the earth but when I observe those who populate My houses, those who love one another for My sake and those who seek forgiveness during the time before dawn, I ward My punishment away from them.'[42]

There are many reports regarding the merits of those who love one another for the sake of Allāh ﷻ but we shall restrict them to this amount.

1.3.1 Other Reports

There are also many reports from the pious predecessors and the practising scholars [on loving others for the sake of Allāh ﷻ].

We shall mention some of them for you, my dear fellow.

As from al-Ḥasan al-Baṣrī[43], Allāh ﷻ have mercy on him, he said:

[38] Ibn Abū ad-Dunyā, *al-Ikhwān*.
[39] Ibn Abū ad-Dunyā, *al-Ikhwān*.
[40] al-Ḥākim, *al-Mustadrak*.
[41] al-Bayhaqī, *Shu'ab al-Īmān*.
[42] al-Bayhaqī, *Shu'ab al-Īmān*.
[43] al-Ḥasan al-Baṣrī (21AH/642CE - 110AH/728CE) was a prominent Successor (*Tābi'ī*).

It is binding upon you to be cordial to every person who pursues the path of obeying Allāh تعالى; one who loves a righteous person is as though he loves Allāh تعالى.

Imām ash-Shāfi'ī[44], Allāh تعالى have mercy on him, said:

I would have disliked to remain in this world had it not been for the company of good people and for the intimate discourses (with Allāh تعالى) made during the time before dawn.

He also said:

According to me, nothing can compare with meeting (righteous) fellows.

Muṭarrif ibn ash-Shakhīr[45] (Allāh تعالى have mercy on him) said:

According to me, the most reliable of my actions is my loving a righteous person.

Abū Naṣr Bishr al-Ḥāfī[46], Allāh تعالى have mercy on him, said:

You must keep the company of righteous people if you want comfort in that world, [and you must] also have a good opinion of bad people and free yourself from the captivity of strangers.

My Master Aḥmad ar-Rifā'ī[47], Allāh تعالى have mercy on him, said:

The companionship of the pious people is a huge favour from among the favours of Allāh تعالى upon the servant.

Abu's-Sa'ūd ibn Abu'l-'Ashā'ir[48], Allāh تعالى have mercy on him, said:

Someone who wishes to be given the optimum rank on the Day of Judgement should keep company for the sake of Allāh تعالى. Someone who wants to have the difficulty of the Station (in the Plain of the Great Gathering (Ḥashr) on the Day of Judgement) averted from him should feed something sweet to his fellow-in-Allāh تعالى.[49]

It is mentioned in a ḥadīth:

Whoever commits to the desire of his fellow will be forgiven.[50]

---

[44] Imām Muḥammad ibn Idrīs ash-Shāfi'ī (150AH/767CE – 204/820CE).

[45] Muṭarrif ibn ash-Shakhīr al-Ḥarashī (d.207AH/822CE) was from among the senior Successors.

[46] Abū Naṣr Bishr al-Ḥāfī (149AH/767CE – 235AH/850CE).

[47] Abu'l-'Abbās Aḥmad ibn Abu'l-Ḥasan ar-Rifā'ī (511AH/1118CE – 577AH/1182CE).

[48] Abu's-Sa'ūd ibn Abu'l-'Ashā'ir (d.644AH/1246CE).

[49] Ibn al-Mubārak, *Kitāb az-Zuhd*.

[50] al-Bazzār , *Kashf al-Astār*; etc.

The Shaykh of the Wafā'iyyah [spiritual path, i.e. Muḥammad Wafā][51], Allāh ﷻ have mercy on him, said:

> *Do not sell a speck of love (that you have) in Allāh ﷻ - or for the sake of Allāh ﷻ, for many quintals of (good) deeds.*
>
> *The Messenger of Allāh ﷺ said: 'A person will be with whom he loves.''*[52]

My Master 'Alī Wafā[53] (Allāh ﷻ have mercy on him) said:

> *If you love a fellow for the sake of Allāh ﷻ, protect him; the love for whom you love will increase by it.*

Shaykh Abu'l-Mawāhib ash-Shādhilī[54], Allāh ﷻ have mercy on him, said:

> *You must increase interacting with the majority group of the people; verily, whoever increases interaction with the majority group of a people is (deemed to be) from among them.*

He also said:

> *When you see your heart diverting away from being cordial to the People of Allāh ﷻ then you must know that you have been expelled from the Gate of Allāh ﷻ.*

He also said:

> *You must adopt the company of the faqīrs (poor)*[55]*; it would be enough (for you) were they merely to hold your hand on the Day of Judgement despite their bearing whatever tragedies they may from their companions in this world. Many poor people have been enlightened in their company; the broken, fixed; the lowly, raised; the unsightly, covered; the oppressors, perished; oppressions, removed. A ḥadīth has been mentioned about them:*
>
> *'It is through them that you are given sustenance, rain and mercy.'*[56]

Shaykh Sulaymān al-Khuḍayrī[57], Allāh ﷻ have mercy on him, said:

---

[51] Muḥammad Wafā (d.764AH/1363CE).

[52] al-Bukhārī, *al-Jāmi' aṣ-Ṣaḥīḥ*; Muslim, *al-Musnad aṣ-Ṣaḥīḥ*.

[53] 'Alī Wafā (761AH/1359CE – 801AH/1398CE) is the son of Shaykh Muḥammad Wafā.

[54] Muḥammad Abu'l-Mawāhib ash-Shādhilī (809AH/1407CE – 881AH/1477CE).

[55] The poor, in this context, means 'those who are independent of the needs of the creation and are only dependent on Allāh ﷻ.'

[56] A similar ḥadīth has been mentioned with regards to the *abdāl* (spiritual substitutes) in aṭ-Ṭabarānī, *al-Awsaṭ*, Aḥmad, *al-Musnad*, etc.

[57] Shaykh Sulaymān al-Khuḍayrī (d. ca. 960AH/1552CE).

Whoever wishes to be given goodness aplenty should accompany the people of self-scrutiny.

My Master 'Alī al-Khawwāṣ[58], Allāh ﷻ have mercy on him, said:

Whoever intends to complete their faith (īmān) and have good opinions of himself ought to accompany the elite [among the righteous people].

My Master Afḍaluddīn[59], Allāh ﷻ have mercy on him, said:

You must have cordiality for the sake of Allāh ﷻ because it has been reported that on the Day of Judgement Allāh ﷻ will say to the servant: 'Did you make a friend for Me or did you make an enemy for Me?'

He also said:

Someone who intends to be among the seniors of those (buried) in cemeteries should accompany (others) for the sake of Allāh ﷻ.

1.3.2 Statement of Imām al-Yāfi'ī (Allāh ﷻ have mercy on him)

I said: "That which al-Yāfi'ī[60] (Allāh ﷻ have mercy on him) mentioned in his book *Rawḍ ar-Rayyāhīn* on the authority of one of the *awliyā'* (Friends of Allāh ﷻ) supports this. He said:

I asked Allāh ﷻ to show me the stations of the people [buried] in cemeteries, and so on one particular night I saw as though the (Day of) Judgement had [already] taken place and the graves had split open. Among them were those sleeping on fine silk; among them were those sleeping on satin and silken brocades; among them were those sleeping on fragrant plants; among them were those sleeping on couches – some of them were laughing and some were crying.' He said, 'I asked, 'O Lord! Had You willed, You could have made it equal for them out of (Your) favour,' and so an announcer from among those in the graves proclaimed, 'O So-and-So! These are the degrees of good deeds: as for those upon fine silk, they are those of noble character; as for those upon satin and silken brocades, they are the martyrs; as for those upon fragrant plants, they are those who used to fast; as for those of laughter, they are the repentant; as for those crying, they are the sinners; and as for

---

[58] 'Alī al-Khawwāṣ al-Burullusī (d.939AH/1532CE) – the spiritual master of Imām ash-Sha'rānī.

[59] Afḍaluddīn al-Aḥmadī (d.942AH/1535CE).

[60] Abū Muḥammad 'Abdullāh ibn As'ad al-Yāfi'ī (d.768AH/1366CE).

> *those of [lofty] degrees, they are those who loved one another for the sake of Allāh ﷻ.'*

Al-Yāfi'ī said:

> *What I have reported from him is what he actually mentioned. In other words, he made mention of those upon the various degrees even though he did not make any mention of the degrees [per sé]. He did mention the couches but he did not explain those [reclining] upon them after [mentioning the couches]. By making mention of the degrees, he probably intended the couches whose mention was made prior to them, because the reality of the degrees are the noble positions and the lofty eminent standings themselves. There is no doubt that those on couches are of a nobler degree and of a loftier rank than those on the ground, even though those on the ground may be on satin, etc., despite the couches that are mentioned are prepared for honour, they are not predominantly without venerated mats, even though the mats may not be mentioned together with them, as Allāh ﷻ has said:*
>
> ﴿ إِخْوَانًا عَلَىٰ سُرُرٍ مُّتَقَـٰبِلِينَ ﴾
>
> *(They shall be) brothers, facing each other, upon couches. (15:47)*[61]
>
> *Allāh ﷻ has not mentioned the mats in this verse, which means that the couches that have been mentioned will have upon them bedspreads that are mentioned in another verse*[62]*. So, when someone says, 'The king sat upon his couch and we sat down with him,' we learn two things:*
>
> 1. *the couch had a mat upon it*
> 2. *even though the king sat upon the couch, whoever was with him was ennobled due to the elevation of the meeting with the majesty of the kingship, and the king would not have consented to anyone else sitting with him on the couch.*

He said:

> *It is based on this that those who love one another for the sake of Allāh ﷻ are superior to all those who are mentioned in this*

[61] Holy Qur'ān, Sūrat al-Ḥijr (15), Verse 47.

[62] Holy Qur'ān, Sūrat ar-Raḥmān (55), Verse 54; Sūrat al-Wāqi'ah (56), Verse 34.

> *narration. A ṣaḥīḥ (sound) ḥadīth has been reported in at-Tirmidhī:*
>
> *Allāh ﷻ has said: 'Those who love one another for the sake of My Majesty will have pulpits of light. The Prophets ﷺ and martyrs will envy them.'*[63]
>
> *What the aforementioned dream supports is evident from this ḥadīth that they are the People of [Lofty] Degrees even though he did not mention the degrees, and that they embrace the nobleness of majestic esteem and tremendous pride. What honourable positions they are! [This is in addition to] whatever [else] they will have, including; Salsabīl*[64] *(fresh cool sweet water) - as Salsabīl is originally mentioned, [as well as] compliments, blazing beauty, and the bliss of residing in the proximity of the Generous Master (Allāh ﷻ).*
>
> *As for the mention of the couches in the aforementioned dream and the mention of the pulpits of light in the famous ḥadīth, there is no contradiction between them and nor with the shining that is [also] mentioned, as the pulpits will be on the [Day of] Judgement and the couches will be in the graves, as is reported in the aforementioned dream.*

The statement of al-Yāfi'ī, Allāh ﷻ have mercy on him, ends."[65]

There are a multitude of reports on the merits of loving one another for the sake of Allāh ﷻ but this amount is sufficient.

All praise is to Allāh ﷻ - the Lord of all the worlds.

[63] at-Tirmidhī, *al-Jāmi'*.
[64] Salsabīl is a river in Paradise. (Holy Qur'ān, Sūrat al-Insān (76), Verse 18).
[65] al-Yāfi'ī, *Rawḍ ar-Rayyāḥīn fī Ḥikāyat aṣ-Ṣāliḥīn.*

CHAPTER 2

The Rights of Companionship

You should know – may Allāh تعالى enable me and you that which He تعالى loves – that there are many rights of companionship. However, we shall mention to you a summary of those that are indispensable in the path of social living and association. You should also know that the Shaykhs have encouraged concern for fellows' rights such that they have said:

> *Someone who neglects the rights of his fellows, Allāh تعالى takes him to task by his rights being neglected; and when Allāh تعالى puts a servant to task He تعالى also dislikes him; and when Allāh تعالى dislikes a servant He تعالى casts him into the Fire [of Hell].*

When you have learnt this, I say, and with Allāh تعالى from Whom comes all ability:

2.1 Overlooking the Defects of Others

It is from among the rights of a person over another person that he should cast a blind eye to his defects.

The Shaykhs have said:

> *Whoever focuses on the defects of people, its benefits will be few and his heart will be ruined.*

They also said:

> *When you see someone who has commissioned himself with the defects of people as if he is well aware of them then you should know that he has been deceived.*

They also said:

> *The servant's focusing on the defects of [other] people but acting blind to his own defects is from among the signs of his being enticed [towards Hell].*

They also said:

> *We have not seen anything more destructive for [noble] deeds; nor more corrupting of hearts; nor more swift in destroying the servant; nor more close to the hatred [of Allāh ﷻ]; nor more affirming to the objective of ostentation, vanity and leadership than the lack of a servant recognising his own defects and his focusing on the defects of [other] people.*

2.2 Observing the Positive in Others

It is from among the rights of a person over another person that he bears what he sees in him in a manner of interpretation that is as beautiful as possible. If he cannot find any [good] interpretation, then he ought to blame himself.

It is mentioned in the counsel of my Master Ibrāhīm ad-Dasūqī[66] (Allāh ﷻ have mercy on him):

> *Do not reproach your fellow because of his state, his clothing, his food, or his drink because criticism gives cause to estrangement and disconnection from Allāh ﷻ. Thus, [there should be] no reproachment of anyone unless he pursues something that is prohibited about which the sacred law (sharī'ah) is explicit. Surely, the people are: i. specific, ii. ultraspecific, iii. beginner, iv. advanced, v. attempting, vi. actualised, vii. strong - who is unable to walk with the weak, viii. opposite to that [i.e. weak - unable to walk with the strong], [because] Allāh ﷻ shows mercy to some [people] through others.*

It is from among the sayings of Imām Sa'īd ibn al-Musayyib[67] (Allāh ﷻ have mercy on him):

> *There is none who is noble or of merit except that there exists a deficiency in him. However, one's deficiency is concealed by his merit when his merit is greater than his deficiency.*

2.3 Wishing the Best for Others

It is from among the rights of a person over another person that he wishes, as he would for himself, the best things for him, forgiveness and acceptance of repentance regardless of what sins he may have committed among [those that do not expel him from] Islām.

[66] Ibrāhīm ad-Dasūqī al-Hāshimī (d.676AH/1277CE).

[67] Sa'īd ibn al-Musayyib - also pronounced al-Musayyab (21AH/642CE – 93AH/711CE).

2.4 Concealing the Past Faults of Others

It is from among the rights of a person over another person that he does not focus on any error [that he has made] in the past and nor expose his fault that has been covered.

It is mentioned in a ḥadīth:

> *Someone who sees a fault (in others) and conceals it is like someone who brings an infant female back to life from her grave.*[68]

The Shaykhs have said:

> *Anyone who does not conceal what faults he sees in his fellows opens the door to his own faults being exposed in accordance to their faults that he reveals.*

They also said:

> *When you see any of your fellows committing a sin which he does not do so openly, you should conceal it; if he does it openly then you should admonish him between yourselves [i.e. in private]; if he is not deterred then you should admonish him among other people as welfare for him and not to embarrass him, and hopefully, he will mend his ways and be deterred. One does not commit the sin openly as long as he does it inside the privacy of his home and has its door closed upon it, unless children are there who will narrate what they see because they are like [grown] men [i.e. it will not be private anymore but public].*

2.5 Not Dishonouring Someone Over a Sin

It is from among the rights of a person over another person that he does not dishonour him over a sin or otherwise because dishonouring cuts off cordiality or [at least] pollutes its purity.

It is from among the sayings of al-Ḥasan al-Baṣrī:

> *If it reaches you that someone has [made] a mistake and it has not been proven with a judge then do not dishonour him by it, but rather, belie the one who publicises it, especially if he is among you. That is because the original state is to be free of any domain until genuine evidence is established with the judge. Thereafter, when it has been established with him, you should*

[68] Abū Dāwūd, *as-Sunan*.

even then not dishonour him for it could be that Allāh ﷻ might relieve him and put you to task.

It is mentioned in a ḥadīth:

Whoever dishonours his fellow due to a sin will not die until he himself has committed that sin.[69]

It is from among the sayings of my Master 'Alī Wafā:

Do not discredit your fellow by what has afflicted him from the afflictions of your world because at that time he is either oppressed and Allāh ﷻ will soon assist him or he is sinful who is being punished and Allāh ﷻ has purified him. It is something of a stupidity for you to pride yourself on something that you cannot protect from being taken away or for you to dishonour anyone over that which is not improbable for you to do while you yourself know that what is possible against someone like you is [also] possible against you.

2.6 Not Being Contemptful

It is from among the rights of a person over another person that he does not see him with an eye of contempt because the Shaykhs have said:

Whoever looks at his fellow with an eye of contempt will [himself] be subject to humiliation and disgrace.

It is mentioned in a ḥadīth:

Allāh ﷻ will forgive someone who looks at his fellow with a loving gaze.[70]

2.7 Blaming Oneself for the Defects in Others

It is from among the rights of a person over another person that when he becomes aware of a defect in him he ought to blame his own self for that and say: "Verily, that is a defect in me," because a Muslim is the mirror of a Muslim[71] and a person merely sees his own image in a mirror.

A man accompanied Abū Isḥāq Ibrāhīm ibn Adham[72] (Allāh ﷻ have mercy on him). When he wanted to part from him, he said to him: "Tell

[69] at-Tirmidhī, *al-Jāmi'*.
[70] at-Tirmidhī, *al-Jāmi'*.
[71] Abū Dāwūd, *as-Sunan*.
[72] Abū Isḥāq Ibrāhīm ibn Adham (d.162AH/778CE).

me about what defects I have in me," and he replied: "My dear fellow! I have not seen any defect in you for I have been observing you with the eye of cordiality and I have considered good whatever I have seen in you. Ask someone else about your defects."

It is in this meaning that they sing:

و عينُ الرضا عن كل عيب كليلةٌ   كما أن عينَ السخط تبدي المساويا

Weak from all defects is the eye of consent

Makes the balance clear does the eye of displeasure.

2.8 Considering Oneself Inferior to Others

It is from among the rights of a person over another person that he always sees himself inferior to him, and that too based on certainty and not on assumption and conjecture, for they [i.e. the Shaykhs] have said:

> *Someone who does not see himself inferior to his fellow will not benefit from his company.*

It is from among the sayings of Shaykh Abu'l-Mawāhib ash-Shādhilī:

> *Ever since the People of Allāh ﷻ (i.e. His friends - the awliyā') have recognised that no plant grows or bears fruit unless it is placed under the earth with feet [treading] over it, they have rendered their selves 'earth' for everyone.*

It is from among the sayings of my Master 'Alī Wafā:

> *The earth has been made an expanse for you in order to teach you humbleness. Thus, be humble and you will expand.*

2.9 Giving Preference to Others

It is from among the rights of a person over another person that he gives preference to him over himself in everything. They [i.e. the Shaykhs] have said:

> *None of you will lead his companions unless he gives them preference over himself, tolerates their harms and does not compete with them in anything they aspire to.*

2.10 Serving Others

It is from among the rights of a person over another person that he serves him when he is ill. They [i.e. the Shaykhs] have mentioned:

Verily, chivalry is in serving others.

It is from among the sayings of Ustādh al-Junayd[73], Allāh ﷻ have mercy on him:

> *A person ought to serve his fellows and then seek pardon from them for not having fulfilled their right and confess to them for having betrayed himself even though he knows that he is free of that domain, as long as it [i.e. his confession] is not liable to ḥadd or ta'zīr (discretionary) punishment, otherwise he would have entered into [the category of] someone who has wronged himself - and that is unlawful.*

It is from among the sayings of Shaykh Abu'l-Mawāhib ash-Shādhilī:

> *Someone who considers himself too haughty to serve his fellows, Allāh ﷻ strikes him with a humiliation from which he will never be able to free himself. [However,] someone who serves his fellows will be given some of [the reward of] their best deeds.*

2.11 Respecting and Revering Others

It is from among the rights of a person over another person that he respects him and reveres him, especially when he deserves it, like being from among the scholars, from among those who bear the Noble Qur'ān or from among the descendants of the Messenger of Allāh ﷺ.

It is mentioned in the counsel of Imām an-Nawawī[74] (Allāh ﷻ have mercy on him):

> *Never belittle anyone because the final state [of any person] is hidden and the servant does not know how his [own] ending will be. Thus, when you see a sinner, do not consider yourself superior to him because it could be that he is of a higher station in the Knowledge of Allāh ﷻ than you are whereas you might be from among the morally corrupt and he could be interceding for you on the Day of Judgement. [Therefore,] whenever you see a minor, decree that verily he is superior to you on account of his being less than you in committing sins; whenever you see someone who is older than you in age, decree that verily he is superior to you on account of his being earlier than you in*

[73] al-Junayd ibn Muḥammad az-Zujāj al-Baghdādī (220AH/835CE - 297AH/909CE).
[74] Abū Zakariyyā Muḥiyyuddīn Yaḥyā ibn Sharaf an-Nawawī (631AH/1233CE - 676AH/1277CE).

migrating into Islām; when you see a non-Muslim, do not determine the Fire [of Hell] for him out of the possibility that he might surely become Muslim and die as a Muslim.

2.12 Praising Others

It is from among the rights of a person over another person that he praises him in his absence and in his presence according to the Islāmic legal manner because it is certainly from among those [acts] that increase the purity of cordiality.

Aṭ-Ṭabarānī and others have reported:

When the Believer - that is the complete Believer - is praised on his face, his faith inside his heart increases,[75]

because when the complete Believer is praised, he thanks Allāh ﷻ on concealing his shortcomings and making his good aspects apparent, and so his faith increases because of it. Then again, it is clear that this is prior to [the attainment of] purity and soundness of cordiality. As for when cordiality is pure and sound then in that case praise cannot be good.

[It is in this meaning that] they sing:

إذا صفت المودّة بين قوم وصحّ ولاءُهم سمج الثناءُ

When cordiality becomes pure among a people

And their friendship has become good

Then praise becomes hostile.

2.13 Honouring Others When Meeting Them

It is from among the rights of a person over another person that he honours him when he encounters him, that he meets him with a greeting, with cheerful countenance, embraces him if he is a male and lays something out for him to protect him from the dirt.

2.14 Making Space for Others in Gatherings

It is from among the rights of a person over another person that he makes space for him in a gathering when he sees him. This is from among those acts that strengthen cordiality.

---

[75] aṭ-Ṭabarānī, *al-Awsaṭ*.

It is mentioned in a ḥadīth:

> *Verily, the Muslim has a right that when his fellow sees him he ought to move up (and make space) for him.*[76]

2.15 Not Calling Others by Only Their Name

It is from among the rights of a person over another person that he does not call him only by his name.

It is mentioned in the counsel of some of them [i.e. the Shaykhs]:

> *When you call out to your fellow, give him honour - it will establish his cordiality [for you]. It is from among [the acts of] unfriendliness to your fellow to call him without mentioning his filial appellation, agnomen or a word of reverence, and likewise [to] his children and his grandchildren, be it in his absence or his presence.*

2.16 Acknowledging the Merits of Others

It is from among the rights of a person over another person that he acknowledges him with merit and expresses his own lack of equality to him, especially if that person has initiated in giving him a gift because he himself is [now] unable to equal his initiating it. This is what Shaykh Muḥiyyuddīn ibn al-'Arabī[77] (Allāh ﷻ have mercy on him) has said.

It is mentioned in a ḥadīth:

> *Someone who has been subjected to good should publicise it; someone who publicises it has been grateful but someone who conceals it has been ungrateful, and he who is not grateful to the people is not grateful to Allāh ﷻ.*[78]

2.17 Paying Visits to Others

It is from among the rights of a person over another person that he visits him every few days for it is mentioned in a ḥadīth:

> *Walk a mile to visit an ill person; walk two miles to reconcile between two people; walk three miles to visit a fellow for the sake of Allāh ﷻ.*[79]

---

[76] al-Bayhaqī, *Shu'ab al-Īmān*.
[77] Muḥiyyuddīn ibn al-'Arabī (d.638AH/1240CE).
[78] al-Bayhaqī, *Shu'ab al-Īmān*.
[79] Ibn Abū ad-Dunyā, *al-Ikhwān*.

On this is also mentioned:

One who visits his fellow in his home - one who eats from his food, is loftier in status than the one who is feeding.[80]

On this is also mentioned:

When any of you visits his fellow and he lays out something to protect him from the dirt, Allāh ﷻ protects him from the punishment of the Fire (of Hell).[81]

On this is also mentioned:

Visit (others) for the sake of Allāh ﷻ because seventy thousand angels escort someone who visits (others) for the sake of Allāh ﷻ.[82]

Al-Yāfi'ī narrated from a *walī* that he said:

I saw the Quṭb (spiritual pole) [of the time] in Makkah upon a golden calf that the angels were driving in the air with golden reins, and so I asked, 'Where are you going?' He replied, 'To one of my fellows whom I long [to meet].' I asked, 'What if I ask Allāh ﷻ that He ﷻ brings him to you,' and he replied, 'In that case, where would lie the reward of visiting, my dear fellow?'

Ends [the statement of al-Yāfi'ī].[83]

It is from among the sayings of my Master Ibrāhīm al-Matbūlī[84] (Allāh ﷻ have mercy on him):

Strive [to visit] your fellows and do not disassociate from them such that they begin to worry [about you] and are made to visit you because all the assistance the faqīr needs in these times does not come by the right of only one path leading to him.

Imām ash-Shāfi'ī would frequently visit his student Imām Aḥmad ibn Ḥanbal[85] (Allāh ﷻ have mercy on him) and the latter too would visit the former likewise. Imām ash-Shāfi'ī was asked regarding that and so he, Allāh ﷻ have mercy on him, said the [following] poem:

قالوا: يزورُك أحمد فتزوره   قلتُ: الفضائل لا تفارق منزلَه

---

[80] al-Khaṭīb, *at-Ta'rīkh*.
[81] aṭ-Ṭabarānī, *al-Kabīr*.
[82] aṭ-Ṭabarānī, *al-Awsaṭ*.
[83] al-Yāfi'ī, *Rawḍ ar-Rayyāhīn fī Ḥikāyat aṣ-Ṣāliḥīn*.
[84] Ibrāhīm al-Matbūlī (d.877AH/1472CE).
[85] Imām Aḥmad ibn Ḥanbal (164AH/780CE - 241AH/855CE).

إن زارَني فبفضله أو زرته فلفضلِه فالفضل في الحالين لَه

They ask, 'Aḥmad visits you and you visit him?'

I replied, 'The merits do not leave his house.

If he visits me, the merit is his, and if I visit him...

The merit is still his. In both cases, the merit is his.'

Imām Aḥmad, Allāh ﷻ have mercy on him, responded:

إن زرتَنا فبفضلٍ منكَ تمنحنا أو نحنُ زرنا فللفضلِ الّذي فِيكا

فلا عدمنا كلا الحالينِ منكَ ولا نالَ الّذي يتمنّى منكَ شانيكا

'If you visit us then it is your grace that you bestow on us

Or if we visit you then it is because of your merit,

For in both cases we must not be deprived of you, and nor...

The influence that one desires from your honour.'

It is from among the sayings of my Master Alī al-Khawwāṣ, Allāh ﷻ have mercy on him:

> *Visiting [one's] fellows increases the faith whereas omitting it decreases it because it is like the pollination of the date-palm tree. Some people [of verity] have said, 'When your wealth diminishes, visit your fellows.'*

I say:

> *Visiting [one's] fellows will not increase the faith unless the etiquettes of visiting are met, but Allāh ﷻ knows best.*

2.18 When Meeting Others

2.18.1 Shaking Hands

It is from among the rights of a person over another person that whenever he meets him he shakes hands with him with the intention of receiving blessings and obeying the command [of Allāh ﷻ] because aṭ-Ṭabarānī has reported:

> *When two Muslims shake hands with one another, their palms do not separate until they are both forgiven.*[86]

[86] aṭ-Ṭabarānī, *al-Kabīr*.

Abu'sh-Shaykh reported:

> *When two Muslims meet and one of them greets the other with peace, the one who is more cheerful of the two to his companion is more beloved to and more excellent with Allāh ﷻ. When they shake hands, Allāh ﷻ showers a hundred mercies upon them both.*[87]

2.18.2 Invoking Blessings and Peace on Prophet Muḥammad ﷺ

It is from among the rights of a person over another person that when he meets him and shakes hands with him, he invokes blessings and peace upon the Prophet [Muḥammad] ﷺ and he reminds him of that.

Abū Ya'lā reported:

> *There are no two servants who love one another (for the sake of Allāh ﷻ) that when one meets his companion and they invoke blessings on the Prophet ﷺ, they do not separate until both their sins, of the past and the future, are forgiven.*[88]

2.19 Exchanging Gifts

It is from among the rights of a person over another person that he gives him a gift every few days, especially when some bitterness has taken place from him.

It is mentioned in a ḥadīth:

> *Exchange gifts with one another - you will love one another, and shake hands with one another - malice between you will go away.*[89]

2.20 Advising to Avoid Seeking Revenge

It is from among the rights of a person over another person that he advises him not to offend anyone who has offended him but to seek the aid of Allāh ﷻ since the advice of an oppressed fellow to seek the aid of Allāh ﷻ and to submit oneself to Him ﷻ is from among the greatest modes of assistance to one's fellow.

It is mentioned in the Zabūr (Psalms) of Prophet Dāwūd (David) ﷺ:

---

[87] Abu'sh-Shaykh, *Kitāb ath-Thawāb*.
[88] al-Bayhaqī, *Shu'ab al-Īmān*.
[89] A ḥadīth with a similar meaning: at-Tirmidhī, *al-Jāmi'*.

O Dāwūd! Do not offend someone who has offended you because My help stays away from someone who offends someone who has offended him.

2.21 Assisting Others in Marriage

It is from among the rights of a person over another person that he assists him in getting married. They [i.e. the Shaykhs] have mentioned that assisting in this respect is more excellent than assisting in battles and prayers since it is the best of supererogatory charities and the reward becomes great due to the greatness of the cause; had there been no marriage, there would be no *mujāhid* and nor anyone who worships Allāh ﷻ.

2.22 Visiting and Serving the Ill

It is from among the rights of a person over another person that he does not neglect visiting him and serving him when he falls ill, especially during the night.

It is mentioned in a ḥadīth:

There is no person who visits someone who is ill in the evening except that seventy thousand angels go out with him - they seek forgiveness for him until morning; and whoever goes to [visit] him in the morning, seventy thousand angels go out with him seeking forgiveness for him until the evening.[90]

The visitor ought to not eat when he is with the ill person as it is mentioned in a ḥadīth:

When one of you visits an ill person, he ought not eat anything when he is with him.[91]

2.23 Advising Another in Making a Bequest

It is from among the rights of a person over another person that he advises him to make a bequest when death approaches him and not to give in to natural shyness in that respect for the benefits therein are well known.

[90] Abū Dāwūd, *as-Sunan*.
[91] ad-Daylamī.

2.24 Staying Overnight with the Moribund

It is from among the rights of a person over another person that he stays up overnight with him until morning when he is in a state that will lead to death as it could be that his time may be up at that very moment and thus he will separate from him while fulfilling his right to him.

2.25 Acknowledging One Who Claims Noble Lineage

It is from among the rights of a person over another person that he acknowledges him if he attributes himself [in lineage] to any of the seniors from among the *awliyā'*, scholars or leaders.

It is from among the counsels of Shaykh Muḥiyyuddīn ibn al-'Arabī:

> *When your fellow attributes himself [in lineage] to any of the seniors [among the predecessors], caution yourself from discrediting his lineage even if that be [secretly] within yourself - otherwise you are intervening between that person, Allāh ﷻ and between the bedridden person - lest you fall into a major sin. In fact, it has been reported, 'Discrediting [another's] lineage is disbelief (kufr).'*

2.26 Not Declaring Apostasy Due to a Sin

It is from among the rights of a person over another person that he does not declare him an apostate due to a sin even though the people relent to it since the lack of godliness in people these days regarding what they say is clear and it is difficult to identify all the words by which a person may become an apostate. *Takfīr* (declaring someone to be a non-Muslim), as Shaykh al-Islām as-Subkī[92] (Allāh ﷻ have mercy on him) has said: "[It is] a horrifying affair," - of which the least is to tell someone that they will remain in the Fire [of Hell] forever and the rules of Islām do no apply to them in their life and nor after their death.

2.27 Not Hating Others Over Inappropriate Acts

It is from among the rights of a person over another person that he does not hate him when he commits something inappropriate.

---

[92] Taqiyyuddīn 'Alī ibn 'Abdulkāfī as-Subkī al-Khazrajī (683AH/1284CE - 756AH/1355CE).

It is from among the sayings of my Master 'Alī al-Khawwāṣ, Allāh ﷻ have mercy on him:

> *Our hostility towards the actions of someone against whom Allāh ﷻ has commanded us to be antagonistic is a legal [form of] hostility and [our] contentedness [with them] is legal and not natural whereas our hostility against their person is a natural [form of] antagonism. However, it is common among the people for their hatred to go against the person of someone about whom they hear has committed an unlawful act whereas if they hear that he has said something against them that they dislike, they begin to hate his children as an extension to his person and, in addition to that, they begin to disparage him. Some of them might even believe that he deserves to be disdained by them and [thus] they forget that it is from [the acts of] absolute ignorance to disparage a servant [of Allāh ﷻ] whom He ﷻ has taken care of and brought into existence from nothingness.*

Be careful of this, dear fellow! Verily, Allāh ﷻ has not commanded you to disdain anyone from His ﷻ creation, but rather He ﷻ has commanded you to oppose their deeds that are contrary to His ﷻ law and nothing else. Thus, you ought to enjoin the sinner [to do good] and forbid him [from unlawful acts] but you must not disparage him. Just ponder over the saying of the Prophet ﷺ on the garlic plant:

It is a plant whose smell I dislike.[93]

The Prophet ﷺ did not dislike it [i.e. the garlic plant] per sé, but rather he ﷺ disliked its smell which is one of its characteristics. Therefore, it is known that our antagonism to disbelievers is a hostility to characteristics with the proof that it will be unlawful for us to have animosity against them if they become Muslim and their condition [against Muslims] becomes good.

2.28 Increasing in Doing Good When an Interposition Takes Place

It is from among the rights of a person over another person that when something interposes between them, he increases in doing good to him more than prior to the interposition, out of the consideration for cordiality.

---

[93] Muslim, *al-Musnad aṣ-Ṣaḥīḥ*.

The pious predecessors would praise their enemies whenever their names were mentioned in their presence such that those who think would presume they are their greatest lovers. Therefore, my dear fellow, emulate them and never withhold yourself from mentioning your fellow in goodness during the days that you are angry with him, and refrain from spoiling his reputation – this could pollute the purity of cordiality [between you] even though reconciliation might take place. Think of the bread you ate with him and the good that took place [between you] even though there are few who do this.

2.29 Giving Preference to the Needs of Others

It is from among the rights of a person over another person that he prioritises the essential needs of the other over his [own] forms of worship that are prescribed by the Sunnah. It is well known that the good whose benefit is transitive is more excellent than that which is limited [only] to the one who does it.

2.30 Seeking Forgiveness for Shortcomings

It is from among the rights of a person over another person that when he does something against the other which reaches him, the former ought to hurry in seeking forgiveness, humbling himself, submitting himself, serving him and expressing remorse on what took place from him against his fellow. He should continue this until his fellow has mercy on him. Then again, if he does not have mercy on him, he ought to blame himself and acknowledge that he [himself] is the wrongdoer - though there are few who do this.

2.31 Accepting Excuses of Others

It is from among the rights of a person over another person that he accepts his excuse even if he is lying. At-Tirmidhī and others have reported:

> *One whose brother comes to him shirking the responsibility of a sin [against him], he should accept his excuse regardless of whether he is truthful or lying. If he does not, he shall not come to the Fountain (Ḥawḍ).*[94]

[94] at-Tirmidhī, *al-Jāmi'*.

It is in reference to this that they sang:

اقبلْ معاذيرَ مَن يأتيك معتذرا   إن برّ عندك فيما قالَ أو فجرا

فقدْ أطاعكَ مَن يَرضيكَ ظاهره   وقد أجلّك مَن يعصيك مستترا

Accept the apology of one who comes to you with an excuse

Irrespective of whether he is sincere in what he says or not.

He has apparently come wanting to please you

Even though he hides what has harmed you.

And they sang:

قيلَ لِي: قد أسا إليك فُلان   ومقام الفتىٰ على الذلّ عارُ

قلتُ: قد أتىٰ و أحدث عذرا   ديةُ الذنبِ عندنا الاعتذارُ

I was told: 'So-and-so has spoken against you,

It is a defect for such a station of chivalry.'

I said: 'He has come and offered an excuse,

The recompense for a sin, with us, is a simple apology.'

And they sang:

إذا اعتذرَ الصديق إليك يوماً   فجاوِز عن مساويهِ الكثيره

فإن الشافعيّ روى حديثاً   بِإسنادٍ صحيحٍ عن المُغيره

عن المختار أنّ الله يمحو   بعذر واحدٍ ألفَي كبيره

When a friend makes an excuse to you one day

Then go forth in assisting him much

For ash-Shāfi'ī has reported a ḥadīth

With a sound chain from al-Mughīrah ﵁

From the Choicest One ﷺ, that Allāh ﷻ forgives

Two thousand major sins with one excuse.

Ibn Mājah reported:

One whose brother offers him an excuse and he does not accept it shall have a sin similar to (that of) the tax-man.[95]

It is from among the sayings of my Master 'Alī al-Khawwāṣ, Allāh ﷻ have mercy on him:

> *When your fellow comes to you with an excuse, accept it, especially when it happened a long time ago. If any of you does not find any tenderness in his heart for his fellow then he ought to blame his own self and say to it, 'Your fellow came to you with an excuse yet you did not accept it!? How many a time have you violated his right when you did not pay any regard to him. As such you are worse than he is!'*

Some of them said:

> *A fellow who compels his fellow to apologise to him is not a true brother and nor a Fellow of the Path [of Verity]. Verily, the Fellows of the Path make excuses for the creatures [of Allāh ﷻ] prior to the creatures apologising to them.*

2.32 Avoiding Envy

It is from among the rights of a person over another person to be immensely happy for him when [people's] obedience to him increases and [also] when the people turn to him in loyalty. The sickness of envy befalls someone who is not like that.

It is mentioned in a ḥadīth:

Envy eats away good deeds like fire eats away firewood.[96]

It is from among the counsels of my Master 'Alī Wafā:

> *You must refrain from being envious of someone whom Allāh ﷻ has selected over you otherwise Allāh ﷻ will deform you as He ﷻ deformed Iblīs from the angelic image to the satanic image when he was envious of Prophet Ādam ﷺ.*

It is mentioned in the virtues of my Master Aḥmad al-Badawī[97], Allāh ﷻ benefit us with his blessings:

---

[95] Ibn Mājah, *as-Sunan.*

[96] Abū Dāwūd, *as-Sunan.*

[97] Abu'l-'Abbās Aḥmad ibn 'Alī al-Fāsī al-Maghribī al-Badawī (596AH/1199CE - 675AH/1276CE).

The landlord of the mansion in Ṭantathanā[98], known due to his moonlike face, was a great walī who suffered with envy when my Master Aḥmad al-Badawī came to Ṭantathanā and the people began turning to him in loyalty. His state was despoiled and his name and any mention was extinguished. His place in Ṭantathanā today is where dogs roam. The speakers of Ṭantathanā assisted him, specified time [to have gatherings of dhikr, etc.] at his place and they also erected a huge minaret at his zāwiyah. However, when my Master 'Abdul'āl[99] (Allāh ﷻ have mercy on him) arrived and destroyed it with his feet, it has been in ruins [ever since] to this time of ours.

2.33 Bidding Farewell when Travelling

It is from among the rights of a person over another person that when one intends to travel he must not leave until after he has bidden farewell to the other by embracing him if he is a man, or with a gesture if he is a minor, for it is mentioned in a ḥadīth:

When any of you leaves on a journey, he should bid his fellows farewell for Allāh ﷻ places blessings in their supplications.[100]

2.34 Visiting Others when They Return from a Journey

It is from among the rights of a person over another person that when one returns from a journey, the other ought to go to him in his home, greet him with salutations and express joy at his [returning in] safety – and [visit] his child also, as well as his relatives, when they return from a journey or when they are cured from an illness. Thus, it is from among his rights that his fellow goes to him and expresses his joy at his safety.

2.35 Consulting with Others

It is from among the rights of a person over another person that he consults with him in all important affairs for the scholars have stated that mutual consultation increases the purity of cordiality.

It is mentioned in a ḥadīth:

---

[98] The city of Tantathana (Ṭantathanā) lies 58 miles (92 kilometres) north of Cairo and 75 miles (120 kilometres) southeast of Alexandria in Egypt.
[99] 'Abdul'āl al-Majdhūb (d. ca. 930AH/1523CE) was a disciple of Aḥmad al-Badawī.
[100] Ibn 'Asākir, *at-Ta'rīkh*.

Whoever intends to do anything ought to consult a Muslim person about it; Allāh ﷻ will enable him to the best means of pursuing his affairs.[101]

My Master ʿAlī al-Khawwāṣ would say:

You must consult your fellows in every important affair for verily [it is mentioned] in the ḥadīth:

One who seeks good will not be destroyed and one who seeks advice will not be embarrassed.[102]

[It is in this meaning that] they sang:

شاوِرْ أخاكَ في الخفيّ المشكلِ　　وأقبلْ نصيحة فاضل متفضل

Consult with your fellow in every secret difficulty,

And to the advice of every generous wise person, agree.

And they sang:

شاوِرْ أخاك إذا نابتك نائبة　　يوماً وإن كنتَ مِن أهل المشوَرات

فالعين تلقى كفاحًا ما نأى ودَنا　　ولا ترى نفسها إلّا بمرآة

Consult with your fellow when something befalls you,

On any day, even when you an adviser may be.

For the eye sees what it encounters, far or near,

And it sees not itself but through a mirror it will see.

2.36 Having Concern for the Other's Dependents

It is from among the rights of a person over another person that one repeatedly shows concern for the dependents and children of the other when that person is away from them.

It is from among their [i.e. the Shaykhs'] sayings:

One who does not show concern for the dependents of his fellow in his absence has betrayed companionship.

---

[101] aṭ-Ṭabarānī, *al-Awsaṭ*.
[102] aṭ-Ṭabarānī, *al-Awsaṭ*.

2.37 Extending Wealth and Time to Others

It is from among the rights of a person over another person that he makes him an equal partner in his own property and other things.

Shaykh Abu'l-Mawāhib ash-Shādhilī said:

> *When the poor person seeks fellowship for the sake of Allāh ﷻ, it is incumbent on him to make his fellow an equal partner in his own wealth as the Anṣār (Helpers), who were themselves poor, did with the Muhājirs (Migrants) when the latter came to them in Madīnah. Thus, anyone who claims fellowship for the sake of Allāh ﷻ, He ﷻ tests them on this scale.*

My Master Abū Madyan at-Tilmisānī[103], Allāh ﷻ benefit us with him, said:

> *Someone who makes a distinction between his own clothes and those of his fellow regarding ownership has not truly fulfilled [the right of] fellowship.*

He also said:

> *Your fellowship is not complete until you expand your heart that your fellow may take everything that you own from you [including] your clothing and your food. You will be a hypocrite in your fellowship as long as you [continue to] feel a constriction in your heart in this regard.*

Some of them [i.e. Shaykhs] said:

> *Fellowship between two is not correct until one of two says to the other, 'O Me!' He is not a fellow who says, 'My bowl,' or, 'My garment.'*

2.38 When Others Dislike Him

It is from among the rights of a person over another person that he does not become perturbed when he says to him: "I hate you." Rather, he ought to probe the reasons for which his fellow hates him, and then remove them – if his fellow's hatred is removed then fine, otherwise he should repeat the investigation again and again.

---

[103] Abū Madyan Shu'ayb ibn al-Ḥusayn al-Maghribī at-Tilmisānī, also known as *al-Ghawth* (509AH/1115CE - 594AH/1197CE).

2.39 Keeping the Secrets of Others

It is from among the rights of a person over another person that he hides his fellow's secret since secrets are like privacy; it is prohibited to disclose them, to look into them or to discuss them.

It is mentioned in a ḥadīth:

> *Allāh ﷻ will conceal the privacy of someone who conceals the privacy of his fellow and He ﷻ will reveal the privacy of someone who reveals the privacy of his fellow."*[104]

It is mentioned in the counsel of Shaykh Abu'l-Mawāhib ash-Shādhilī:

> *Refrain from disclosing the secret of your fellow to anyone else because Allāh ﷻ might dislike you because of that and you might suffer loss in this world and the Hereafter [as a consequence].*

2.40 Rejecting Talebearers

It is from among the rights of a person over another person that he never accepts anyone who bears tales about him.

Ḥujjat al-Islām[105], Imām al-Ghazālī[106] (Allāh ﷻ have mercy on him) mentioned:

> *[The following] six points are incumbent on someone to whom tales are borne:*
>
> 1. *that he does not believe him, i.e. the talebearer*
> 2. *that he forbids him from doing that*
> 3. *that he hates him for the sake of Allāh ﷻ*
> 4. *that he does not think bad of what has been transmitted from him*
> 5. *that he does not investigate to verify that [tale]*
> 6. *that he does not narrate [to anyone] the tales that have been borne about him.*[107]

[104] A ḥadīth with a similar meaning: Ibn Mājah, *as-Sunan*.

[105] Translated as 'The Proof of Islām', the title *Ḥujjat al-Islām* is given to Imām Muḥammad al-Ghazālī for his authoritative stance on the true teachings of Islām.

[106] Abū Ḥāmid Muḥammad ibn Muḥammad al-Ghazālī (450AH/1058CE - 505AH/1111CE).

[107] al-Ghazālī, *Iḥyā' 'Ulūm ad-Dīn*.

It is from among the sayings of Shaykh Abu'l-Mawāhib ash-Shādhilī:

> *When someone transmits to you a saying of one of your fellows, say [to him], 'Oi! I am in the companionship and cordiality of my fellow based on conviction whereas your saying is based on speculation, and conviction is not abandoned for speculation!'*

It is from among the sayings of Shaykh Afḍaluddīn:

> *When someone transmits to you a saying from someone against your reputation, reprimand him even if he is from among the most honoured of your fellows. Say to him, 'If you believe the matter between us is such then you and from whom you transmit are the same. In fact, you are worse than he is for he did not make us hear it whereas you have made us listen to it. Had you believed this matter between us to be void and far from us to have done like so then what benefit is there in transmitting it to us?!'*

Ends [the statement of Shaykh Afḍaluddīn].

We have mentioned in [a place] other than this epistle:

> *Whoever wants the cordiality for their fellows to last long must repel the saying of the talebearer at the onset of [its] mention.*

2.41 Defending Another's Reputation

It is from among the rights of a person over another person that he defends his reputation but [only] with a noble intention and in the best policy.

It is mentioned in a ḥadīth:

> *Someone who defends the reputation of his fellow, Allāh ﷻ will keep the Fire (of Hell) away from him on the Day of Judgement.*[108]

It is from among the sayings of Imām ash-Shāfiʿī:

> *It is from among the signs of someone who is honest in fellowship with his fellow that he accepts his defects, complements his deficiencies and forgives his lapses.*

[108] at-Tirmidhī, *al-Jāmiʿ*.

2.42 Waking Others for Prayers

It is from among the rights of a person over another person that he wakes him prior to the time [for prayer, etc.] so that when the time begins and he is on alert, his regular sunnah units [of ritual prayer] prior to the obligatory units are not missed – not even the consecratory *takbīr* (i.e. *taḥrīmah*)!

Likewise, it is from among his rights that he wakes him prior to dawn because taking care of the affairs of the *dīn* (religion of Islām) [i.e. spiritual life] are superior to and more excellent than taking care of the affairs of the material world [i.e. mundane life]. This ought to be done with gentleness because the ego might become active when awoken with harshness.

2.43 Wise Counsel and Irresponsible Flattery

It is from among the rights of a person over another person that he does not act irresponsibly with him.

It is mentioned in a ḥadīth:

Religion is to counsel.[109]

The People [of Verity] said:

> *Fellows are in goodness as long as they advise one another. When they make peace with one another [by not reforming each other,] they shall perish.*

2.43.1 The Difference Between Wise Counsel and Irresponsible Flattery

Among the differences between irresponsible flattery (*mudāhanah*) and wise counsel (*mudārāh*) is that the latter is when you intend welfare for your fellow whereas the former is something you resolve to do that is based on egotistic passions.

2.44 Self-Accusation on Another's Being Burdensome

It is from among the rights of a person over another person that he accuses his own self of arrogance and hypocrisy when he experiences a burden from him, and he ought to strive to remove it from within himself.

---

[109] Muslim, *al-Musnad aṣ-Ṣaḥīḥ*.

A man accompanied Abū Bakr al-Kattānī[110] (Allāh ﷺ have mercy on him) and he was a burden to his heart. He said:

> *I gave him something as a gift with the intention that it would remove his being burdensome to me but it did not go away. So, I was alone with him one day and said to him, 'Place your foot on my cheek!' but he refused, but then I said to him, 'It is imperative,' and so he did that. Thus, what was inside of me against him was removed.*[111]

2.45 Accepting the Counsel of Others

It is from among the rights of a person over another person that he accepts his advice. They [i.e. the Shaykhs] have said:

> *Someone who guides you to that which saves you from the anger of Allāh ﷻ has interceded for you; if you obey him and accept his advice then his intercession for you has been accepted and it will benefit you, otherwise [i.e. if you do not accept his advice] ...! We seek refuge with Allāh ﷻ from a people whom the intercession of interceders does not benefit such that they turn away from reminders.*

2.46 Awaiting One's Fellow When Entering Paradise

It is from among the rights of a person over another person that he firmly resolves not to enter Paradise when Allāh ﷻ admits him into it unless his fellow enters [it] - even if the duration in [the process of] accountability is long, and that he allows his [fellow's] partaking in his good deeds on the Day of Judgement.

2.47 Abstaining from Food and Drink

It is from among the rights of a person over another person that he does not eat or drink when his fellow falls into a sin or a calamity until Allāh ﷻ turns to him [in forgiveness] or He ﷻ relieves him of that calamity. Ibn Adham abstained [from eating and drinking] for forty days when a calamity fell upon a fellow, and he continued his abstention until it was removed from him.

---

[110] Abū Bakr Muḥammad ibn 'Alī ibn Ja'far al-Kattānī (d.322AH/933CE).

[111] Abu'l-Qāsim 'Abdulkarīm ibn Hawāzin al-Qushayrī (376AH/986CE - 465AH/1072CE), *ar-Risālat al-Qushayriyyah*, Bāb aṣ-Ṣuḥbah, p.327.

2.48 Abstaining from Minor Sins

It is from among the rights of a person over another person that he guides him in honouring the prohibitions of Allāh ﷻ and distancing himself from trespassing His ﷻ limits (*ḥudūd*), such that when he falls into the minutest of sins, he sees that minor sin to be from among the major sins being in complete opposition [to the commands of Allāh ﷻ]. Thus, he should continue doing that until he deems even a moment of being oblivious to Allāh ﷻ worse than committing unlawful sexual intercourse (*zinā*) or killing a person.

Thereafter, once the *sālik* (traveller to Allāh ﷻ) is accomplished, he turns to something more perfect than that and that is to take trespassing the limits (*ḥudūd*) of Allāh ﷻ with serious respect, according to what is mentioned in sacred law, because the servant obeys what has been legally prescribed; he holds the major sin graver than the minor sin, the minor sin worse than the disliked (*makrūh*) and the disliked worse than the unorthodox (*khilāf al-awlā*). The Lawgiver [i.e. the Messenger of Allāh] ﷺ has only explained the ranks of the limits (*ḥudūd*) [of Allāh ﷻ] to teach us their disparity, and so we honour them according to their ranks.

And likewise is the saying with regards to the division of the prescriptions; we honour the obligatory (*farḍ* and *wājib*) more than the optional (*mandūb*) and the optional more than the punctilio (*adab*). We act upon each of these according to the emphasis of the Lawgiver upon it. Thus, in his final state, the *sālik* returns to his initial form and the objective varies in status with regards to the disparity of the prescriptions and the prohibitions. In the beginning, the equality of the prescriptions and the prohibitions demand from the *sālik* intense honour for Allāh ﷻ and thus he honours His ﷻ prescriptions and His ﷻ prohibitions out of fear and in order to shut the door of opposing [Allāh ﷻ] while not paying attention to the wisdom behind their disparity, as has been reported in sacred law. That is where lies a high status and then a status that is even higher.

The saying of al-Junayd is mentioned in reference to what has been established:

> *I do not have a sin graver than being heedless of Allāh ﷻ.*

Surely, backbiting is a sin greater than heedlessness. However, it could be that he saw the reason for a servant's falling into sin was due to heedlessness of Allāh ﷻ.

2.49 Preventing Others from Expressing Their Spiritual Status

It is from among the rights of a person over another person that he orders him not to express the status [of saintliness] when he expects him to incline towards disclosure. Someone who likes to reveal [his own status] becomes the slave of disclosure. Anyone who proceeds to [be known to] the people prior to having the authority that is specific to him shall be taken to task and become a laughingstock to them. The *awliyā'* would not go out to the created beings except after they were warned of demotion if they did not.

Thus, the intelligent person is he who conceals his own status until Allāh ﷻ takes it upon Himself ﷻ to reveal him without his own ambition.

2.50 Being Apparently Hostile to the One Who is Hostile to Others

It is from among the rights of a person over another person that he demonstrates [outward] hostility towards someone who is unjustly hostile to his fellow. As for inward hostility, well that is not permitted, even [towards] the enemy of one's shaykh – inward hostility is not permitted against him. In fact, it is incumbent upon him merely to express his hostility towards him just as it is incumbent upon him to avoid someone with whom his shaykh is angry.

2.51 Standing for the Comer

It is from among the rights of a person over another person that he stands for him when he appears before him even if he dislikes it and especially in gatherings. Thus, they [i.e. the Shaykhs] have said:

> *You must not refrain from standing for your fellow in gatherings because resentment and malice may arise from [omitting] it and you will be unable to remove it afterwards.*

2.52 Not Lying to Others

It is from among the rights of a person over another person that he does not engage him in a conversation with lies because there is disparagement in it for him.

It is mentioned in a ḥadīth:

> *It is a huge disloyalty that you converse in a discussion with your fellow in which he is truthful to you but you are lying to him.*[112]

2.53 Supplicating for Others

It is from among the rights of a person over another person that he does not forget to pray for his forgiveness, pardon and mercy whenever he finds time exclusive with his Lord تعالى regardless of whether it is during the night or day, in prostration or otherwise.

2.54 Not Harbouring Malice

It is from among the rights of a person over another person that he does not harbour malice against him for [it is mentioned] in a ḥadīth:

> *Three are those that if they exist in any person Allāh تعالى will forgive him other than those; i. someone who dies without ascribing partners to Allāh تعالى, ii. he was not a sorcerer following magic, iii. he harboured no malice against his fellow.*[113]

The People [of Verity] said:

> *Anyone who harbours malice, deception, plotting or cheating against any of the people is an imposter in the Path of the People [of Verity]. It is not permitted for him to be a caller towards Allāh تعالى.*

2.55 Listening Well to Others

It is from among the rights of a person over another person that he raises his eyes towards him whenever his fellow speaks to him until he completes his conversation because that increases the purity of cordiality, just like being distracted away from the speaking of his

[112] Abū Dāwūd, *as-Sunan.*
[113] aṭ-Ṭabarānī, *al-Kabīr.*

fellow or by interrupting what he is saying prior to his completing it gives rise to aversion.

2.56 On Testing Others

It is from among the rights of a person over another person that he does not test him because testing is from the genus of exposing nakedness. They [i.e. the Shaykhs] said:

> *You must refrain from testing your fellows because Allāh does not test His servants unless He is sure of their fulfilling [it] so as not to embarrass them by revealing whatever of theirs is covered.*

It was said to al-Kubrā[114] (Allāh have mercy on him): "Do you not test your companions?" He replied: "In such case we will all appear with defects."

2.57 Meeting Others Honourably

It is from among the rights of a person over another person that he prepares to meet him with devotion and honour whenever he separates from him.

Shaykh Muḥiyyuddīn [ibn al-'Arabī] said: "... even if the duration of the separation is short," out of goodwill thinking that Allāh has presented him with a gift or placed him in a position to reach the hearts of His servants during any particular moment of the day or night, and so he reaches a status that is loftier than before. Thus, if that act is correct then he has fulfilled his [fellow's] right but if it is not correct then he has been good-mannered in the sight of Allāh. This is such that his dealing with that affair according to what the divine status requires of him is achieved by his honouring any person who comes to it.

He [also] said:

> *This affair is such that rarely does anyone immerse himself in it [and that is] because of the stronghold of heedlessness over the hearts.*

---

[114] Najmuddīn Aḥmad ibn 'Umar ibn Muḥammad al-Kubrā (540AH/1145CE – 618AH/1221CE).

2.58 Allowing Others to Repent

It is from among the rights of a person over another person that when he sees him doing something inappropriate, he should believe that he has repented since that time and is internally ashamed. Some of the predecessors used to say:

> *I am ashamed with Allāh ﷻ that I disrupted the repenting of someone who disobeyed his Lord ﷻ in front of me and then he screened himself from me behind a wall.*

They [also] said:

> *Whoever disrupts the repentance of any sinner, seeing himself to be essentially better than him, and every person who thinks himself to be more excellent than any of the [other] Muslims is a deluded ignoramus [regardless of] whatever honours he may have been given.*

2.59 Preserving Cordiality with Others

It is from among the rights of a person over another person that he preserves his cordiality out of respect for it even if the other becomes disloyal or goes astray.

Ibn al-Khaṭṭāb (Allāh ﷻ have mercy on him) said:

> *I saw the Mighty Lord ﷻ in a dream and I said, 'O Lord! Teach me something that I can take from You directly.' He ﷻ said: 'O Ibn al-Khaṭṭāb! One who does good to someone who has done bad to him, his gratitude to Allāh ﷻ is sincere. One who does bad to someone who has done good to him, he has repaid the favour of Allāh ﷻ with ingratitude.' Then, I said, 'O Allāh! It is enough for me!' and He ﷻ replied: 'It is enough for you.'*

Ends [the statement of Ibn al-Khaṭṭāb].

This matter has become very rare in this age; none but dogs remain its upholders – as is mentioned in the book *Faḍl al-Kilāb 'alā Kathīrin mi'm-Man Labisa ath-Thiyāb – The Superiority of Dogs Over Many Who Wear Clothes.*[115]

---

[115] The author of this book is Abū Bakr Muḥammad ibn Khalaf ibn Marzubān (d. ca. 309AH/921CE).

2.60 Not Reminding of Favours

It is from among the rights of a person over another person that he does not remind him of the favour that he has done to him when the other argues with him and has forgotten that favour. Reminding of favours during a quarrel is an indication of the lack of sincerity in it and a proof of lowly essence; [someone of] noble essence never reminds of the favour that he has done to his fellow, but rather, he sees the superiority in the fellow who ate with him, for instance, or accepted a gift from him.

It is mentioned in a ḥadīth:

> *Three are whom Allāh ﷻ will not look at on the Day of Judgement nor purify them - and they will have a painful punishment; i. one who trails his garments, ii. one who reminds of favours, and iii. one who sells his goods with a false oath.*[116]

Some of them said:

> *Reminding of favours during a quarrel is an abscess that never heals, i.e. it is not forgotten. In fact, it continues to pollute the companionship each time one mentions it.*

2.61 Avoiding Disputes

It is from among the rights of a person over another person that he does not dispute with him because disputation severs cordiality. They [i.e. the Shaykhs] have said:

> *Nothing is found to be more destructive to the dīn (i.e. religion of Islām) and more distracting to the heart than disputation.*

From arguing emerge anger, envy and deception, such that one may be in prayer whereas his mind might be stuck in disputes. It is clear what [dangers] lie therein.

It is mentioned in a ḥadīth:

> *It is enough as a sin for you that you remain disputative.*[117]

They sang:

[116] Muslim, *al-Musnad aṣ-Ṣaḥīḥ*.
[117] at-Tirmidhī, *al-Jāmi'*.

تجنبْ قرين السوء واصرمْ حبالَه فإن لم تجد عنه مُحيصا فدارِه

وأحبب قرين الصّدق واتركْ مراءَه تنلْ منه صفوَ الوُد ما لم تمارِه

Avoid the supporter of evil and sever ties with him.

If you find no refuge from him then be amicable with him.

Love the supporter of honesty and avoid disputing with him,

You'll gain purity of cordiality from him as long as you do not argue with him.

2.62 Avoid Hastening Abandonment

It is from among the rights of a person over another person that he does not hasten to abandon him because haste in something like this is not good; its mistake is greater than what is correct about it. We have mentioned the conditions of the permissibility of abandonment in [a place] other than this epistle.

2.63 Avoid Taking to Task

It is from among the rights of a person over another person that, out of regard for cordiality, he does not take him to task if he falls short in [fulfilling] his right.

It is from among the counsels of my Master 'Alī al-Khawwāṣ:

> *Leave as much of your right as you can for your fellow and forgive the missteps of the people of moral nobility and of decency from among your fellows. You must refrain from being offensive to someone who caused offence to you; Allāh ﷻ has not permitted causing offence without the condition of it being equal and to be equal is very difficult - you might be excessive, or the mistake might have a bigger impact on the dispute than it did on you. Thus, this consideration [for the retaliation to be equal] includes a dispensation for the weak.*

2.64 Compassion to the Children of Others

It is from among the rights of a person over another person to be continuously compassionate to his [fellow's] children and to stand [as their guardian] after his death. The People [of Verity] said:

> *One who is not compassionate to his fellow's children in his absence and does not stand [guard] for them after his death is not honest in his fellowship.*

2.65 Opposing Others on Innovations

It is from among the rights of a person over another person that he does not support him in any [religious] innovation. If he does not turn away from it, one must abandon him out of fear for his own self lest its ill-fortune might [also] affect him. The pious predecessors used to avoid sitting with the people of innovation and they would say:

> *Avoid keeping company with someone who has even the smallest form of innovation in him for whoever is lax in that its ill-fortune will affect him though maybe after a while.*

2.66 Avoiding to Marry a Fellow's Divorcée or Widow

It is from among the rights of a person over another person that he does not marry someone who had been his [fellow's] wife whom he had divorced or whom he left as his widow – even if he bequeathed that [request] and said: "You have more of a right than anyone else."

Conclusion to Chapter 2

Thus, my dear fellow, reflect your own self in what is mentioned in this chapter. If you see that it fulfils [the rights] then thank Allāh ﷻ or else seek forgiveness, day and night, for falling short in [fulfilling] the rights of your fellows.

All praise is to Allāh ﷻ - the Lord of all the worlds.

CHAPTER 3

The Etiquettes of the People [of Verity]

- Allāh ﷻ be pleased with them -

You should know – may Allāh ﷻ enable me and you that which He ﷻ loves – that the etiquettes of the People [of Verity] cannot be encompassed because they are a combination of what is in the Divine Books, Prophetic Reports, Narrations of the Companions ﷺ and of the Predecessors. However, we shall mention to you a portion of their etiquettes as a source of blessings and an opening of the door [to them]. Thus, we say, with the assistance of Allāh ﷻ:

3.1 Rushing to Allāh ﷻ for Help

It is from among the etiquettes of the People [of Verity] that they rush to Allāh ﷻ for all of their needs prior to [asking from] any of the created beings – based on their knowledge of revelation and witnessing that the sovereignty of all things is in the Power of Allāh ﷻ – as opposed to others who do not resort to Allāh ﷻ except after turning to his created beings [and not having their needs fulfilled].

3.2 Having the Presence of Heart

It is from among their etiquettes to bring the senses and the heart together when doing something. It has been reported in some of the Divine Scriptures:

> *Allāh ﷻ says to His angels – the Kirāman Kātibīn (Honourable Scribes): 'Record the deed of My such-and-such a servant. Record where his heart was during his deed so that he may take his reward from the One with Whom his heart was present.'*

It is from among the sayings of my Master 'Alī al-Khawwāṣ:

> *Every action where the servant is not present with his Lord ﷻ - it is like carrion! And it resembles hypocrisy! All that is*

> *because the people thought he was with Allāh ﷻ during his intimate discourses whereas he was with the created beings. The Path [of Verity] has become long [and difficult] for the people because of their heedlessness of it and so they have been screened off with [their] deeds from the objective for what they are done. Had they been focusing on the objective for what they are done they might have preoccupied themselves with it instead of the deeds.*

3.3 Refraining from Seeking Status and Reward

It is from among their etiquettes that they do not seek a station, [spiritual] state or divine proximity by their worship. They [i.e. the Shaykhs] have said:

> *Whoever serves Allāh ﷻ to acquire a station has in fact sought estrangement with Him ﷻ and whoever serves Him ﷻ to acquire a reward or out of the fear of punishment has in fact displayed his own greed and manifested his own ignobility.*

They also said:

> *The most wretched of created beings to Allāh ﷻ is someone who adulates Him ﷻ with obedience prior to dawn seeking therewith proximity to Him ﷻ.*

They also said:

> *Fulfil what you can of what the sacred law has commanded you, provided it is in accordance to its legal permissibility and command and not out of any other reason. Abandon all motives for all your actions and [spiritual] states and do not look at any reward because whoever looks at any reward for his actions, be it immediate or delayed, he has left the qualifications of servitude; there is no reward for servitude except for the pleasure of Allāh ﷻ.*

3.3 Investigating the State of the Limbs

It is from among their etiquettes to investigate their outward and inward limbs in the morning and in the evening; did they honour or transgress the limits set for them by Allāh ﷻ; did they or did they not uphold with sincerity what they have been instructed with regards to lowering the gaze, protecting the tongue, the ear, the heart and other aspects? If they see any of their limbs being obedient, they thank Allāh ﷻ because they do not consider themselves capable of that, but if they see them stained with any sin, they begin to seek forgiveness and express remorse followed by their being grateful to Allāh تعالى that He تعالى did not enable them [to commit] more sins than those, and that their limbs that sinned were not taken to task during their state of sinning; surely, every limb that sins deserves calamity to befall it when it is sinning.

3.4 Investigating the Inner Self

It is from among their etiquettes that they do not neglect to investigate their inner selves as there are secret base characteristics inside the servant [of Allāh تعالى]. It is well known that as the *faqīrs* make progress through the [spiritual] stations, their falling into apparent sin is mostly non-existent. However, if any of them do fall into [an apparent sin] and forget to investigate their inner selves, it is a decline in status for the People of Divine Gnosis (*Ahl al-'Irfān*). Anyone who believes that base characteristics have ended in him is fantasising.

Allāh تعالى says:

﴿ وَمَن يُوقَ شُحَّ نَفْسِهِۦ فَأُو۟لَٰٓئِكَ هُمُ ٱلْمُفْلِحُونَ ﴾

And those who are saved from the stinginess of their selves, it is they who are successful. (59:9)[118]

He تعالى did not say: "And those who have ended the stinginess of their selves," because He تعالى lets stinginess remain inside the self, except that, despite it being there, the servant fulfils the act with protection from Allāh تعالى.

It is from among the sayings of Shaykh Afḍaluddīn:

> *Surely, Allāh تعالى has placed all of the opposites of all the base and praiseworthy characteristics in the natural disposition of humans that they appear and disappear in them. However, as long as divine protection surrounds the servant, all of the base characteristics are silent [and] inactive [i.e. they are dormant]. However, when [divine] protection leaves him, the base characteristics stir into [being subject to] exploitation and his good characteristics become silent.*

[118] Holy Qur'ān, Sūrat al-Ḥashr (59), Verse 9.

Then again, it is clear that Allāh ﷻ has purified the natural disposition of the Prophets ﷺ of all basenesses by providing protection. [Dear fellow!] Understand and avoid mistakes!

3.5 Refraining from Making Promises

It is from among their etiquettes not to attach themselves to promises, and thus they do not make a promise to anyone except in rare cases because they know well that true promises only come from Prophets ﷺ due to their being free of sin. As for others, they sometimes might make promises and then break them, and [consequently] one trait of hypocrisy will appear within them.

3.6 Being the Teacher's Servant

It is from among their etiquettes that when they are asked of their shaykh they ought to say: "I am his servant," or "... from among those who go to him," and not say, "I am his companion," for the status of companionship is surely something great since the companion of a person is 'he who drinks from the same ocean' – as has already passed [mention] at the beginning of this epistle.

3.7 Elevating the Status of Colleagues in their Absence

It is from among their etiquettes that if any of his colleagues is mentioned in absentia in his presence, he does not say: "He is one of my colleagues," or [even] "... from among my senior colleagues," unless he [i.e. the colleague] is lower than them by many ranks. If he is equal or superior to them [in rank], he should say: "I am from among his followers," or "... [from among] his servants."

3.8 Not Claiming the Seniors to Have Perished

It is from among their etiquettes that they do not say: "The seniors and the honest have gone [i.e. they no longer exist]," for in reality they have not gone [i.e. they do exist]; they are like the treasure of the 'owner of the wall'.[119]

Allāh ﷻ bestows upon whoever comes later in time what He ﷻ had concealed from the people of the previous age; Allāh ﷻ bestowed

[119] It is said that Khaḍir ﷺ knows of this treasure.

upon our Prophet Muḥammad ﷺ what He ﷻ did not bestow upon the Prophets عليهم السلام prior to him ﷺ, and then He ﷻ praised him ﷺ prior to them عليهم السلام.

It is from among the sayings of the author of *al-Ḥikam*[120]:

> *Instead of your saying, 'Where are the awliyā'? Where are the righteous?' say, 'Where is insight?' Is it appropriate for the defiler of virgins to see the daughter of the King?*

Ends [the statement of Ibn 'Aṭā'ullāh (Allāh ﷻ have mercy on him)].

Words like these do not come [from anyone] except one who has no belief in the *awliyā'* and scholars of his time. It is clear what [dangers] lie therein.

3.9 Not Seeking the Absence of Opposition

It is from among their etiquettes that they do not seek not to have someone who envies them because entification into existence (*al-ḥukm al-wujūdī*) necessitates an opposition to blessings through envy. Thus, someone who desires not to have an envier is essentially seeking not to have any blessings [at all].

3.10 Not Stating the Power of Allāh ﷻ When They Mention Their Own Sins

It is from among their etiquettes that when they mention their [own] sins, they do not say upon them: "*lā ḥawla wa-lā quwwata illā bi'Llāh* – There is no ability or power except through Allāh ﷻ," because it entails the sense of seeking proof from Allāh ﷻ. Rather, they say:

﴿ رَبَّنَا ظَلَمْنَآ أَنفُسَنَا وَإِن لَّمْ تَغْفِرْ لَنَا وَتَرْحَمْنَا لَنَكُونَنَّ مِنَ ٱلْخَٰسِرِينَ ﴾

Our Lord! We have wronged our selves, and if You do not forgive us and have mercy on us, we shall certainly be from among the losers. (7:23)[121]

Individually [one says]:

[120] Tājuddīn Aḥmad ibn 'Aṭā'ullāh al-Iskandarī (658AH/1259CE – 709AH/1310CE).
[121] Holy Qur'ān, Sūrat al-A'rāf (7), Verse 23.

رَبِّ ظَلَمْتُ نَفْسِيْ فَاغْفِرْ لِيْ، إِنَّكَ أَنْتَ الْغَفُوْرُ الرَّحِيْمُ.

My Lord! I have wronged myself. Forgive me! Verily, You are the Most-Forgiving, the Ever-Merciful.

3.11 Not Being Congenial with Allāh تعالى

It is from among their etiquettes that they do not say: "We are sociable with Allāh تعالى," because humans cannot be sociable with other than their own species. There is no sociability between Allāh تعالى and His تعالى servants in any respect. Thus, if you see in the expression of any of the people that the servant is sociable with Allāh تعالى then you should know that he has not done any research. However, had he investigated he would have found his sociability to be with that which is from Allāh تعالى and not with Allāh تعالى Himself – due to the absence of homogeneity.

It is likewise that the jinn (spirits) are not amiable with any of us [humans]. Rather, every human hair stands on end when one sees a jinn!

Just as it is not correct to be sociable with Allāh تعالى, it is likewise not correct to delight in Him تعالى. The People [of Verity] said:

> *Such is the command for us in both the worlds. The Lawgiver [i.e. the Messenger of Allāh] ﷺ has not explained the reason behind the delight when the Beatific Vision takes places for us but rather he ﷺ has said: 'They have not been given any delight compared to that of their beholding their Lord تعالى,' and this is a delight that we cannot currently comprehend.*

3.12 Seeking Divine Gnosis

It is from among their etiquettes that they do not say: "We seek Allāh تعالى," because seeking is only for something lost whereas Allāh تعالى is present; reaching Him تعالى cannot be sought as there is no extent to Him تعالى. Rather, we seek the path to the cognisance of Allāh تعالى.

3.13 Seeking Divine Protection

It is from among their etiquettes that they do not seek protection with Allāh تعالى from anything [per sé] other than from its evil. Likewise, they do not say: "O Allāh تعالى! Free us from all of Your created beings," but they say: "(O Allāh ﷻ!) Free us from the evil of Your created beings."

3.14 Avoiding Embellished Statements

It is from among their etiquettes not to embellish the messages that they write to their fellows out of the fear of falsity.

It is from among the counsels of Abū Naṣr Bishr al-Ḥāfī:

> *When any of you writes a letter to someone, he ought not embellish it with wonderful words because once I wrote a letter and it occurred to me that I should write something that, had I written it, it would have adorned the letter but it would have been a lie, and if I omitted it, the letter would have been dull but it would have been truthful. So, I decided to mention dull honest words, when a caller proclaimed from the side of the house:*

﴿ يُثَبِّتُ اللّٰهُ الَّذِيْنَ اٰمَنُوْا بِالْقَوْلِ الثَّابِتِ فِى الْحَيٰوةِ الدُّنْيَا وَفِى الْاٰخِرَةِ ﴾

Those who believe, Allāh ﷻ keeps them firm in the life of this world as well as in the Hereafter with this Firm Word.(14:27)[122]

3.15 Seeking Divine Forgiveness when People Trust Them

It is from among their etiquettes that when the people have faith in them they seek forgiveness [from Allāh ﷻ] abundantly because they are secretly opposed to it.

It is mentioned in a ḥadīth:

Blessed are those in whose records seeking an abundance of forgiveness is found.[123]

They [i.e. the People of Verity] have encouraged concerning oneself with seeking forgiveness night and day irrespective of whether or not he mentions the sins specifically.

3.16 Seeking Divine Forgiveness when People Praise Them

It is from among their etiquettes that when they are praised, they express gratitude and seek forgiveness [from Allāh ﷻ] abundantly, and they say:

---

[122] Holy Qur'ān, Sūrat Ibrāhīm (14), Verse 27.
[123] Ibn Mājah, *as-Sunan*.

O Allāh تعالى*! You know about us more than they do. O Allāh* تعالى*! Make us better than what they think [of us] and do not take us to task for what they say. Forgive us regarding what they do not know [about us].*[124]

3.17 Avoiding Reliance on Earnings

It is from among their etiquettes that they do not rely on what they earn; reliance on one's earnings is associating partners with Allāh تعالى. We have mentioned in [a place] other than this epistle[125] how to identify the manner of ridding oneself of this [form of] associating partners with Allāh تعالى, and that anyone who rids himself of it is the Believer to whom come provisions whence he cannot even imagine.

3.18 Not Making Claim of Good Deeds

It is from among their etiquettes not to attribute anything of good deeds to their own selves except only to the extent of ascribing responsibility.

The People [of Verity] said:

> *A deed is not acceptable when its witnessing is attributed to the servant. Thus, one whose deed is witnessed, his such deed is from himself and not from his Lord* تعالى*. One who sees truly will know that doing something that must be done has no effect on the created beings, but rather, it only has a ruling upon it. Most people do not differentiate between the ruling and the effect.*

It is from among the sayings of my Master 'Alī al-Khawwāṣ:

> *The servant will remain screened as long as he continues to attribute affairs to his own self as his own passion and knowledge being Allāh's* تعالى*. Thus, when the screen is removed, he will see all his deeds as created beings of Allāh* تعالى *but not his own passion. The [spiritual] state of the disciple is not complete until he witnesses all his deeds as creations of Allāh* تعالى *as [His* تعالى*] passions. As for his [merely] knowing that they are the creation of Allāh* تعالى*, it is insufficient for him since knowledge is not like passion.*

He also said:

---

[124] al-Bayhaqī, *Shu'ab al-Īmān*.
[125] ash-Sha'rānī, *Laṭā'if al-Minan wa'l-Akhlāq*.

For most of the disciples, firm-footedness in the monotheism of their deeds is not established. Likewise, they seek reward from Allāh ﷻ for what good deeds took place at their own hands. They also seek reward from the people when Allāh ﷻ renders by their [i.e. the disciples] hands favours to them [i.e. the people]. Had they not ascribed that [favour] to their own selves they would not seek reward from Allāh ﷻ and nor from the people. The gnostic would never say:

﴿ اِيَّاكَ نَعْبُدُ وَاِيَّاكَ نَسْتَعِيْنُ ﴾

We worship only You, and we ask for help only from You.
(1:4)[126]

other than merely on the basis of recitation and not on the basis of it being a partnership in the works [of Allāh ﷻ]. The works of Allāh ﷻ are above and beyond being associated to. Understand!

3.19 Withdrawing from Status and Wealth

It is from among their etiquettes to withdraw from [social] status and wealth, and to attribute oneself to lowliness and poverty whenever they turn their attention to Allāh ﷻ in the affairs of this world or of the Hereafter so that they are not hindered from [receiving] a response [from Allāh ﷻ].

It is from among their sayings:

Whenever you turn your attention to Allāh ﷻ, then do so as if you are a lowly beggar because your wealth and your [glorious] status, though they are from Allāh ﷻ, deprive you from the [anticipated] response; wealth and glory are two attributes with which the servant ought never approach Allāh ﷻ because the presence of Allāh ﷻ is of [divine] inherent position that does not accept the glorious [person] and nor the wealthy.

3.20 Asking Allāh ﷻ by Proxy

It is from among their etiquettes that they do not ask from Allāh ﷻ anything regarding the affairs of either of the two worlds but by proxy and by referring the knowledge back to Allāh ﷻ. This is in observance of the general [meaning of the] saying of Allāh ﷻ:

---

[126] Holy Qur'ān, Sūrat al-Fātiḥah (1), Verse 4.

﴿ وَعَسَىٰٓ أَن تَكۡرَهُواْ شَيۡـٔٗا وَهُوَ خَيۡرٞ لَّكُمۡۖ وَعَسَىٰٓ أَن تُحِبُّواْ شَيۡـٔٗا وَهُوَ شَرّٞ لَّكُمۡۚ وَٱللَّهُ يَعۡلَمُ وَأَنتُمۡ لَا تَعۡلَمُونَ ﴾

It may be that you do not like something when it is good for you, and it may be that you like something when it is bad for you. Allāh ﷻ knows but you do not know. (2:216)[127]

Thus, when asking [from Allāh ﷻ], any one of them can say: "O Allāh! Give me such-and-such if there is any good in it for me, and remove from me such-and-such if there is any bad in it for me."

It is from among the counsels of my Master 'Abdulqādir al-Jīlī[128] (Allāh ﷻ have mercy on him):

> *Beware of asking anything from Allāh ﷻ without a proxy. If He ﷻ bestows something upon you without [your] asking then it is blessed and its end will be a fine one, and if Allāh ﷻ wills, you will not be held accountable for it since it came without self-ambition.*

3.21 Not Being Preoccupied with Benefits

It is from among their etiquettes not to be preoccupied with a favour from the Benefactor ﷻ since it is disgraceful for the servant to be attached to the favour, or to incline to it, without [attaching or inclining to] the Benefactor ﷻ; surely, inclining to anything other than Allāh ﷻ is loathsome, other than [in connection] to the rights and commands of Allāh ﷻ.

It is from among the counsels of my Master 'Abdulqādir al-Jīlī:

> *You must avoid preoccupying yourself with whatever wealth Allāh ﷻ has bestowed upon you lest He ﷻ should veil you by it from Him ﷻ in this world and the next. It is possible for that wealth to despoil you as a lesson to you. However, if you preoccupy yourself in His ﷻ obedience using that wealth, it shall be praiseworthy wealth rather than loathsome.*

---

[127] Holy Qur'ān, Sūrat al-Baqarah (2), Verse 216.
[128] 'Abdulqādir al-Jīlānī - al-Ghawth al-A'ẓam (470AH/1077CE – 561AH/1166CE).

3.22 Being Reclusive in the Early Stages of Seeking

It is from among their etiquettes to prefer reclusion in the early stages [of this path] but not in the later stages. This is because, owing to his weakness, something minor might distract the beginner away from Allāh ﷾ whereas such is not the case with the advanced [seeker] since he has recognised Allāh ﷾ with the gnosis that is well known among the People [of Verity] – he has become someone whom nothing distracts away from Allāh ﷾. However, created beings are not independent from him in [one of] two circumstances:

1. if any of [the created beings] are wayward, it is incumbent on him to get close to them in order to correct their waywardness
2. but if they are on the straight [path], then he may seek benefit from them in knowledge and etiquettes.

We never said: "The created beings are not independent from him in *three* circumstances, [the third] of which we regard the created beings to be equal to him in two connections," [because in reference] to their [i.e. the People of Verity's] saying: "There are no two existing things equal in every respect, and nothing is left out but the excess or the deficiency." Likewise, the statement about [enduring] extreme hunger at the initial stages of embarking on this path when they have food with them is a struggle against their egos. As for the state of their being accomplished, they do not feel any hunger unless they lose the food because they are required to fulfil the rights of what their limbs need, and they are taken to task for their oppressing their own selves against the wishes of Allāh ﷾ after accomplishment. This is opposed to their responsibilities at the initial stages of their affair [i.e. in pursuing the Path of Verity].

It is from here that it is said:

> *The hunger of the seniors is incumbent and not optional, as opposed to their initial stages when they remain hungry out of choice, with the presence of food, in order to punish their egos so as to render them obedient when they are called to the wishes of Allāh ﷾. Prior to training and disciplining (riyāḍah), egos are like wild beasts.*

3.23 Showing Mercy to Muslims

It is from among their etiquettes to show mercy to Muslims, [as] it is mentioned in a ḥadīth:

> *The Divinely-Compassionate (Allāh) ﷻ is merciful to those who show mercy.*[129]

It is from among the counsels of my Master 'Alī al-Khawwāṣ:

> *You must be merciful to Muslims if you wish to be shown mercy to. That you bear their sorrows is from being merciful to them.*

He [also] said:

> *You must know that our bearing the sorrows of our fellow Muslims does not oppose submitting [oneself to the decree of Allāh ﷻ], unlike what some people think. The servant bears the sorrow of his fellow in accordance to their having earned sins - for which they are liable to the calamity that has befallen them, and he acknowledges in accordance to the divine decree for which the knowledge has come to pass. Thus, it is impossible to repel something like that. Understand!*

A group of ignorant shaykhs are mistaken in this regard - believing they themselves are submitting to Allāh ﷻ while they reject anyone whom they see bearing the sorrow of his fellows. They say: "Why is so-and-so opposing divine decrees,"- and they think that which they follow is more correct but it is ignorance.

It is mentioned in a ḥadīth:

> *Someone who does not bear the interests of Muslims is not from among them.*

In [different] words, [it is mentioned]:

> *Someone who is not concerned with the affairs of the Muslims is not from among them.*[130]

Imām 'Umar ibn al-Khaṭṭāb[131] ؓ would not laugh at all after a calamity had befallen the Muslims until that calamity had been

---

[129] Abū Dāwūd, *as-Sunan*.
[130] aṭ-Ṭabarānī, *al-Awsaṭ*.
[131] 'Umar ibn al-Khaṭṭāb, the second Caliph of Muslims (38BH/586CE - 23AH/644CE).

removed, and likewise 'Umar ibn 'Abdul'azīz[132], Sufyān ath-Thawrī[133] and 'Aṭā' as-Sulamī[134] (Allāh ﷻ have mercy on them all).

He [i.e. 'Alī al-Khawwāṣ) said:

> *It is of the status of the Quṭb (Spiritual Pole) that he can bear calamities that even mountains cannot endure. Thus, all the calamities against the inhabitants of the earth fall on him first and then they transfer from him on to the two Imāms, thereafter to the Abdāl (Substitutes). They continue to transfer until they become widespread among the companions of [ṣūfī] circles and of [spiritual] stations. Thus, when they have covered everything after that, they are apportioned between the general Muslim populace. One might be seen to be in a difficult and constricted [situation] such that he might perish whereas its reason may not be known. Well, this is its reason!*

It is from here that they [i.e. the People of Verity] say:

> *Mercy is specific and calamity is common, because it is [all] from the mere mercy of Allāh ﷻ upon the sinners; if all of their calamity descended on them with regards to what they deserve in accordance to their sins, Allāh ﷻ would wipe out their existence. Therefore, it is apportioned among the people such that each is afflicted with [such] a small amount that he hardly notices it.*

3.24 Having Concern for Muslims

It is from among their etiquettes to be concerned about Muslims in the evening and the morning, according to what has been narrated in [Qur'ānic] verses and [Prophetic] reports [on what we ought] to be concerned about: their crops from [the harms of] caterpillars [and other pests], their bridges from rebels [and offenders], the River Nile [or other flowing body of water] until its normal [beneficial] extent is reached, and fruits when [intense] heat or intense cold is experienced that hurls the blossom [afar].

---

[132] 'Umar ibn 'Abdul'azīz (d.101AH/719CE).
[133] Sufyān ath-Thawrī (d.261AH/874CE).
[134] 'Aṭā' as-Sulamī (d.132AH/749CE).

3.25 Refraining from Complaining to Created Beings

It is from among their etiquettes to not make complaints to created beings of calamities and afflictions, etc., that befall them.

It is from among the counsels of my Master 'Abdulqādir al-Jīlī:

> *Refrain from complaining to your Lord تعالى when you are physically healthy or when you have the strength to bear that calamity with the power that Allāh تعالى has strengthened you. If you say, 'I have no power or ability [to bear it],' or if you complain of it to the created beings when you have so many favours that Allāh تعالى has bestowed upon you, and with that complaint you seek more from the created beings when you yourself have been blessed with favours and relief, then you must refrain from complaining to created beings of your struggle even if it rips apart your flesh. Verily, most calamities that descend upon humans are because of their complaints. How can any servant complain to the One تعالى Who is more Merciful to him than his [own] compassionate mother!?*

3.26 Being Profusely Grateful

It is from among their etiquettes to be profusely grateful for the favours in obedience to the [divine] command and not for seeking more [of them].

It is from among their [i.e. the People of Verity's] sayings:

> *You must be grateful for the favours [of Allāh تعالى upon you]; someone who is not grateful for the favours is prepared to lose them. Refrain from expressing gratitude for your own sake, but rather, make your gratitude in obedience to the command of your Lord تعالى. It is thus that Allāh تعالى has said:*

﴿ أَنِ اشْكُرْ لِي ﴾

That you must be grateful to Me. (31:14)[135]

Understand!

[135] Holy Qur'ān, Sūrah Luqmān (31), Verse 14.

3.27 Concealing One's Spiritual Station

It is from among their etiquettes to be highly secretive when concealing their [spiritual] station. They [i.e. the People of Verity] have said:

> *The accomplished is he who breaks his ego down such that his Lord ﷻ purifies it.*

They also said:

> *Excellent is the tiller's sowing what he sows and then covers it up after he has sown it that it grows inside the belly of the earth. What grows on top of [the land] is bad because there is no firmness in it.*

They also said:

> *The veracious should not pay importance to expressing his status that entails him to acquire assistance from created beings. If he is within the Light of Verity then it will shine [of its own accord,] with the permission of Allāh ﷻ:*
>
> ﴿ وَكَفَىٰ بِاللَّهِ وَلِيًّا وَكَفَىٰ بِاللَّهِ نَصِيرًا ﴾
>
> *Allāh ﷻ is enough as a guardian, and Allāh ﷻ is enough as a helper. (4:45)*[136]
>
> *If, however, he is in a void darkness and it results in the expression of his status and publicising it, he will not [be able to] utilise it even if it is given to him for utilising, except a little:*
>
> ﴿ وَاللَّهُ أَشَدُّ بَأْسًا وَأَشَدُّ تَنكِيلًا ﴾
>
> *Allāh ﷻ is strongest in power and firm in punishment. (4:84)*[137]

3.28 Avoiding Mundane Planning

It is from among their etiquettes to avoid planning. [Planning] is of two kinds: i. commendable planning, and ii. blameworthy planning.

1. Commendable [planning] is that which leads you closer to Allāh ﷻ - such as planning to free oneself from blame regarding the rights of the servants [of Allāh ﷻ] - be they

---

[136] Holy Qur'ān, Sūrat an-Nisā' (4), Verse 45.
[137] Holy Qur'ān, Sūrat al-Baqarah (2), Verse 216.

to fulfil [rights] or to legitimise [something],- and [such as] to render repentance valid and anything that leads to the subduing of desire and [also the influence of] Shayṭān.

2. Blameworthy [planning] is the planning of the mundane to acquire the mundane, planning to amass it to show pride in it or to increase it. Each time any portion of it increases, heedlessness and delusion increase [with it]. Its sign is that it distracts one from being attune [to divine commands] and it leads to him opposing [them].

As for planning this world for the Hereafter, there is no harm in it, such as someone planning to be a profiteer in order that he may consume the wholesome lawful of it and give it to the famine-stricken that they may preserve their dignity from begging. Its signs are that there is no seeking abundance or hoarding, but [rather providing] relief and altruism with it.

3.29 Leaving Choices with Allāh تعالى

It is from among their etiquettes to leave the choice with Allāh تعالى. They [i.e. the People of Verity] have mentioned that when the Banū Isrā'īl were given a choice with Allāh تعالى they were covered with dishonour and misery.

They [i.e. the People of Verity] said:

> *You must refrain from fleeing from any situation in which Allāh تعالى places you because goodness lies in that which Allāh تعالى chooses for you. Ponder over when Prophet 'Īsā عليه السلام fled from the Banū Isrā'īl after they venerated him عليه السلام - how he عليه السلام was worshipped besides Allāh تعالى, and he عليه السلام ended up in a situation worse than that whence he عليه السلام had fled.*

They also said:

> *The essence of the choice [given] to the servant is for him to believe that he himself is a created being and that Allāh تعالى did not create him but for Himself تعالى. Therefore, He تعالى does not bestow anything upon His تعالى servant unless it is valid for it to be for Himself تعالى.*

They also said:

> *You must not place your confidence in anything and nor seek refuge from anything with Allāh's تعالى plan - or even from nothing at all, and nor should you exercise a choice as you do*

> *not know whether or not you will achieve what you have chosen. Thereafter, if you do achieve it, you will not know whether or not there is any good in it for you. If you do not acquire it then be grateful to whoever hindered you from it as they have not hindered you out of miserliness. When Allāh ﷻ selects you for a matter then choose 'not to choose' and do not depend on anything. Do not grieve over anything that leaves you for had it been for you it would not have left you, and do not rejoice over anything that comes to your possession from among the matters of [either of] the two worlds - except for Allāh ﷻ; anything other than Allāh ﷻ is nothing.*

They also said:

> *Do not choose to attract favours and nor to dispel calamity; favours will come to you through fate [regardless of] whether you attract them or dispel them, and calamity will disengage from you [regardless of] whether you dispel it or dislike it. Thus, you must submit to Allāh ﷻ in everything - He ﷻ does as He ﷻ wills. If favours come to you then busy yourself in dhikr (remembrance) and shukr (gratitude), but if calamity afflicts you then hold firmly to patience and compliance - or consent, and enjoy them according to the situations that are given to you - until you meet the Supreme Friend [i.e. Allāh] ﷻ, and you are made to stand at the station of the utmost honest [servants of Allāh ﷻ] who have gone ahead.*

3.30 Being Content Without Desires

It is from among their etiquettes that they are pleased with the lowest that the ego likes from the desires of this world and that they remain firm when Allāh ﷻ constricts them financially. Thereafter, it is clear that someone who is pleased with the lowest that the ego likes from the desires of this world, there will be no dispute or animosity between him and anyone else, and his heart and soul will be at ease against the fatigue of seeking to acquire more than what is needed. He will be content if he is given [merely] a piece of barley and he will be grateful to Allāh ﷻ for it, and he will [also] be content if he is given [merely] a grain and he will be grateful to Allāh ﷻ for it. If any extra matter comes to him after that, he will express further gratitude [to Allāh ﷻ] in word and in deed.

3.31 Attributing to Oneself with the Presence of Mind

It is from among their etiquettes that they do not attribute anything to themselves except with the presence [of mind] that it is from the favours of Allāh ﷻ upon them – they do not heedlessly attribute it to themselves and nor claim ownership [of it].

3.32 Not Repulsing Those in Need

It is from among their etiquettes that they do not say to those who seek them in need: "Go away and come to us at another time."

They do not hold [anything] back from a beggar – not due to a grudge and nor out of miserliness, unless it be due to a logical reason.

3.33 Not Attaching Themselves to Places

It is from among their etiquettes that they do not attach themselves to any place in which the people honour them and from which they fear tribulation.

3.34 Speaking Less Over Food

It is from among their etiquettes to speak less when eating for they are in reality sitting at the dining-spread of Allāh ﷻ; Allāh ﷻ is observing them, their etiquettes, their altruism for one another and their gratitude to Him ﷻ.

3.35 Not Eating from the Middle

Likewise, it is from among their etiquettes that they do not eat from the middle of the container – in observance of the ḥadīth:

Surely, blessings emerge from the middle of the container. Therefore, you should eat from its edges and you must not eat from its middle.[138]

3.36 Accepting Invitations of the Devout

It is from among their etiquettes to accept when their devout fellow invites them to his food.

It is from among the sayings of my Master 'Alī al-Khawwāṣ:

---

[138] at-Tirmidhī, *al-Jāmi'*.

> *You should accept and please your devout fellow when he invites you to his food. Do not accept [the invitation of] a wrongdoer or a sinner, someone who deals in usury (ribā') or of someone who specifies his invitation to the wealthy without [inviting] the poor. When you have eaten, do not move away until the dining-spread is lifted as this is the practice of the Pious Predecessors. When you wash your hand, pray for blessings and seek permission to leave.*

3.37 Not Eating Alone

It is from among their etiquettes that they do not eat alone as it is reported that the worst of people is someone who eats on his own.

It is in the counsels of my Master 'Alī al-Khawwāṣ:

> *Do not eat on your own or in the dark, do not waste anything from the food; it is only presented to you that you eat it and not that you drop it on the ground. So, turn to that which has fallen on the ground and eat it for it has been mentioned in a report:*
>
> *Surely, someone who eats what has dropped, Allāh تعالى will remove insanity, leprosy and leucoderma from him, as well as from his child and his grandchild, until the fourth [generation] from his household.*

3.37.1 Not Turning the Face Away when Drinking

However, it is not from among their etiquettes to turn their faces away from those present when drinking.

Shaykh Najmuddīn al-Kubrā said:

> *When any of you drinks, he should do so with his face towards the people. He should not turn his face away from them as some people do with the intention of showing respect. When any of you have finished washing their hand, they should pray for whoever poured [the water] for them in the manner, 'Allāh تعالى purify you of sins.'*

3.38 When Cleansing Oneself

It is from among their etiquettes that when they cleanse [after relieving] themselves they use their hand from inside the cloth and they apprehend their right hand touching their private part – all out of honour for the Holy Qur'ān, books of knowledge and the rosary that they use when glorifying [Allāh تعالى].

It is from among the sayings of Shaykh Afḍaluddīn:

> *I feel ashamed of entering the lavatory in the clothes that I performed ritual prayer or to recite the Qur'ān when I have spoken a bad word. I will probably refrain from reciting [the Holy Qur'ān] for a long time when [after] I have spoken a bad word - until I have forgotten that [bad] word. Likewise, I feel ashamed to touch my private part with my right hand.*

He [also] said:

> *It has reached us from one of the [Prophetic] Companions ﷺ that, until he died, he did not touch his private part with his right hand ever since he pledged allegiance with the Messenger of Allāh ﷺ.*
>
> *It has also reached me regarding one of the disciples of Shaykh Najmuddīn al-Kubrā that his hand touched his private part while [he was] in privacy, and so it became difficult for him to open [the door of the room]. After it opened and he came out, his Master [i.e. Shaykh Najmuddīn al-Kubrā] said to him, 'My dear son! I knew that your hand had touched your private part while you were in privacy, and so your opening [the door] was delayed because of that. How can any of you sit before Allāh ﷻ while having placed his hand on his private part? Nevertheless, I know [with certainty] that someone who is in private is in the presence of Allāh ﷻ.'*

3.39 Curtailing the Garments

It is from among their etiquettes to curtail their garments. Shaykh al-Baṣrī said concerning the saying of Allāh ﷻ:

﴿ وَثِيَابَكَ فَطَهِّرْ ﴾

Keep your clothes clean. (74:4)[139]

meaning: curtail [them].

3.40 Praising Allāh ﷻ When Putting on New Clothes

It is from among their etiquettes, when they don new clothes, they do not forget to say:

> *All praise is to Allāh ﷻ Who clothed me in this and provided me with it without there being any ability or strength in me -*

[139] Holy Qur'ān, Sūrat al-Muddathir (74), Verse 4.

according to what Abū Dāwūd has reported from Mu'ādh ibn Anas ﷺ, who said:

> *The Messenger of Allāh ﷺ said: 'Someone who eats food and says, 'All praise is to Allāh ﷻ Who provided me with this without there being any ability or strength in me,' his previous sins are forgiven, and someone who dons new clothes and says, 'All praise is to Allāh ﷻ Who clothed me in this and provided it to me without there being any ability or strength in me,' his previous and future sins are forgiven."*[140]

3.41 Honouring the People of Spiritual Transmission

It is from among their etiquettes to honour the People of the Legally Qualified Spiritual Transmission, and to respect them in compliance to the sacred law because they are shaped by etiquettes with Allāh ﷻ and with the world [itself] even though they may not be aware of it.

3.42 Respecting the Scholars

It is from among their etiquettes to respect, out of love for the Messenger of Allāh ﷺ, the scholars and those who bear the Holy Qur'ān because they carry the sacred law.

3.43 Not Passing One's Teachers while Mounted

It is from among their etiquettes that they do not pass while mounted by someone who taught them anything from the Holy Qur'ān, even though they [themselves] may have become the shaykhs of the age. [Moreover,] they do not walk in front of him; they do not forget to give him presents, to express gratitude [to him] or to make supplications [for him]; they do not marry the woman he divorced or his widow; they do not take up any office from which he has been deposed even if they are requested to – all because he is a spiritual father.

When Shaykh Shamsuddīn ad-Dīrūṭī[141] (Allāh ﷻ have mercy on him) – the man of the tower at Dimyat[142], would pass by a jurist, he would alight from his mount, drive it in front of him and kiss his hand,

[140] Abū Dāwūd, *as-Sunan*.

[141] Shaykh Shamsuddīn Aḥmad ibn Muḥammad ad-Dīrūṭī ad-Dimyāṭī (d.921AH/1515CE) was one of the teachers of Imām ash-Sha'rānī.

[142] Dimyat (Dimyāṭ) is a city approximately 200 kilometres (125 miles) northeast of Cairo.

even though he himself might have reached the extents of knowledge or even commented on the *Minhāj*, etc. Thereafter, he would not remount until he was very far from him or if he disappeared from him behind a wall, etc. His jurist [i.e. the one whom he had respected], who is someone in the ruling of the jurists of the academies, might not have exceeded beyond memorising the Holy Qur'ān other than the essential. There are few who do likewise in these times [of ours].

3.44 Not Seeking Leadership

It is from among their etiquettes that, even though its conditions do exist in them, they do not take up the seat of being a shaykh except by approval from Allāh ﷻ, from its Greatest Doorway [i.e. the Holy Prophet] ﷺ or from a shaykh who is a gnostic and gives good counsel. There are certainly blessings in approval as well as protection from future calamities. Approval from Allāh ﷻ means *true inspiration.*

3.45 Not Relinquishing the World

It is from among their etiquettes that they do not relinquish [anything of] the world, so as [to seek] physical comfort or a reduction in accountability, unless it is disliked with Allāh ﷻ and not for any other reason. Likewise, they do not relinquish that which people possess except in compliance with the [divine] command and so that the people [continue to] love them and seek intercession for them with their Lord ﷻ when reproach for sins takes place and not for any other reason, like seeking [social or political] status or widespread fame among them.

3.46 Having No Goods of Material Value

It is from among their etiquettes that they do not acknowledge any property for themselves in [either of] the two worlds. Here, the status of being dispossessed in the inward state becomes real as there is no connection that they might seek of this world and nor its loss that they would regret. If any of them was to remove their outer customary clothing, place merely a white cotton skullcap upon his head, around his waist a rag that merely conceals his private part or a sack that barely dispels the suffering of heat and cold, he will not be subject to censure for that because his outward assimilates his inward. This is opposed to his wearing suchlike clothing prior to his [condition of] being dispossessed in the inward state. Thus, if his outward [appearance] does not assimilate his inward [state], he ends up in the form of a hypocrite since the hypocrite is he who reveals the opposite to what he conceals.

3.47 Distancing from Non-Practising Scholars

It is from among their etiquettes to adopt distance from whichever scholar they see not practising according to their knowledge, while also having a good opinion of him.

It is from among the sayings of my Master 'Alī Wafā:

> *Evil scholars are more harmful to the people than Iblīs; when Iblīs whispers to the Believer, the Believer recognises him to be an open deceiving enemy. Thus, if he follows his whispers, he will recognise that he has sinned, and so he will hasten to repent from his sin and to seek forgiveness from his Lord سبحانه وتعالى. Evil scholars dress the Truth with falsehood and they conceal the commands according to their own agendas and desires. Thus, the effort of someone who follows them will be lost while he continues to think that he is doing something good. Stay away from them and be with those who are truthful; you will gain the benefit of acting on religious commands from them, as opposed to pedants from whom you will not benefit in anything other than claiming to have knowledge and being arrogant against [fellow] Muslims.*

3.48 When They see Something Unlawful

It is from among their etiquettes, out of altruism to Allāh سبحانه وتعالى and compassion to the doer, to depress their own selves whenever they see something against the sacred law.

It is not from among their etiquettes to say: "This is an act of Allāh سبحانه وتعالى so there ought not be any depression from it," because that would be ignorance; the Messenger of Allāh سبحانه وتعالى would become angry when the prohibitions of Allāh سبحانه وتعالى were violated.

They [i.e. the People of Verity] said:

> *The Believer ought to have two eyes or many eyes; i. an eye with which he looks at the communicated command in the divine act so that he would be safe from falling into an objection against*

> *[Allāh ﷻ] the Wise, the All-Knowing, and ii. an eye with which he looks at the servants opposing the commands of their Lord ﷻ and so he becomes estranged to Allāh ﷻ. Thus, he learns [or it is known] that rejecting what is forbidden is not vilified at the station of [absolute] submission because both [the aforementioned] are legally instructed. Understand!*

3.49 Lowering the Gaze from Futile Vision

It is from among their etiquettes to lower the gaze away from futile vision, to be swift in walking with calmness, to reconcile [when there is] hostility, to turn a blind eye to people's flaws and conceal them while publicising their good acts – except for the [evil] innovators [in religion] (*Mubtadiʿah*); to expose their evil deeds and warn against them is being merciful to Muslims so that the punishment of the [evil] innovator [in religion] does not increase because of the people following him in his [evil] innovation and nor does anyone become sinful because of it.

3.50 Not Abusing the Leaders

It is from among their etiquettes not to abuse the [political] leaders even if they are oppressive because in most cases they govern the masses according to the deeds and the intentions of the masses.

3.51 Not Seeking Assistance from Anyone

It is from among their etiquettes not to seek assistance for their own selves; seeking assistance for one's own self are from among the matters that are completely futile. [However,] someone who submits his affair to his Lord [i.e. Allāh] ﷻ, He ﷻ will help him without [assistance from] kin or family.

It is from among their [i.e. the People of Verity's] sayings:

> *When the ṣūfī seeks assistance for his own self and he pleads for it then he and dust are alike.*

3.52 Not Cursing Others

It is from among their etiquettes that they do not pray against someone who wrongs them and nor do they seek help against him, knowing that Allāh ﷻ dislikes it from them, even though seeking help against the wrongdoer is from among the inner desires.

3.53 Respecting the Masjid

It is from among their etiquettes that they do not enter the masjids with the intention of sleeping or seeking rest and therein: they do not break wind without an excuse, they do not speak of anything from the affairs of the world, they do not outstretch their legs and they do not raise their voices.

3.54 The Blessed Hands of the Prophet ﷺ

It is from among their etiquettes that they do not speak of the [blessed] hand of the Prophet [Muḥammad] ﷺ as 'the left-hand', but they rather say 'the primary right hand,' and 'the secondary right hand,' or 'the right hand to his ﷺ front,' and 'the right hand to his ﷺ back.'

They do not mention his ﷺ noble name without [mentioning] the title of lordship, [i.e. *Sayyidunā* – Our Master,] at all places, other than during recitation [of the Qur'ān] and the *adhān* (call to congregational ritual prayer). It is well known that to honour the Prophet ﷺ is obligated upon the Muslim Community (*Ummah*), and to mention his ﷺ noble name without the title of lordship is contrary to expressing honour, because it has bad manners and little modesty in it. This is clear to the enlightened.

3.55 Prayers for the Prophet ﷺ

It is from among their etiquettes that they do not say, for example, "*Al-Fātiḥah* for the Prophet ﷺ," or, "O Allāh ﷻ! Render the reward of such-and-such into the records [of deeds] of the Messenger of Allāh ﷺ," – because the deeds of the Ummah are essentially for him ﷺ.

3.56 Loving Their Fellows

It is from among their etiquettes to love their fellow Muslims with the love of fellowship and faith and not with natural love and nor as a favour.

It is from among the counsels of my Master 'Abdulqādir al-Jīlī:

> *When you experience grudge against or love for any person in your heart then analyse his deeds against the Qur'ān and the Sunnah; if they are disapproved of in them both then you [too] must dislike him; if they are commendable in them both then you [too] must love him, so that you do not [end up] loving him or begrudging him out of your [own] desire.*

Allāh ﷻ said:

﴿ وَلَا تَتَّبِعِ الْهَوٰى فَيُضِلَّكَ عَنْ سَبِيْلِ اللّٰهِ ﴾

Do not follow (selfish) desire; it will lead you astray from the Path of Allāh ﷻ. (38:26)[143]

We have mentioned in [a place] other than this epistle that the reality of love for the sake of Allāh ﷻ is 'neither to exceed in righteousness and nor to fall short out of futility.'

3.57 Securing Cordiality with Whom They Eat

It is from among their etiquettes to secure cordiality for someone whom they ate bread with or [even] tasted salt with.

My Master 'Alī al-Khawwāṣ, Allāh ﷻ have mercy on him, mentioned that this used to be from the among the manners of burglars during the days of Sulṭān Qā'itbāy[144]. He narrated a story about the intelligent Ḥamūr, the burglar leader, that once he and his group entered upon a merchant next to the Ghamrī Masjid in Egypt.

> *They stood over the merchant's head and began searching the house. The merchant awoke and saw the burglars standing over his head, and so Ḥamūr said to him, 'Do not fear for your life, sir, for the children only want food from you.' The merchant asked, 'How many are you?' He replied, 'Ten.' The merchant stood up and brought them a thousand dīnārs, and he added four hundred dīnārs behind their backs. Ḥamūr said to him, 'May Allāh ﷻ bless you for your generosity, sir. We did not expect all this from you.'*

[143] Holy Qur'ān, Sūrah Ṣād (38), Verse 26.

[144] Sulṭān Qā'itbāy (also spelt Qā'itbā'ī, Kait Bey, Qaytbay, Qaitbai): He is Sulṭān Abu'n-Naṣr Sayfuddīn al-Ashraf Qā'itbāy (818AH/1416CE – 901AH/1496CE), the Burji Mamluk ruler of Egypt, who was known for his piety, justice, religious devotion and love for the poor, the scholars and fine architecture.

> *Each put his share into their pockets but one of them saw a white pot shining upon the shelf of the house. He took it and his ego told him to open it, while he was outside at the threshold of the house, and see what was inside. He opened it and saw something soft inside it and so he tasted it and said, "Salt!"*
>
> *Ḥamūr heard him and said [to his comrades], 'Return whatever you have got because your colleague has tasted this gentleman's salt. No wickedness shall be seen with us for the rest of our lives. Return all the goods.' The gentleman pleaded them to take a hundred dīnārs [at least] but they refused.*

3.58 Disassociating from Thieves and Cheats

It is from among their etiquettes to disassociate from the thief and the deceiver and expel them from among themselves. The difference between the thief and the deceiver is that the deceiver is someone who steals that which is entrusted to him whereas the thief is someone who steals that which is not entrusted to him. They [i.e. the People of Verity] said:

> *Surely, deception removes blessings from the wealth and the life of a person.*

[Their] saying regarding theft is similar, as we have never seen a thief except that his property and his life are bereft of blessings.

3.58.1 Disassociating from Liars

It is likewise from among their etiquettes to disassociate from the liar. 'Ā'ishah ﵂ said:

> *There is nothing more hateful to the Messenger of Allāh ﷺ than a liar. He ﷺ would avoid a person for two or three months due to a word of falsity.*[145]

3.59 Expressing Magnanimity

It is from among their etiquettes to express as much magnanimity as possible from their own selves. Its standard depends on the affair of the person; if one who presents it the same out of seriousness in the *dīn* (religion) of Allāh ﷻ as well as other than the *dīn* of Allāh ﷻ then that is personal magnanimity, but if he presents it out of seriousness in the *dīn* (religion) of Allāh ﷻ only, it is from the magnanimity of faith.

---

[145] A ḥadīth with a similar meaning: at-Tirmidhī, *al-Jāmi'*.

3.60 Being True without Pretence

It is also from among their etiquettes to give priority to one who is a simple jurist over the jurist who pretends to be on the Path [of Verity] because the simple jurist is free of the hypocrisy that exists in the pretender even though the latter has the added [attribute] of Islāmic legal knowledge. In fact, the common person [, or the sinful person,] who worships Allāh ﷻ and asks the scholars regarding the confusions he faces in his *dīn* (religion) is in a better state than the one who pretends to be on the Path of the People [of Verity].

3.61 Etiquettes of Visiting

It is from among their etiquettes not to go out to visit anyone until they have acquired the etiquettes of visiting. They are:

1. an interest in the one being visited
2. perfect certainty of his high merit and his being free from apparent and unperceivable sins, while believing themselves to be contrary to it
3. earnest request for his prayers and consideration
4. consecrating the intention, such that the motive to visit is nothing more than compliance to the [divine] command
5. guarding the tongue from falling into exposing [other] people
6. omitting to mention [their own] favours [to him].

These are [the etiquettes] that the visitors and the one visited partake in.

There is no benefit and nor any reward if the visit is devoid of these etiquettes, but rather, it becomes a burden and hypocrisy. Moreover, it is clear that it is incumbent on the visitor that if the one being visited mentions something that is from among his favours upon him, he ought to believe that he only mentioned it for a purpose allowable in sacred law.

3.62 Honouring Bread

It is from among their etiquettes to give due right to bread by honouring it, exalting it, kissing it and placing it on the eyes.

It is from among the sayings of my Master 'Alī al-Khawwāṣ:

> *You must refrain from placing bread on the floor without a support; in such an act lies humiliation to the favour of Allāh ﷻ.*

It is reported from 'Ā'ishah ﵂ who said:

> *Once, (when) the Messenger of Allāh ﷺ came to me, he ﷺ saw a dry piece of bread on a wall that was covered in dust. The Messenger of Allāh ﷺ took it, kissed it, placed it upon his eye and then said: 'O 'Ā'ishah! Make good [your] proximity to the favours of Allāh ﷻ; verily, favours that are driven away from the people of a household rarely return to them.'*[146]

It is from among the sayings of my Master Aḥmad ar-Rifā'ī:

> *Paucity in honouring bread is ingratitude to the favours of the Provider of favours ﷻ. You must exert yourselves in venerating as much as you can what you seek to eat and pick up what falls [on the floor] as soon as it falls and do not leave it until after you have finished your meal, because to honour the favours of Allāh ﷻ is surely like honouring Allāh ﷻ. Expenses do not befall a people until they despise the grain out of its cheapness.*

It is mentioned in some non-Prophetic reports:

> *The loaf (of bread) is not eaten until three hundred and sixty created beings alternate it between themselves - the first of which is Angel Mīkā'īl ﵇ and the last of whom is the baker.*[147]

He [also] said:

> *It is enough for us to honour bread because the Messenger of Allāh ﷺ has rendered it commensurate with the Beatific Vision in the [following] ḥadīth:*
>
> *There are two joys for someone who is fasting - a joy when he duly breaks his fast and a joy when he meets his Lord ﷻ.*[148]

---

[146] Ibn Mājah, *as-Sunan*.
[147] al-Ghazālī, *Iḥyā' 'Ulūm ad-Dīn*.
[148] al-Bukhārī, *al-Jāmi' aṣ-Ṣaḥīḥ*.

3.63 Praising Allāh سبحانه وتعالى after Eating

It is from among their etiquettes that when they have concluded eating what was offered to them they say:

اَلْحَمْدُ لِلّٰهِ رَبِّ الْعَالَمِيْنَ عَلىٰ كُلِّ حَالٍ، اَلْحَمْدُ لِلّٰهِ الَّذِيْ بِنِعْمَتِهِ تَتِمُّ الصَّالِحَاتُ وَ تَعُمُّ الْبَرَكَاتُ.

All praise is to Allāh سبحانه وتعالى in all circumstances. All praise is to Allāh سبحانه وتعالى with Whose favours good deeds are completed and blessings become widespread.

They [also] recite Sūrah Quraysh[149] and Sūrat al-Ikhlāṣ[150].

3.64 To Drink Something when at Another's Invite

It is from among their etiquettes that when they eat with someone they do not leave him until after they have had something to drink. They [i.e. the People of Verity] say:

It is of miserliness from the ṣūfī if he eats but does not drink.

3.65 Encouraging Others to Partake in Their Food

It is from among their etiquettes that when they eat they welcome anyone who is present to partake in that food.

It is from among the sayings of my Master 'Alī al-Khawwāṣ:

When you eat food, give some of it to anyone who is present if you wish for a continuation of favours upon you. If someone eats when there are eyes staring at him and he does not offer them food, Allāh سبحانه وتعالى inflicts on him an illness that is called 'the ego'.

3.66 Honouring the Rights of Parents

It is from among their etiquettes to honour the rights of parents out of fear of stumbling into bad manners towards them or being undutiful to them. In sacred law, there is no set procedure against [parental] disobedience; it is generic in covering everything that goes against the wishes of parents in all that is permitted. After the rights of Allāh سبحانه وتعالى

---

[149] Holy Qur'ān, Sūrah Quraysh (106).
[150] Holy Qur'ān, Sūrat al-Ikhlāṣ (112).

and of the Messenger of Allāh ﷺ, there is nothing greater than the rights of parents.

It is from among the sayings of my Master 'Alī al-Khawwāṣ:

> *It is from among the rights of your parents over you that you: i. listen to what they say, ii. stand up when they stand, iii. follow their orders, iv. do not walk in front of them, v. do not raise your voice over theirs, vi. humble yourself to them, vii. do not mention the favours of your kindness to them - or of [your] fulfilling their command, vii. do not glance at them sideways [i.e. out of contempt], ix. do not express anger in their presence, x. do not go ahead of them in [taking] the best food when you eat with them but you should rather give them preference over yourself, and xi. [always] be greedy in earning their pleasure.*

The mother's right is twice as much as that of the conventional father. As for the father-in-*dīn* [i.e. the Shaykh], he is probably higher in status and in rights than the mother.

It is also from among their rights that you do not call them by their names; someone who calls either of his parents by their names is disrespectful to them.

3.67 Loving Their Own Dependents

It is from among their etiquettes to love their dependents with lawful love and not with natural spousal love. Surely, natural [spousal] love is lust of the ego – all the while the servant is [influenced] by it, he remains behind a screen from Allāh ﷻ.

Know that surely Allāh ﷻ made women attractive to us [men] by the order of natural disposition. Thereafter, He ﷻ enjoined upon us a vigorous struggle against the ego so that it abandons its natural love for the love that is prescribed by sacred law. There are [only] a few who can bear the vigorous struggle of their ego so that it leaves that [natural love]. It is because of this that the Shaykhs have cautioned against marrying a beautiful woman; her harm is greater than that of a malformed woman.

It is from among the sayings of my Master Afḍaluddīn:

> *Someone who frequents the company of women: i. his intellect becomes corrupt, ii. his merits are lost, iii. Allāh ﷻ refuses to*

enter his heart, and iv. Shayṭān settles in his heart where he germinates.

3.68 Honouring Every *Faqīr*

It is from among their etiquettes to honour every *faqīr* who is lethargic in making *dhikr* [of Allāh ﷻ] with consistency more than [their honouring] the *faqīr* who is famous for making miracles because the world is not the realm of consequences but rather it is the realm of burden.

3.69 Not Persisting in Sin

It is from among their etiquettes that they do not persist in committing sin as persistence is from among destructive agents, and because of it the minor sin becomes a major sin. Some shaykhs have defined persistence as 'that when a person delays repenting such that the time for the next prayer from the five [obligatory] prayers begins.'

3.70 Conferring Reward to the Backbitten

It is from among their etiquettes that whenever they have bad thoughts about anyone, or they have backbitten [them], and the latter do not find out, they recite Sūrat al-Fātiḥah[151], Sūrat al-Ikhlāṣ[152], Sūrat al-Falaq[153] and Sūrat an-Nās[154], and confer the reward of [all] that to the records of whom they have had bad thoughts about or whom they have backbitten.

The manner of conferring [the reward] is for you to say:

اَللّٰهُمَّ صَلِّ وَسَلِّمْ عَلىٰ نَبِيِّكَ وَحَبِيْبِكَ سَيِّدِنَا مُحَمَّدٍ وَآلِهِ، وَأَثِبْنِي عَلىٰ مَا قَرَأْتُهُ،

وَاجْعَلْهُ فِيْ صَحَائِفِ عَبْدِكَ فُلَانٍ.

O Allāh ﷻ! Bless and grant peace to Your Prophet, Your Beloved, Our Master Muḥammad ﷺ and his family. Reward

---

[151] Holy Qur'ān, Sūrat al-Fātiḥah (1).
[152] Holy Qur'ān, Sūrat al-Ikhlāṣ (112).
[153] Holy Qur'ān, Sūrat al-Falaq (113).
[154] Holy Qur'ān, Sūrat an-Nās (114).

me for what I have recited and confer it to the records of Your servant So-and-So [mention his name].

3.70.1 Note

If someone knows that he himself has people's rights in wealth and honour to fulfil and he finds it difficult to gain their pleasure, he ought to recite with the presence [of mind] Sūrat al-Ikhlāṣ twelve times, Sūrat al-Falaq and Sūrat an-Nās every night, and confer their reward to the records of those people.

The manner of conferring [the reward] is for him to say:

اَللّٰهُمَّ صَلِّ وَسَلِّمْ عَلىٰ نَبِيِّكَ وَحَبِيْبِكَ سَيِّدِنَا مُحَمَّدٍ وَآلِهٖ، وَأَثِبْنِي عَلىٰ مَا قَرَأْتُهُ،

وَاجْعَلْهُ فِيْ صَحَائِفِ مَنْ لَهُ عَلَيَّ تَبِعَةٌ مِنْ عِبَادِكَ، مِنْ مَالٍ وَعِرْضٍ.

O Allāh ﷻ! Bless and grant peace to Your Prophet, Your Beloved, Our Master Muḥammad ﷺ and his family. Reward me for what I have recited and confer it to the records of anyone among Your servants who has a right over me in wealth or honour.

3.71 Seeking Divine Assistance when Taking a Loan

It is from among their etiquettes that when any of them intends to take a loan they ought to turn their heart's attention to Allāh ﷻ and verbally say:

اَللّٰهُمَّ عَلَيْكَ التَّدَايُنُ، فَخُذْ بِيَدِيْ صَدَقَةً مِنْ صَدَقَاتِكَ عَلَيَّ.

O Allāh! The [taking of my] loan is [dependent] on You. Take my hand in charity in exchange for Your favours to me.

3.72 Loving the Descendants of the Messenger ﷺ

It is from among their etiquettes to love the descendants of the Messenger of Allāh ﷺ because they are a part of him ﷺ – even if they might not be upright; cordiality, reverence and admiration for the part is the same as that for the whole.

Some scholars have said:

> *Among the rights upon us of the sharīfs (descendants of the Prophet Muḥammad ﷺ) - even if their relationship [to him ﷺ] is distant - is that we bear their pleasure over our own wants and desires, that we respect them and admire them, and that we do not sit upon couches when they are [sitting] on the floor - out of [respect for] the flesh and blood of the Messenger of Allāh ﷺ flowing through them.*

My Master 'Alī al-Khawwāṣ used to say:

> *It is from among the rights of the sharīfs upon us that we sacrifice our souls for them and that we commit our hands [i.e. efforts] for them due to their proximity with the Messenger of Allāh ﷺ. It is among etiquettes that none of us marries a sharīfah unless he recognises that he will be subject to her commands and indications, presenting her shoes to her, standing for her whenever she comes to him and not acting skimpily in expenses for her unless she [herself] chooses it.*

3.73 Not Forgetting to Visit the Prophetic Household

It is from among their etiquettes that they do not neglect visiting the Prophetic Household (*Ahl al-Bayt*).

The People of *Kashf* (the disclosure of true realities and secrets) have verified that:

> Lady Zaynab ﵂, daughter of Imām 'Alī ﵁, is buried at Qanāṭir as-Sabā' without doubt
>
> her sister Lady Ruqayyah ﵂ in the mausoleum close to the house of the Caliph - Leader of the Believers ﵁, near Jāmi' ibn Ṭūlūn (Masjid), and many members of the Prophetic Household with her
>
> Lady Sukaynah ﵂, daughter of Imām al-Ḥusayn ﵁ in the *zāwiyah* at Darb, close to the mausoleum of her paternal aunt and to the house of the Caliph
>
> Lady Nafīsah ﵂ in this very place without doubt
>
> Lady 'Ā'isha ﵂, daughter of Imām Ja'far aṣ-Ṣādiq ﵁, in the masjid with the low minaret, to the left if someone wants to leave Rumaila towards the Gate of al-Qarāfah
>
> the [blessed] head of Imām al-Ḥusayn ﵁ in the grave that is recognised by the mausoleum, close to Khān al-Khalīlī without doubt. Ṭalā'i' ibn Ruzzīk, the Governor of Egypt,

placed it here inside a green pouch of green silk on a platform made of ebony wooden strips, laying musk and perfume under it. He and his army brought it here barefooted when they arrived from non-Arab lands to Egypt

Muḥammad al-Anwar ﵁, the paternal uncle of Lady Nafīsah ﵂, in the mausoleum close to the Jāmi‘ ibn Ṭūlūn (Masjid), adjacent to the house of the Caliph, inside the *zāwiyah* that is situated there. He had settled there

his ﵁ brother, al-Ḥasan ﵁, father of Lady Nafīsah ﵂, in the famous grave close to Jāmi‘ ‘Amr (Masjid)

the [blessed] head of Imām Zaynul‘ābidīn ﵁ and the [blessed] head of Zayd ﵁ in the dome close to the passageways to the fort

the head of Ibrāhīm ibn Zayd ﵁ in the masjid on the way to al-Matriyyah, adjacent to the *khānqah*.

This is what has appeared to me at this time regarding those who are buried in Egypt from among the Prophetic Household. It is thus, my dear fellow, imperative to visit them and to prioritise it over visiting any other *walī* in Egypt, contrary to what most people do. It is uncommon that you will see anyone interested in visiting any of those who are [afore]mentioned like their interest in visiting some of those who are madly attracted to Allāh ﷻ (*majdhūbs*). This is out of complete ignorance.

3.74 Not Inclining to their Spiritual States

It is from among their etiquettes that they do not incline towards anything in their [spiritual] states.

It is from among the sayings of my Master Ibrāhīm al-Matbūlī:

> *What the Believer fears most is his own self inclining to his own good deeds in order to affirm sincerity in them even if that is by way of kashf (disclosure) or dhawq (taste).*

It is from among the sayings of my Master ‘Alī al-Khawwāṣ:

> *Do not rejoice over what favours [or miracles], spiritual states, knowledge and spiritual gnosises you have been bestowed until the coverings are removed for you as to whether you are entitled to them or whether they are [yours] by way of pledge. Surely, the sane ought not rejoice over bestowals made by way*

of pledge unless they are definite. You have nothing except by way of pledge and only optimism.

3.75 Testifying to the Perfection in Others

It is from among their etiquettes to acknowledge perfection in their colleague and deficiency in their own selves. Someone who testifies to that dislikes reclusion from people unless [it be] due to another legal objective such as his fearing they might acquire from him something by which they would be harmed.

3.76 Testifying to Divine Mercy Being Supreme

It is from among their etiquettes to perpetually testify that Allāh ﷻ is more merciful to them than they themselves are. Likewise, they do not despair in the mercy of Allāh ﷻ at any time.

3.77 Having Equal Love for the Prophetic Companions ﵁

It is from among their etiquettes to be wary of having bias in their love for any of the Companions ﵁ or for any of their ﵁ descendants since it is incumbent on everyone to love the Companions ﵁ of the Messenger of Allāh ﷺ in compliance to the love for the Messenger of Allāh ﷺ. One must love their ﵁ descendants in a similar manner but prioritise the descendants of Lady Fāṭimah ﵂ over the descendants of the [other] Companions ﵁.

Shaykh 'Abdulghaffār al-Qawṣī[155] (Allāh ﷻ have mercy on him) mentioned that he had a colleague who was one of the greatest scholars. When he died, he saw him and asked him about the *dīn* of Islām, and the latter stuttered in response. He said:

> *I asked him, 'Is it the Truth?' He replied, 'Yes. It is the Truth.' I looked at his face and it was pitch black, though he used to be a man of a white complexion. So I asked him, 'If the dīn of Islām was the Truth then why is your face black?' He replied in a low voice, 'I used to prioritise some of the Companions ﵁ over others out of prejudice and bias.'*

---

155 Shaykh 'Abdulghaffār ibn Aḥmad al-Qawṣī, also known as Ibn Nūḥ (d.708AH/1308CE).

3.78 Benefitting Anyone Who Associates with Them

It is from among their etiquettes to provide benefit to anyone who associates with them even though he may not be worthy of the benefit. Some of them [i.e. the People of Verity] were such that no person would sit next to them except that he would make *dhikr* [of Allāh ﷻ] - it would be only him and the other in a gathering of *dhikr*. After that, he would turn him away and say: "One who is not good enough to gain benefit from knowledge is [still] good enough to make *dhikr* of Allāh ﷻ."

3.79 Not Visiting the Heedless

It is from among their etiquettes that they do not visit anyone and nor eat from his food unless they know well that he is cautious regarding the deeds of his contemporaries and concerned about the fermenting dough [i.e. the source of the food].

3.80 Not Responding to Aspirants of Discipleship

It is from among their etiquettes that they are not interested in responding to someone who seeks to be their disciple - subjecting [himself] to their indications and training. They have said in the past:

> *If there was genuinely only one true disciple for the shaykh in his entire life, he would be more precious than red sulphur.*

3.80.1 Qualities of the True Disciple

There are, in summary, four qualities of the true disciple:

1. having true love for his shaykh
2. obedience to his command
3. not objecting to him, and
4. dispossessing [his own] authority [when he is] with him.

The oath-taking of every disciple who incorporates these four qualities [within himself] is valid. He thus becomes desiccated tinder for the firelock.

The spark of the firelock will not ignite if the tinder of someone who seeks to administer an oath to his disciples is damp. In fact, any spark that falls upon it dies.

3.81 Persisting in Doing Good

It is from among their etiquettes to charge themselves with persisting in doing good and in having gatherings of *dhikr* as there are few who persist in doing good while the people also find them doing good. They remain safe from calamities.

It is from the nature of the self that when it becomes attune to exalting [Allāh تبارك وتعالى] for its worship that abandoning it might become a fault and not for the sake of seeking by it the proximity with Allāh تبارك وتعالى, the *sālik* ought to test himself; if he finds shyness in it when he omits to express that worship, he should know well that all of that was ostentation and that repenting and seeking forgiveness is binding upon him; if he does not find any shyness in it, he should be grateful to Allāh تبارك وتعالى who saved him and then he should not seek any [other] refuge.

It happened to one of the predecessors that he would perform the five [daily] prayers in the front row. One day he stayed back [from the front row] and felt ashamed within himself. So, he repeated all of those prayers and said: "Surely, my persistence was ostentation and prestige."

It is from among the sayings of my Master 'Alī al-Khawwāṣ, may the mercy of Allāh تبارك وتعالى be upon him:

> *Anyone who feels ashamed within himself when he omits to express his devotional prayers from the Holy Qur'ān, [his] fasting, [his practising] ascetism or silence, his deeds - all of them - are ostentation and prestige, and he will not find anything from them in his Record [of Deeds] on the Day of Judgement.*

It is from among the sayings of my Master 'Alī al-Marṣafī[156] (Allāh تبارك وتعالى have mercy on him):

> *It behoves not the faqīr to assemble the people to a gathering of dhikr except [after] he has abandoned the love for leadership otherwise he destroys his own self. I have known faqīrs and*

---

[156] 'Alī ibn Khalīl al-Marṣafī (d. 930AH/1523CE).

> *none would dare to sit with any group [to lead them] in a gathering of dhikr except after the demise of his shaykh, or his [shaykh] authorising him after he has acknowledged him to be accomplished.*

3.82 Not Taking Pleasure from Own Submissiveness

It is from among their etiquettes that none of them take pleasure in what is achieved for them in the forms of submissiveness (*khushū'*) and quivering, joining the shoulders and drooping the head on the ground. They do not allow themselves to do that unless they are overwhelmed.

Imām 'Umar ibn al-Khaṭṭāb ﵁ saw a man praying who had joined his shoulders and so he struck him and said: "Submissiveness is not like this because submissiveness is in the heart." Ends [the statement of 'Umar ibn al-Khaṭṭāb ﵁].

Therefore, my dear fellow, flee from falling into something like that, but if you see anyone doing it then take it that he is overwhelmed.

3.83 Being Inwardly Angry at False Claimants

It is from among their etiquettes that they are inwardly angry at anyone who makes a false claim with them though they may smile outwardly. Then they make him aware of his lie in secret if they see him bearing something similar to that [false claim]. In this etiquette is a combination of ardency to Allāh تعالى as well as counsel to that servant [of Allāh تعالى]. Few are those who combine these two qualities.

3.84 Seeking Needs from Allāh تعالى

It is from among their etiquettes to seek from the door of Allāh تعالى all that they need and not from the door of any of His تعالى servants. They must not even look at the door of anyone else other than for the state that created beings are like a waterway in which water flows and nothing else. The excellence is in the one who makes the water flow in the waterway and not the waterway itself.

It is from among the sayings of my Master 'Abdulqādir al-Jīlī:

> *Feign blindness, my dear fellow, to all contacts when you seek your needs from your Lord تعالى and the door of His تعالى grace will open for you, otherwise it won't as He تعالى is ardent.*

If someone does not reach that [state] then it is from among his obligations to rely on the means and to depend on them because ingratitude for the means is in obedience to the command, and that [i.e. ingratitude] is *shirk* (associating partners with Allāh ﷻ).

You must refrain from omitting the medium of the Messenger of Allāh ﷺ in any need you seek as it is disrespectful to him ﷺ. In such a case you would be an innovator [in the *dīn*] and not a follower. Understand!

3.85 Seeking Permission in the Heart

It is from among their etiquettes that when they are reciting the Holy Qur'ān or the Noble Ḥadīth and they wish to speak to any person for something they need, they do not speak until they have sought permission in their heart and on their tongue from Allāh ﷻ and His Messenger ﷺ to speak to that person. However, if they spoke to someone after having neglected to seek permission, they beg forgiveness from Allāh ﷻ until Allāh ﷻ inspires to them in their hearts that He ﷻ has accepted their plea for forgiveness.

It so happened that while Shaykh Afḍaluddīn was reading a ḥadīth, he spoke to someone prior to seeking permission from the Prophet ﷺ. He thus sought forgiveness from Allāh ﷻ seventy times!

3.86 Not Preoccupying Oneself During *Adhān*

It is from among their etiquettes that, out of courtesy to Allāh ﷻ, they do not preoccupy themselves with anything during *adhān*.

Some of them [i.e. the People of Verity] narrated regarding a woman from among the female rebels that she was seen [in a dream] in a beautiful form after she had died. She was asked: "Why is this?" and she replied: "Once the *mu'adhdhin* (caller of the *adhān*) called the *adhān* while we were in circumstances in which it was improper to raise the voice, and so I ordered my comrades to be silent until the *mu'adhdhin* had finished. So, Allāh ﷻ forgave us because of that."

3.87 Not Stretching the Legs Without Divine Permission

It is from among their etiquettes that when their legs ache out of squatting, they do not stretch them until they have sought permission from Allāh ﷻ. It is likewise the ruling on stretching them in the direction of the Noble [city of] Madīnah or in the direction of any of the *awliyā'* – they do not stretch them [in those respective directions] until they have sought permission from the Prophet ﷺ or from that *walī*.

All of this is their testimony that they are, whether they are aware of it or not, always in the presence of Allāh ﷻ and of His Messenger ﷺ. If that had not been *kashf*, it [definitely] is *īmān* (faith).

It so happened that Abū Isḥāq Ibrāhīm ibn Adham outstretched his leg, when it ached out of squatting, prior to seeking permission [from Allāh ﷻ and His Messenger ﷺ]. Thus, he was admonished for it, and so he did not outstretch his leg after that until he died.

Likewise, it so happened that Abū Muḥammad al-Jarīrī[157] (Allāh ﷻ have mercy on him) stretched his leg prior to seeking permission and he was admonished for it. He did not stretch his leg [again] until he died.

3.88 Persisting in Devotional Recitation

It is from among their etiquettes to persist:

in seeking forgiveness thrice, in reciting the Qur'ān, Āyat al-Kursī (the Verse of the Chair)[158], the last [ten verses] of Sūrat al-Kahf[159], Sūrat al-Kāfirūn[160], Sūrat al-Ikhlāṣ[161], Sūrat al-Falaq[162] and Sūrat an-Nās[163] when retiring to sleep

in glorifying [Allāh ﷻ by saying "*subḥān-Allāh*"] thirty-three times, praising [Him ﷻ by saying "*al-ḥamdu li'Llāh*"] thirty-three times and exalting [Him ﷻ by saying "*Allāhu Akbar*"] thirty-four times – according to what is reported in Abū Dāwūd and at-Tirmidhī:

> *Two acts are such that the servant cannot guard over except that he will enter Paradise. They are easy but few are those*

[157] Abū Muḥammad al-Jarīrī (d.311AH/923CE).
[158] Holy Qur'ān, Sūrat al-Baqarah (2), Verse 255.
[159] Holy Qur'ān, Sūrat al-Kahf (18), Verses 99-110 – though they total 12, the number 10 has been mentioned in ḥadīths (Muslim, *al-Musnad aṣ-Ṣaḥīḥ, Kitāb faḍā'il al-qur'ān wa mā yata'allaqu bi-hī*, Ḥadīth 1884).
[160] Holy Qur'ān , Sūrat al-Kāfirūn (109).
[161] Holy Qur'ān, Sūrat al-Ikhlāṣ (112).
[162] Holy Qur'ān, Sūrat al-Falaq (113).
[163] Holy Qur'ān, Sūrat an-Nās (114).

who do them; that he glorifies Allāh ﷻ ten times at the end of every ritual prayer, praises Him ﷻ ten times and exalts Him ﷻ ten times. This (amounts to) one hundred and fifty on the tongue but one thousand and five hundred on the Mīzān (Divine Weighing-Scales). When he goes to his bedspread and glorifies (Allāh ﷻ) thirty-three times, praises (Him ﷻ) thirty-three times and exalts (Him ﷻ) thirty-four times, it is one hundred on the tongue but one thousand on the Mīzān. Which one of you does a bad deed two thousand and five hundred times during a day and its night? It was asked, 'O Messenger of Allāh ﷺ, how can one not guard over them?' and He ﷺ replied, 'Shayṭān comes to each one of you while you are in prayer and says, 'Remember such-and-such, remember such-and-such,' or he comes to you when you are about to sleep and makes you fall asleep.'[164]

3.89 Detesting to Sleep when Ritually Impure

It is from among their etiquettes to severely detest sleeping in [the states of] major or minor ritual impurity.

It is from among the sayings of my Master 'Alī al-Khawwāṣ, Allāh ﷻ have mercy on him:

> *You must refrain from sleeping when in [the states of] outward or inward impurity – from the love for this world and its desires. It could be that Allāh ﷻ might take your soul that night and you might meet Allāh ﷻ with Him ﷻ being angry with you out of disgust for the sin that you slept in.*

It is mentioned in a ḥadīth:

> *A person will be made to rise (on the Day of Judgement) upon the dīn of his friend. Thus, each of you should observe whom he befriends.*[165]

It is also mentioned in a ḥadīth that:

> *Allāh ﷻ has not looked upon this world ever since He ﷻ created it, i.e. out of pleasure or love for it*[166]

except that He ﷻ does look upon it with organisational observation because had it not been for that, it [i.e. this world] would

---

[164] Abū Dāwūd, *as-Sunan*; at-Tirmidhī, *al-Jāmi'*.
[165] Abū Dāwūd, *as-Sunan*; at-Tirmidhī, *al-Jāmi'*.
[166] at-Tirmidhī, *al-Jāmi'*.

have perished into the Knowledge of Allāh ﷻ and nothing of it would have remained in existence. Understand!

So, whoever sleeps with the love for this world [in his heart] and dies that night, he will be made to rise [on the Day of Judgement] with the anger of Allāh ﷻ upon him - He ﷻ will not look at him, even though He ﷻ created him, unless he repents. There are few in these times who are aware of this matter that they turn away from it [i.e. love for the world] but an overwhelming number of people do not [even] consider the love for this world to be a sin.

Mālik ibn Dīnār[167] (Allāh ﷻ have mercy on him) used to assemble his companions and say to them:

> *Come! Let us seek forgiveness from the sin that people have forgotten. It is love for this [mundane] world.*

3.90 Cleansing Deception from Their Hearts

It is from among their etiquettes to strive in cleansing their hearts of deception so that they become worthy of entering the Divine Presence, which is nobler and more excellent than Paradise [itself], for surely its entry is forbidden to whoever's heart harbours deception against any of the created beings.

It is mentioned in a ḥadīth on the authority of Anas ibn Mālik ؓ who said:

> *The Messenger of Allāh ﷺ said: 'My dear son! If you are able to (witness) the morning and the evening with there being no deception in your heart for anything then do so.' Then he said: 'My dear son! That is from my Sunnah; whoever revives my Sunnah has revived me, and whoever revives me will be with me in Paradise.'*[168]

The Shaykhs have said:

> *Enduring hunger and tolerating it is easy but treating manners and ridding them of trivial affairs is intensely difficult.*

---

[167] Mālik ibn Dīnār al-Baṣrī (d.131AH/748CE).

[168] at-Tirmidhī, *al-Jāmi'*. Our references mention the words 'أَحَبَّنِي - he has loved me,' and not the words 'أَحْيَانِي - he has revived me.'

The intended meaning of '*ghishsh* – deception' is: grudge, spite, hatred, envy, and having a bad opinion. One is incapable of cleansing his heart of these despicable [emotions] without renouncing this [mundane] world and leadership because the source of that [i.e. deception] is love for this world and love for leadership. Here is where the superiority of the Ṣūfīs and the magnificence of their lofty status over others becomes clear – [it is] their renouncing the [mundane] world as well as any fondness for status among its inhabitants, and because of their attachment to piety through the strongest links. It is well known that anyone who renounces the [mundane] world and adheres to piety, his self becomes firmly safe from grudge, spite, hatred, envy and all contemptible [emotions]. This is the state of the ṣūfī.

Some of them [i.e. the People of Verity] said [that] the combination of the state of the Ṣūfīs is of two things, and both are the qualities of Ṣūfīs, to which Allāh ﷻ has indicated in His ﷻ saying:

﴿ اَللّٰهُ يَجْتَبِيٓ اِلَيْهِ مَنْ يَّشَآءُ وَيَهْدِيٓ اِلَيْهِ مَنْ يُّنِيْبُ ﴾

Allāh ﷻ chooses for Himself whom He ﷻ wills and guides to Himself anyone who turns to Him. (42:13)[169]

3.90.1 The Two Qualities

One group of Ṣūfīs have been specified with being merely selected and [another] group of them have been specified with guidance on the condition of already having turned [to Allāh ﷻ].

1. Mere selection is not based on the servant's hard work. This is the state of the intentionally concealed – whom Allāh ﷻ calls to due to his devotions and his abilities without his any prior earning. His *kashf* overtakes his efforts.

2. As for the People of Guidance for whom Allāh ﷻ has stipulated they turn [to Him ﷻ when], He ﷻ says:

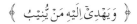

﴿ وَيَهْدِيٓ اِلَيْهِ مَنْ يُّنِيْبُ ﴾

---

[169] Holy Qur'ān, Sūrat ash-Shūrā (42), Verse 13.

(Allāh ﷻ) guides to Himself anyone who turns to Him, (42:13)[170]

Striving has been demanded from them.

Allāh ﷻ says:

﴿ وَالَّذِيْنَ جَاهَدُوْا فِيْنَا لَنَهْدِيَنَّهُمْ سُبُلَنَا ﴾

As for those who strive for Us, We will certainly guide them onto Our paths. (29:69)[171]

Allāh ﷻ advances them gradually through the ranks of achievement by various kinds of [spiritual] exercises and self-exertion, sleeplessness during times of gloom and thirst of midday; they twist and turn in the scorching heat of [divine] will and they abandon everything that is conventional and customary. This is the 'turning [to Allāh ﷻ]' that He ﷻ has stipulated for them and by which He ﷻ has rendered guidance to be recognised. This guidance is also a special [kind of] guidance as it is guidance to Him ﷻ and not common guidance – that which leads to His ﷻ commands and His ﷻ prohibitions by necessitating primal gnosis. This is the [spiritual] state of the lover *sālik* whose efforts overtake his *kashf*. This is more profitable and more complete than the first [i.e. mere selection].

3.91 Performing Night Vigil Ritual Prayer

It is from among their etiquettes that they commence night vigil [praying] with two short units [of ritual prayer] in which they recite the verse:

﴿ وَلَوْ اَنَّهُمْ اِذْ ظَّلَمُوْٓا اَنْفُسَهُمْ جَآءُوْكَ فَاسْتَغْفَرُوا اللّٰهَ

وَاسْتَغْفَرَ لَهُمُ الرَّسُوْلُ لَوَجَدُوا اللّٰهَ تَوَّابًا رَّحِيْمًا ﴾

And, (O Beloved Prophet Muḥammad ﷺ,) if they, having wronged their souls, had come to you and sought the forgiveness of Allāh ﷻ, and the Messenger ﷺ had also asked

[170] Holy Qur'ān, Sūrat ash-Shūrā (42), Verse 13.
[171] Holy Qur'ān, Sūrat al-'Ankabūt (29), Verse 69.

forgiveness for them, they would certainly have found Allāh ﷻ accepting repentance much, Ever-Merciful. (4:64)[172]

in the first unit after [Sūrat] al-Fātiḥah[173], and in the second unit [they recite]:

﴿ وَمَنْ يَّعْمَلْ سُوْٓءًا اَوْ يَظْلِمْ نَفْسَهٗ ثُمَّ يَسْتَغْفِرِ اللّٰهَ يَجِدِ اللّٰهَ غَفُوْرًا رَّحِيْمًا ﴾

And someone who does evil or wrongs his own soul and then seeks Allāh's forgiveness will find Allāh ﷻ Most Forgiving, Ever-Merciful. (4:110)[174]

It is very dear for me to say in my heart and on my tongue after the salutation [ending ritual prayer]:

يَا سَيِّدِيْ! يَا رَسُوْلَ اللهِ! اِسْتَغْفِرْ لِيْ رَبَّكَ ، صَلَّى اللهُ عَلَيْكَ وَسَلَّمَ .

يَا سَيِّدِيْ! يَا رَسُوْلَ اللهِ! اِسْتَغْفِرْ لِيْ رَبَّكَ ، صَلَّى اللهُ عَلَيْكَ وَسَلَّمَ .

يَا سَيِّدِيْ! يَا رَسُوْلَ اللهِ! اِسْتَغْفِرْ لِيْ رَبَّكَ ، صَلَّى اللهُ عَلَيْكَ وَسَلَّمَ .

My Master! O Messenger of Allāh ﷺ! Ask your Lord ﷻ to forgive me – Allāh ﷻ bless you and grant you peace!

thrice or more, [and]:

اَللّٰهُمَّ عَمِلْتُ سُوْءًا وَّ ظَلَمْتُ نَفْسِيْ فَاغْفِرْ لِيْ صَدَقَةً مِّنْ صَدَقَاتِكَ عَلَيَّ ، يَا أَرْحَمَ الرَّاحِمِيْنَ .

اَللّٰهُمَّ عَمِلْتُ سُوْءًا وَّ ظَلَمْتُ نَفْسِيْ فَاغْفِرْ لِيْ صَدَقَةً مِّنْ صَدَقَاتِكَ عَلَيَّ ، يَا أَرْحَمَ الرَّاحِمِيْنَ .

اَللّٰهُمَّ عَمِلْتُ سُوْءًا وَّ ظَلَمْتُ نَفْسِيْ فَاغْفِرْ لِيْ صَدَقَةً مِّنْ صَدَقَاتِكَ عَلَيَّ ، يَا أَرْحَمَ الرَّاحِمِيْنَ .

O Allāh ﷻ! I have done evil and wronged my soul. Forgive me out of the bounty of your bounties upon me, O He ﷻ Who is the Most Merciful of those who show mercy!

thrice or more.

---

[172] Holy Qur'ān, Sūrat an-Nisā' (4), Verse 64.
[173] Holy Qur'ān, Sūrat al-Fātiḥah (1).
[174] Holy Qur'ān, Sūrat an-Nisā' (4), Verse 110.

3.91.1 Disliking to Sleep in the Last Third of the Night

Know well that the *faqīrs* abhor sleeping in the last third of the night more than their repugnance of outward sins. Ibn al-Mu'adhdhin (Allāh ﷻ have mercy on him) lived in the region of Abū 'Abdullāh for forty years during which he did not rest his side [i.e. body] on the ground at night. My Master Muḥammad as-Sarawī[175] (Allāh ﷻ have mercy on him) used to say: "Bravo to Ibn al-Mu'adhdhin! He did not miss out on the assistance that descends from the sky at night; he had a share in it!"

3.92 Praising Allāh ﷻ Excessively When in Hardship

It is from among their etiquettes to praise Allāh ﷻ excessively if they are struck with something that generally harms them for they know well that fates from Allāh ﷻ to His ﷻ servants are not through wisdom but rather they are wisdom per sé. Had they [struck] through wisdom then the acts of Allāh ﷻ would have been subject to the dictates of wisdom. From here [we know that] being displeased with something due to His ﷻ actions is never permissible, so anyone who is displeased [with wisdom-based fate] is ignorant. However, if something is disclosed to the servant regarding what Allāh ﷻ has prepared for him as an illustration of his bearing patience to the calamities of the body, property, children, [etc.,] he would ask Allāh ﷻ about their affecting him. Moreover, everything that takes effect in existence through divine will, assent to it is essential – it is incorrect to change it, as is already known.

3.93 Not Treating Illnesses when Complete Worship is Compromised

It is from among their etiquettes not to treat an illness unless it becomes so intense that tending to it diverts them away from complete presence with Allāh ﷻ. They do not treat [their illness] as long as relative presence in worship is easy enough for them.

Then again, it is essential to treat illnesses on the condition of having consideration for the intention of the treatment, such that one ought to treat an illness as an obligatory fulfilment of the right of the bondmaid of Allāh ﷻ [i.e. the human body] since Allāh ﷻ is the Owner

---

[175] Muḥammad as-Sarawī (d.932AH/1525CE).

of the body whereas the gnostic only treats the illness because his own essence is the bondmaid of Allāh ﷻ and it does not belong to him. The difference between someone who treats the illness as an obligatory fulfilment of the right of his Lord ﷻ and someone who treats it as a fulfilment with regards to the obligation of his own self is:

﴿ وَمَا يَعْقِلُهَآ إِلَّا الْعٰلِمُوْنَ ﴾

And none understands them except those who have knowledge. (29:43)[176]

An illustration of this is their love of being pardoned by Allāh ﷻ; had they no knowledge of the love of Allāh ﷻ for it [i.e. pardon], they would not have sought it from Him ﷻ. Understand!

3.94 Detesting Divine Conversations when Ritually Impure

It is from among their etiquettes to severely detest intimate discourses with Allāh ﷻ when their clothes or bodies are sullied with ritual filth – even if from an illness, out of reverence for the intimate discourse with Allāh ﷻ, especially when any of them suffers from diuresis or diarrhoea. Anyone who intimately converses with Allāh ﷻ when his body or clothes are defiled is deprived of respect from elders.

It is from here that the elders have acquired fine prayer-mats for ritual prayer – out of reverence for the presence of the Divine Word [i.e. intimate discourse with Allāh ﷻ during ritual prayer] and out of fear that someone might tread on a place where they believe the proximity of Allāh ﷻ to be experienced and not for any other personal reason.

3.95 Advising Sincerely Someone Who is Seeking a Spiritual Master

It is from among their etiquettes that when someone seeks their counsel to take [an oath of allegiance with] any of the contemporary shaykhs, they advise him and they do not deceive him. They say to him: "If you wish to follow the Path [of Verity] then you ought to take So-and-So [as your shaykh] and avoid associating with So-and-So." This

[176] Holy Qur'ān, Sūrat 'Ankabūt (29), Verse 43.

must be told in secrecy lest anything disorderly might emerge from it, although he is telling the truth, otherwise it might be deceptive to the servants of Allāh ﷻ. The manner of truthfulness in it is when that shaykh is unaccomplished with no grounding in the Path, and hence there would be no share for this disciple with that shaykh.

My Master 'Alī al-Khawwāṣ would never mention anyone in an ill manner. Moreover, he would often say to his associates:

> *You must refrain from associating with Shaykh So-and-So for he [falsely] seats himself [on the throne of spiritual leadership] without the authorising of a shaykh.*

He would mention his name without giving him an appellation, as an indication to the Muslims, and he would say:

> *The [following] suffices someone who does not find an honest counselling shaykh in his age to train him: love for Allāh ﷻ, love for the Messenger of Allāh ﷺ, sound beliefs and being pleased with fulfilling needs with the intention of benefitting the servants [of Allāh ﷻ] as well as himself.*

When you associate with any of the contemporary shaykhs who [falsely] seat themselves [on the thrones of spiritual leadership] and your foot slips [because of it], then you must take care not to connect him to the Spiritual Polarity (*Quṭbiyyah*) and not to add [the words] 'My Shaykh So-and-So' when describing him. After accompanying him, you must take care not to constrict your faces [out of arrogance] to your fellows, scrunch your noses, or lower your necks, but you should be as you were prior to accompanying him. He who does that with his fellows will harbour between himself and them something that has no good in it, such as mutual disconnection, hostility and hatred. They will become with each other as if they are of separate *dīns*. The Shaykhs do not prohibit the disciple from associating with bad company with his very first repenting unless it is for fear that by associating with them he might return to do something from which he has repented.

3.96 Expressing Remorse on Failing to Omit a Prohibition

It is from among their etiquettes to be remorseful when they commit something that is prohibited more than when they miss something that is obligated.

They [i.e. the People of Verity] said:

> *The station of ṣiddīqiyyah (utmost honesty) is more perfect and loftier than the station of shahādah (testimony).*

In their terminology, *ṣiddīqiyyah* is the term for 'omitting proscriptions' and *shahādah* is the term for 'upholding prescriptions'.

3.97 Not Seeking *Wilāyah* through Solitude

It is from among their etiquettes that they do not preoccupy themselves in disciplining the soul (*riyāḍah*) and solitude (*khalwah*) seeking to gain *wilāyah* (sainthood).

My Master 'Alī al-Khawwāṣ used to say:

> *The ruling pertaining to these shaykhs who administer the oath of hunger and disciplining the soul to the disciples that they become awliyā' is [like the] ruling pertaining to someone who wants the acacia to produce grapes or the sycamore to grow apples. This will never be right for him.*

One particular individual retired into solitude, made an abundance of *dhikr* [of Allāh ﷻ] and exerted his hunger in seeking *wilāyah*. So, he [i.e. 'Alī al-Khawwāṣ] went to him and said:

> *O fortunate one! Come out of solitude. It is essential to acquire that which has been apportioned for you.*
>
> *Specific wilāyah cannot be reached with effort and there are no apparent means by which it may be sought. It is an embrace that captures the servant in any state he might be, and thus he himself becomes a pure walī quicker than the glance of an eye. It is a rank specified for peoples who are specified, [and it is based on] a number that is specified, but the number is according to ranks rather than individual persons; sometimes there are two, four or more persons upon a single rank, sometimes a single person upon two ranks and sometimes two people upon the rank of a single person.*
>
> *As for general wilāyah, it may be reached with effort - as the saying of Allāh ﷻ indicates:*
>
> *My servant continues to come closer to Me by supererogatory deeds that I begin to love him.*[177]
>
> *The love of Allāh ﷻ is not gained by this servant until after he makes his own efforts, and that is conditional according to the specified people [of Allāh ﷻ]. It is favourable to others because*

---

[177] al-Bukhārī, *al-Jāmi' aṣ-Ṣaḥīḥ*.

> *there is no one to guide them to the reality of the matter with regards to the path of the specified people.*
>
> *So, my dear fellow, remove yourself from solitude! Repent to Allāh ﷻ and seek to acquire the station of ṣiddīqiyyah and shahādah through your [own] deeds.*

[Alas!] The station of *wilāyah* did not ensue, he refused [to come out of solitude] and he died two days later.

It is from among the sayings of my Master Afḍaluddīn:

> *In this age, those who marry during the days of inactivity [i.e. periods] are in a better state that these who seclude themselves; these [latter] people stipulate conditions in their solitude that those who marry do not stipulate, such as excessive hunger, absolute silence, sleep deprivation, etc., that weaken their bodies, by which their imaginations increase and their beliefs become corrupt when appear to them whatever light and darkness, beautiful and horrendous images such as dogs, snakes, etc., [and] of those that are latent within human nature. Surely, the body of a human is a comprehensive transcript of that which exists in the upper as well as the lower realms.*

Thereafter, it is clear that what we have mentioned in denouncement of solitude is with regards to someone who seeks a worldly affair by his solitude. However, there is no objection against someone seeking to clarify the relationship with Allāh ﷻ in legally permitted affairs.

3.98 Considering Oneself to be the Most Sinful in Gatherings

It is from among their etiquettes to see their own selves as the most sinful in every gathering where they sit with Muslims, especially [among] the *faqīrs*.

It is very dear for me to say in every gathering wherein I sit with Muslims:

اَللّٰهُمَّ إِنِّيْ اِعْتَرَفْتُ بَيْنَ يَدَيْكَ بِأَنِّيْ أَكْثَرُ هٰؤُلَاءِ ذُنُوْبًا ، وَأَقَلُّهُمْ حَيَاءً ، وَ أَسْوَؤُهُمْ أَدَبًا ،

فَبِحَقِّ أَسْمَائِهِم الظَّاهِرَةِ اغْفِرْ لِيْ .

O Allāh ﷻ! I have surely acknowledged in Your presence that I am indeed more sinful than all of these [people], lesser than them in modesty and worse than them in etiquette. Thus, by virtue of their manifest names, forgive me!

3.99 Consecrating the Intention

It is from among their etiquettes that when they wish to order someone to do good they ought to consecrate their intention as there could be a cause behind it that is detrimental to sincerity (*ikhlāṣ*). Therefore, the one who claims sincerity ought to examine himself that if his group left him for one of his adversaries, if he is [adversely] affected by it, then his command and his inviting was for his own self and not in compliance to the command of Allāh ﷻ.

That is why, in the past, only the senior *awliyā'* - who had broken free from the possessions of their own selves – would invite to Allāh ﷻ. As for the likes of us, if one invites [to Allāh ﷻ], he might destroy himself as well those who follow him.

3.100 Returning Property to the Rulers

It is from among their etiquettes to return all property that comes to them from the rulers as it is mingled with the unlawful and the doubtful.

3.101 Not Eating Food from the Wayward

It is from among their etiquettes not to eat any food from the wayward.

It is from among the sayings of my Master Ibrāhīm al-Matbūlī:

> *It behoves not a faqīr to eat from anyone's food unless it be such that if he informs him of all his previous mistakes that he has committed between himself and Allāh ﷻ his trust in him does not change. In any other case it is unlawful for him to eat.*

3.102 Praying for Whom One Eats With

It is from among their etiquettes that when they eat or drink with anyone they say:

اَللّٰهُمَّ إِنْ كَانَ مَا أَكَلْنَاهُ عِنْدَ عَبْدِكَ أَوْ شَرِبْنَاهُ حَلَالًا فَوَسِّعْ عَلَيْهِ ، وَاجْزِهِ خَيْرًا ، وَإِنْ

كَانَ حَرَامًا أَوْ شُبْهَةً ، فَاغْفِرْ لَنَا وَ لَهُ ، وَ أَرْضِ عَنَّا أَصْحَابَ التَّبِعَاتِ يَوْمَ الْقِيَامَةِ ،

صَدَقَةً مِنْ صَدَقَاتِكَ عَلَيْنَا ، يَا أَرْحَمَ الرَّاحِمِيْنَ .

O Allāh ﷻ! If what I have eaten and drank with your servant is lawful, expand it for him and reward him well. If it was unlawful or doubtful, forgive us and him and make the followers happy with us on the Day of Judgement out of the bounty of your bounties upon us, O He ﷻ Who is the Most Merciful of those who show mercy!

3.103 Praying When Intending to Do Good

It is from among their etiquettes that when they intend to pursue any righteous deed they say in their heart or on their tongue:

نَعْمَلُ ذٰلِكَ . . .

We shall do that...

or:

نَقُوْلُ ذٰلِكَ امْتِثَالًا لِأَمْرِكَ ، يَا مَوْلَانَا وَ مَوْلَى كُلِّ مَوْجُوْدٍ ، وَأَنْتَ خَالِقُهُ .

We shall say that in obedience to Your command, our Lord and the Lord of all that exists ﷻ - You are its creator.

These words are highly effective.

When they have completed it, they praise Allāh ﷻ since it is He ﷻ Who enabled them to do it. They seek His ﷻ forgiveness thrice for their shortcomings in it.

It is very dear for me to say:

اَسْتَغْفِرُ اللهَ الْعَظِيْمَ مِنْ تَقْصِيْرِي فِيْ كُلِّ عِبَادَةٍ عَدَدَ أَنْفَاسِيْ .

I seek forgiveness from Allāh the Great for my shortcomings equal to the number of my breaths in every form of worship.

Conclusion to Chapter 3

The etiquettes of the People [of Verity] are many, as aforementioned, but this amount is sufficient.

All praise is to Allāh ﷻ - the Lord of all the worlds.

Conclusion

The Agreed Upon Etiquettes for the *Dhikr* [of Allāh سبحانه وتعالى]

You should know – may Allāh سبحانه وتعالى enable me and you to make perpetual remembrance of Him سبحانه وتعالى – that the etiquettes of *dhikr* (remembrance [of Allāh سبحانه وتعالى]), when they are made on the tongue, are twenty-six. Some of them are pre-*dhikr*, some of them are during *dhikr* and some of them are post-*dhikr*.

4.1 Etiquettes Pre-*Dhikr*

Pre-*dhikr* [etiquettes] are five:

1. earnest repentance – that one turns away from anything that does not concern him in [his] sayings, doings and intentions. It is from among their [i.e. the Shaykhs] sayings:

   Someone who claims to repent but inclines to something from the permissible desires of this world is a liar!

2. bathing or ablution (*wuḍū'*)
3. perfuming one's clothes and mouth
4. consecrating the intention – for the incentive to make *dhikr* in compliance to nothing but the command [of Allāh سبحانه وتعالى]
5. associating honour for the One سبحانه وتعالى Who is remembered.

4.2 Etiquettes During *Dhikr*

As for the [etiquettes] during *dhikr*, [they are] sixteen:

1. sitting in a clean place, like sitting during the *tashahhud* position in ritual prayer
2. placing palms on thighs

3. facing the *qiblah* (direction towards the Ka'bah in Makkah), if one is making *dhikr* on his own. If they are a congregation, they form a circle
4. perfuming the gathering of *dhikr*
5. continued sincerity
6. [continued] honesty
7. the food and clothing to be lawful
8. the place to be darkened
9. closing the eyes during the *dhikr*
10. making oneself aware of the meaning of the *dhikr*
11. that one does not hold a partner with Him ﷻ [in the *dhikr*]
12. negating everything in the heart other than the One ﷻ Who is remembered
13. that it is audible
14. that it is with full strength
15. that one imagines his shaykh in front of his eyes
16. avoiding melody.

4.3 Etiquettes Post-*Dhikr*

As for the post-*dhikr* [etiquettes], [they are] five:

1. blaming the self for a while
2. not to drink until two or three degrees have passed him by
3. to remain silent for a long duration
4. remain attentive to the one who was involved in [i.e. leading] the *dhikr*
5. gratitude for ease and seeking forgiveness for shortcomings.

These are the agreed upon etiquettes of remembrance.

As for those that are not agreed upon, [they are] many. They [i.e. the Shaykhs] have conveyed them [to be] a hundred etiquettes but I have not seen any shaykh in this age who could identify [even] ten etiquettes for *dhikr*.

4.3.1 Note 1:

The best words for remembrance are to repeat the words of *ikhlāṣ* (sincerity)[178] as it has a tremendous effect – such that is not found in any of the other words of remembrance.

4.3.2 Note 2:

Some of them [i.e. the People of Verity] have mentioned three etiquettes for the aforementioned silence:

1. the servant's making himself aware that he is in the presence of Allāh ﷻ and that He ﷻ is well aware of him
2. combining the senses such that not even a hair of his moves, like the state of a cat when hunting a mouse
3. negating all mental thoughts and applying the meaning of the *dhikr* over the heart.

4.3.3 Note 3:

It is known to be favourable for the one making the *dhikr* that when he is silent and is listening to the devotional singer (*qawwāl*) singing the words of the People [of Verity] that he does not move, pronounce [the words] or praise the Prophet ﷺ, but invoke blessings inaudibly and not audibly.

This is the conclusion to the epistle that the need for bringing knowledge into action has entailed. [I swear] by my age, despite its short duration, [that this epistle] is of immense benefit from which none shall turn away but an enemy or an envier. It encompasses what many large books do not encompass; it is worthy of being named *The*

[178] This includes all words and phrases that refer to the oneness of Allāh ﷻ, His ﷻ omnipotence, His ﷻ omnipresence, His ﷻ attributes and qualities, as well as Sūrat al-Ikhlāṣ itself.

Epistle of Lights; its reports are compendious; its etiquettes are uniquely remarkable.

I ask Allāh ﷻ to benefit by it whoever writes it, reads it or hears it, to reward with goodness whoever informs [me] of any error that I may correct it, that He ﷻ blesses and grants peace to our Master and Leader Muḥammad - the Generous, the Trustworthy, ﷺ - all the Prophets ﵊ and Messengers ﵊, all their descendants and companions – the amount [equal to] those who make *dhikr* do make *dhikr* and the heedless ones forget. Allāh ﷻ bless our Master Muḥammad ﷺ, his ﷺ descendants, his ﷺ Companions ﵃, and grant them an abundance of peace until the Day of Judgement.

[This epistle] ends with the praise of Allāh ﷻ, His ﷻ assistance and His ﷻ bestowing strong ability.

All praise is to Allāh ﷻ – the Lord of all the worlds.

THE ARABIC TEXT

رسالة الأنوار

في آداب الصحبة عند الأخيار

للإمام عبد الوهاب أحمد الشعراني

رحمه الله تعالى عليه

مقدمة المؤلف

الحمد لله رب العالمين، وأُصلي وأُسلّم على سيدنا محمدٍ النور المبين، وعلى سائر الأنبياء والمرسلين، وعلى آلهم وصحبهم أجمعين

هذه رسالة اقتضتها البطالةُ، تشتمل على ثلاثة فصول وخاتمة، أسألُ الله أن ينفعَ بها جاهلَ العصر وعالمه

الفَصْلُ الأَوَّلُ

فِي ذكر شيء مِن فضل الصحبَة فِي الله تعالى

اعلمْ - وفقني اللهُ وإياك إلى ما يحب - : أن الصحبة في الله تعالى من أوثق عرى الإسلام، ومن أكبر أبواب الخير، وقد رغَّب العلماء فيها سلفا وخلفا، وأما من حذَّر منها، وقال: إن العزلة أقربُ للسلامة من الآفات، وأبعدُ من تحمل الحقوق في المخالطات، وأحزم للاشتغال بالطاعات... فإنما ذلك في حق المريد ما دام قاصراً، فإذا انتهى سلوكه وكَمُل حاله، بأن صار يشهد الله مع خلقه... كان الأفضل في حقه الخلطة، بل الخلطةُ في حق مثل هذا واجبةٌ كما قال بعضهم، لكن العارف في أواخر عمره يحنُّ إلى الوحدة كالبداية، فلا يصير له وقت يسع الناس، كما وقع لرسول الله ﷺ حين أنزلت عليه سورة النصر، فعلم أنه لا يقال: العزلةُ أفضل مطلقاً ولا الخلطة أفضل مطلقاً

ثم لا يخفى أن صحبة الأدنى للأعلى ليست بصحبة في الحقيقة، وإنما هي تعليم وخدمة؛ إذ صاحب الإنسان: هو من يشرب من بحره ويحيط بمقامه

فإطلاق الصحبة بين المريد والشيخ، والصحابي والرسول إطلاقٌ مجازي لا حقيقي

إذا علمت ذلك... فنورد عليك شيئاً من الأخبار الواردة في فضل المتحابين في الله؛ لأن القلب يقوى بالاطلاع على الدليل

فروى الشيخان في ((صحيحيهما)) : ((سبعةٌ يظلهمُ اللهُ في ظلِّهِ يومَ لا ظلَّ إلا ظلُّهُ : إمامٌ عادلٌ، وشابٌّ نشأَ في عبادةِ اللهِ، ورجلٌ قلبه معلَّقٌ بالمساجد، ورجلان تحابَّا في اللهِ - اجتمعا عليهِ وتفرَّقا عليه؛ ورجل دعتْهُ امرأةٌ ذاتُ منصبٍ وجمالٍ فقال: إنِّي أخافُ اللهَ؛ ورجلٌ تصدَّقَ بصدقةٍ فأخفاها حتّى لا تعلمَ شمالُهُ ما تنفق يمينُهُ؛ ورجل ذكرَ اللهَ خالياً ففاضتْ عينَاهُ))

وروى مسلمٌ : ((والذي نفسي بيدِهِ؛ لنْ تدخلوا الجنَّةَ حتّى تؤمنوا، ولنْ تؤمنوا حتّى تحابُّوا. أوَلا أدلُّكُمْ على شيءٍ إذا فعلتُمُوه تحاببْتم؟ أفشوا السلامَ بينَكُم))

وروى أيضاً : ((زارَ رجلٌ أخاً له في اللهِ، فأرسلَ اللهُ له ملكاً على مدرجتِهِ، قال : أينَ تريدُ؟ قال: أريد أخاً لي في هذهِ القريةِ، قال: فهلْ لكَ عندَهُ من نعمةٍ تربُّها؟ قال: لا، غيرَ أنِّي أحببتُهُ في الله، قال أبشر؛ فإني رسولُ اللهُ إليك: أنَّ اللهَ قد أحبَّكَ كما أحببتَهُ))

وروى ابن عساكر وغيره: ((سبعةٌ في ظلِّ العرشِ يومَ لا ظلَّ إلا ظلُّهُ: رجلٌ ذكرَ اللهَ فَفَاضَتْ عيناه، ورجلٌ يحبُّ عبداً لا يحبُّهُ إلا للهِ، ورجلٌ قلبُهُ معلَّقٌ بالمساجدِ؛ من شدَّةِ حبِّهِ إيَّاها، ورجلٌ يعطي الصدقةَ بيمينهِ فيكادُ أن يخفيها عن شمالِهِ، وإمامٌ مقسطٌ في رعيتِهِ ورجل عَرَضَتْ عليه امرأةٌ نفسَها فتركَها لجلالِ اللهِ، ورجلٌ كان في سريَّةٍ مع قومٍ فلقوا العدوَّ، فانكشفوا، فحمى آثارهم حتى نَجَوا ونجا أو استشهد))

وروى البيهقي في ((الأسماء)): ((سبعةٌ يظلُّهُمُ الله تحتَ ظلِّ عرشِهِ يومَ لا ظلَّ إلا ظلُّهُ: رجلٌ قلبُهُ معلَّقٌ بالمساجدِ، ورجل دعتهُ امرأةٌ ذات منصبٍ وجمالٍ فقال: إنِّي أخافُ اللهَ، ورجلان تحابَّا في اللهِ، ورجلٌ غضَّ عينَيهِ عن محارم الله، وعينٌ حرسَتْ في سبيل اللهِ، وعينٌ بكتْ من خشية اللهِ))

وروى أيضا في ((شعب الإيمان)): ((رأسُ العقلِ بعدَ الإيمانِ باللهِ التودُّدُ إلى الناسِ، وأهلُ التودُّدِ في الدنيا لهم درجةٌ في الجنَّة، ومَنْ كانتْ له درجةٌ في الجنَّة... فهوَ في الجنةِ))

وروى أيضا: ((رأسُ العقلِ بعدَ الإيمانِ التحبُّبُ إلى الناسِ، واصطناعُ الخيرِ إلى كلِّ برٍّ وفاجرٍ))

وروى الدارقطني: ((المؤمنُ يألفُ ويُؤلفُ، ولا خير فيمن لا يألفُ ولا يؤلفُ، وخيرُ الناسِ أنفعهمُ للناسِ))

وروى أبو داود: ((من أحبَّ للهِ، وأبغضَ للهِ، وأعطى للهِ ومنعَ للهِ... فقد استكملَ الإيمان))

وروي أيضا: ((أفضل الأعمال الحب في الله، والبغض في الله))

وروي أيضا: ((أفضل الإيمانِ أن تحبَّ للهِ، وتبغضَ للهِ، وتستعملَ لسانَكَ في ذكرِ اللهِ، وأن تحبَّ للناسِ ما تحبُّ لنفسِكَ، وتكرَهَ لهم ما تكرَهُ لنفسِكَ وأن تقولَ خيراً أو لتصمُتْ))

وروى الإمام أحمد: ((إن اللهَ يقول يومَ القيامة: (أين المتحابونَ لجلالي؟ اليومَ أظلُّهُم في ظلّي)))

وروى أيضا: ((المؤمن الذي يخالطُ الناسَ ويصبرُ على أذاهم... أفضلُ من المؤمن الذي لا يخالطُ الناسَ ولا يصبرُ على أذاهم))

وروى أيضا: ((إنَّ أوثقَ عُرى الإسلامِ أنْ تحبَّ في اللهِ وتبغضَ في الله))

وروى أيضا بسند صحيح: ((إِن المتحابينَ في اللهِ لَتُرى غرفُهُم في الجنَّةِ كالكوكبِ الطالعِ الشرقيِّ أو الغربيِّ، فيقالُ: مَنْ هؤلاءِ؟ فيقالُ: هؤلاءِ المتحابونَ في اللهِ))

وروى أيضا: ((أحبّ الأعمالِ إلى اللهِ الحبُّ في اللهِ والبغضُ في الله))

وروى أيضا: ((مَنْ سرَّه أن يجدَ حلاوةَ الإيمانِ... فليحبَّ المرءَ لا يحبّهُ إلا للهِ))

وروى الطبراني: ((رأسُ العقلِ بعدَ الإيمانِ باللهِ التحبُّبُ إلى الناسِ))

وروى أيضا: ((إنَّ المتحابينَ في اللهِ في ظلِّ العرشِ))

وروى أيضا: ((ثلاثةٌ في ظلِّ العرشِ يومَ القيامةِ يومَ لا ظلَّ إلا ظلُّه: رجلٌ حيثُ توجَّهَ علم أنَّ اللهَ معهُ، ورجلٌ دعتْه امرأةٌ إلى نفسِها فتركَها من خشيةِ اللهِ، ورجلٌ أحبَّ لجلالِ اللهِ))

وروى أيضا: ((المتحابونَ في اللهِ على كراسيَّ من ياقوتٍ حولَ العرشِ))

وروى أيضا: قال الله تعالى: ((وَجَبت محبَّتي للمتحابينَ فيَّ، والمتجالسينَ فيَّ، والمتباذلين فيَّ، والمتزاورين فيَّ))

وروي أيضا: ((لو أن عبدينِ تحابّا في اللهِ، واحدٌ في المشرقِ، وآخرُ في المغربِ... لجمعَ اللهُ بينهما يومَ القيامةِ، يقولُ: هذا الذي كنتَ تحبُّهُ فيَّ))

وروى أيضا: ((ما تحابَّ رجلانِ في اللهِ... إلّا وضعَ اللهُ لهما كرسياً فأُجلِسَا عليه حتّى يفرغَ اللهُ من الحساب))

وروي أيضا: ((مَنْ أحبَّ قوماً... حُشِرَ في زمرتِهم))

وروى أيضا: المتحابونَ في الله في ظلِّ اللهِ يومَ لا ظلَّ إلا ظلُّهُ، على منابرَ من نورٍ، يفزعُ الناسُ ولا يفزعونَ))

وروى أيضا: ((إن للهِ عباداً ليسوا بأنبياء ولا شهداء، يغبطهمُ النبيونَ والشهداءُ على منازِلِهم وقربِهِم من اللهِ، قيلَ: مَنْ هُم يا رسولَ اللهِ؟ قال: ناس من بلدانٍ شتّى لم تصلْ بينهم أرحامٌ متقاربةٌ، تحابُّوا في اللهِ، وتصافحُوا، يضعُ اللهُ لهم يومَ القيامةِ منابرَ من نورٍ قُدّامَ الرحمٰن فيجلسهم عليها، يفزعُ الناسُ ولا يفزعونَ))

وروى أيضا: ((ليبعثنَّ اللهُ أقواماً يومَ القيامةِ، في وجوهِهم النورُ، على منابرِ اللؤلؤِ، يغبطُهم الناسُ، ليسوا بأنبياء ولا شهداء، قيلَ: مَنْ هم؟ قال: المتحابّونَ في اللهِ، من قبائلَ شتّى وبلادٍ شتّى، يجتمعونَ على ذكرِ اللهِ يذكرونَهُ))

وروى أيضا: ((إنَّ في الجنَّةِ غُرفاً، يُرى ظواهرُهَا من بواطِنِها وبواطنُها من ظواهرِها، أعدَّها اللهُ للمتحابينَ فيه، والمتزاورينَ فيه، والمتباذلينَ فيه))

وروى البزار وأبو الشيخ عن أبي هريرة: ((إن في الجنَّةِ لَعُمُداً من ياقوتٍ، عليها غرفٌ من زبرجدٍ لها أبوابٌ مفتَّحةٌ، تضيءُ كما يضيءُ الكوكبُ الدريُّ، قلنا: يا رسولَ الله من يسكنُها؟ قال: المتحابونَ في الله، والمتباذلونَ في الله، والمتلاقونَ في الله))

وروى الترمذي –وقال: حديث حسن صحيح –: ((قال الله تعالى: المتحابونَ في جلالي لهم منابرُ من نورٍ يغبطهمُ النبيونَ والشهداءُ))

وروى أيضا: ((المرءُ مع من أحبَّ، وله ما اكتسبَ))

وروى أيضا: ((ثلاثٌ من كنَّ فيه وجدَ حلاوةَ الإيمانِ: أن يكونَ اللهُ ورسولُهُ أحبَّ إليه مما سواهما، وأن يحبَّ المرءَ لا يحبُّه إلا للهِ، وأن يكرَهَ أن يعودَ في الكفرِ بعدَ أَنْ أنقذَهُ اللهُ مِنْهُ كما يكرَهُ أن يلقى في النارِ))

وروى أيضا: ((المؤمنُ للمؤمنِ كالبنيانِ يشدُّ بعضُهُ بعضاً))

وروى ابن النَّجار: ((استكثروا من الإخوانِ؛ فإنَّ لكلِّ مؤمنٍ شفاعة يومَ القيامةِ))

وروى الحكيم: ((نظرُ الرجلِ لأخيهِ عن شوقٍ خيرٌ من اعتكافِ سنةٍ في مسجدي هذا))

وروى ابنُ أبي الدنيا: ((قال الله تعالى: حقتْ محبَّتي للمتحابينَ فيَّ، اليومَ أظُلُّهُم في ظلِّ العرشِ يومَ القيامةِ يومَ لا ظلَّ إلا ظلِّي))

وروى أيضا: ((مَا أحدثَ رجلٌ إخاءً في اللهِ إلا أحدثَ اللهُ لهُ درجةً في الجنَّةِ))

وروى أيضا: ((أصبْ بطعامِكَ مَنْ تحبُّ في اللهِ))

وروى الحاكم وغيره: ((قال الله تعالى: المتحابونَ فيَّ على منابرَ من نورٍ، يغبطُهُم بمكانهم النبيُّونَ والصدِّيقون والشهداءُ))

وروى البيهقي: ((من أحبَّ أن يجدَ طعمَ الإيمان... فليحبَّ المرءَ لا يحبُّهُ إلا للهِ))

وروى أيضا: ((أن الله تعالى يقول: إنّي لأهمُّ بأهلِ الأرضِ عذاباً، فإذا نظرتُ إلى عُمَّارِ بيوتي والمتحابين فيّ والمستغفرينَ بالأسحارِ... صرفتُ عذابي عنهم))

والأخبار في فضل المتحابين في الله كثيرة، ونقتصر منها على هذا القدر

وأما الآثار عن السلف الصالح، والعلماء العاملين: فكثيرة أيضاً، ونذكر لك — يا أخي — شيئاً منها:

فعن الحسن البصري - رحمه الله تعالى - قال: كل من اتَّبع طريقة طاعة الحق تعالى... لزمتك مودَّتُه، ومن أحبَّ رجلاً صالحاً... فكأنما أحبَّ اللهَ عز وجل

وقال الإمام الشافعي - رحمه الله -: لولا صحبة الأخيارِ، ومناجاةُ الحق تعالى بالأسحار... ما أحببتُ البقاء في هذه الدار

وقال أيضا: لقاء الإخوان ليس يعدلُه عندي شيء

وقال مطرِّف بن الشخِّير: أوثق أعمالي عندي، حُبّي للرجل الصالح

وقال أبو نصر بشر الحافي - رحمه الله -: عليك بصحبة الأخيار، إن أردت الراحةَ في تلك الدار،وأن تحسنَ ظنَّك بالأشرار، وتنفكَّ من رقِّ الأغيار

وقال سيدي أحمد ابن الرفاعي - رحمه الله -: مصاحبة أهل التقوى، نعمةٌ عظيمةٌ من نعم الله على العبد

وقال أبو السعود بن أبي العشائر - رحمه الله -: من أراد أن يعطى الدرجة القصوى يوم القيامة... فليصاحبْ في الله، ومن أحبَّ أن تصرفَ عنه مرارةُ الموقف... فليطعم أخاً في الله شيئاً من الحلوى

وفي الحديث: ((من وافق من أخيه شهوة... غفر له))

وقال شيخ الوفائية - رحمه الله -: لا تبع ذرة من الحب لله، أو في الله بقناطير من الأعمال، قال رسول الله ﷺ: ((المرءُ معَ مَنْ أحبَّ))

وقال سيدي علي وفا: إذا أحببت أخاً في الله... فاحفظْه، تزددْ به ممن أحببته من أجله

وقال الشيخ أبو المواهب الشاذلي - رحمه الله -: عليك بتكثير سوادِ القومِ؛ فإن ((من كثَّرَ سوادَ قوم... فهو منهم))

وقال أيضا: إذا رأيت نفسك معرضة عن موادَدَة أهلِ الله... فاعلم أنك مطرودٌ عن باب الله

وقال أيضا: عليك بصحبةِ الفقراء؛ فإنه لو لم يكن إلا أخذهم بيدك يوم القيامة مع ما يحملون عن أصحابهم في دار الدنيا من المصائب... لكان في ذلك كفاية، وكم استضيءَ لصحبتهم فقير، وجُبِرَ كسير، وارتفع وضيعٌ، وسُتِرَ شنيعٌ، وهلك ظالم، وارتفعت مظالم، وفيهم ورد الحديث: ((بهمْ ترزقونَ وتمطرونَ وترحمونَ))

وقال الشيخ سليمان الخضيري - رحمه الله -: من أراد أن يعطى الخير الكثيرَ... فليصاحب أهل المراقبة

وقال سيدي علي الخواص - رحمه الله -: من أراد أن يكمل أيمانه وأن يحسن ظنه... فليصاحب الأخيار

وقال سيدي أفضل الدين - رحمه الله -: عليك بالودِّ في الله؛ فقد ورد أن الله يقول لعبده يوم القيامة: ((هل واليت لي ولياً، أو عاديت لي عدواً؟))

وقال أيضا: من أراد أن يكون من أكابر أهل المقابر... فليصاحب في الله

قلت: يؤيده ما حكاه اليافعي في كتابه ((روض الرياحين)) عن بعض الأولياء أنه قال: سألت الله تعالى أن يريني مقاماتِ أهل المقابر، فرأيت في ليلة من الليالي كأن القيامة قد قامت، والقبور قد انشقت، وإذا منهم النائمُ على السندس، ومنهم النائمُ علي الحرير والديباج، ومنهم النائم على الريحانِ، ومنهم النائم على السرر، ومنهم الضاحك، ومنهم الباكي، قال: فقلت: يا رب! لو شئت ساويت بينهم في الكرامة، فنادى منادٍ من أهل القبور: يا فلان! هذه منازل الأعمال:

أما أصحاب السندس: فهم أهل الخلق الحسن، وأما أصحاب الحرير والديباج: فهم الشهداء، وأما أصحاب الريحان: فهم الصائمون، وأما أصحاب الضحك: فهم التائبون، وأما أصحاب البكاء: فهم المذنبون، وأما أصحاب المراتب: فهم المتحابون في الله تعالى

قال اليافعي: هكذا ذكر في الأصل الذي نقلت منه، أعني فسّر أصحاب المراتب ولو لم يتقدم للمراتب ذكر، وتقدم ذكرُ السرر ولم يفسر أصحابها بعد (منهم) فلعله أراد بالمراتب السررَ المتقدمَ ذكرها؛ لأن حقيقة المراتب هي المناصبُ الشريفة، والمقاماتُ العالية المنيفة، ولا شك أن أصحاب السرر أشرف مرتبة، وأعلى منزلة ممن على الأرض، وإن كان أهل الأرض على الحرير وغيره، مع أن السرر المذكورة المعدة للإكرام لا تخلو من الفرش العزيزة غالباً، وإن لم تذكر معها كما قال الله تعالى: ﴿إِخْوَانًا عَلَىٰ سُرُرٍ مُّتَقَٰبِلِينَ﴾ [الحجر: ٤٧] فلم يذكر سبحانه الفرش في هذه الآية، ومعلوم أن السرر المذكورة عليها الفرش المذكورة في آية أخرى، وإذا قال قائل: جلس الملك على سريره، وجلسنا عنده... علم من ذلك شيئان:

أحدهما: أن السرير مفروش

الثاني: أن الملك إنما جلس علي السرير ليرتفع على من عنده برفعة المجلس، مع رفعة المملكة ولا يرضى أن يجلس معه على السرير غيره

قال: فعلى هذا يكون المتحابون في الله أفضلَ من سائر المذكورين في هذه الحكاية، وقد ورد حديث الترمذي الصحيح: قال الله تعالى: ((المتحابونَ في جلالي لهم منابرُ من نور يغبطُهم النبيّونَ والشهداءُ))، فقد ظهر من هذا الحديث ما يؤيد المنام المذكور، أنهم أصحاب المراتب، وناهيك بها من مراتب، وأكرمْ بها من مناصب، احتوت على شرفٍ جلَّ قدره وعظم فخره، مع ما لهم من السلسبيل — كذا في الأصل السلسبيل — الأهنا، والجمال الأسنى، والنعيم المقيم في جوار المولى الكريم، وأما ذكر السرر في المنام المذكور، وذكر منابر النور في الحديث المشهور: فليس بينهما تناقض، ولا قادح مذكور؛ فالمنابر تكون في القيامة، والسرر تكون في القبور، كما روي في المنام المذكور. انتهى كلام اليافعي - رحمه الله تعالى

والآثار في فضل المتحابين في الله كثيرة، وفي هذا القدر كفاية

والحمد لله رب العالمين

الفَصْلُ الثَّانِي

فِي ذكر شيء من حُقوقِ الصحبة

اعلم - وفقني الله وإياك إلى ما يحب - أن حقوق الصحبة كثيرة، ولكن نذكر لك جملة من الحقوق التي لا بُدَّ منها في طريق العشرة والمخالطة، واعلم أيضاً: أن المشايخ قد حثُّوا على الاعتناء بحقوق الإخوان، وقالوا: من ضيَّعَ حقوق إخوانه... ابتلاه الله تعالى بتضييع حقوقه، وإذا ابتلى الله عبداً بذلك... مقتَهُ، وإذا مقت الله عبداً... طرحه في النار

إذا علمت ذلك... فأقول وبالله التوفيق:

من حق الأخ على الأخ: أن يتعامى عن عيوبه؛ فقد قال المشايخ: من نظر إلى عيوب الناس... قلَّ نفعه وخرب قلبه. وقالوا: إذا رأيتم الرجل موكلاً بعيوب الناس، خبيراً بها... فاعلموا أنه قد مُكِر به

وقالوا: من علامات الاستدراج للعبد، نظره في عيوب الناس، وعماه عن عيوب نفسه

وقالوا: ما رأينا شيئاً أحبط للأعمال، ولا أفسد للقلوب، ولا أسرع في هلاك العبد، ولا أقرب من المقت، ولا ألزم لمحجة الرياء والعجب والرياسة... من قلة معرفة العبد عيوبَ نفسه، ونظره في عيوب الناس

ومن حق الأخ على الأخ: أن يحمل ما يراه منه على وجهٍ من التأويل جميل ما أمكن، فإن لم يجد تأويلاً... رجع على نفسه باللوم

وفي وصية سيدي إبراهيم الدسوقي: لا تنكروا على أخيكم حاله، ولا لباسه، ولا طعامه، ولا شرابه؛ فإن الإنكار يورث الوحشةَ والانقطاعَ عن الله تعالى، ولا إنكار على أحد إلا إن ارتكب محظوراً صرحت به الشريعة المطهرة، فإن الناس خاص، وخاص الخاص، ومبتدئ، ومُنْته، ومتشبه، ومتحقق، والقوي لا يقدر على المشي مع الضعيف، وعكسه، والله تعالى يرحم البعض بالبعض

ومن كلام الإمام سعيد بن المسيِّب: ما من شريف، ولا ذي فضل... إلا وفيه نقص، ولكن من كان فضله أكثر من نقصه، وُهِب نقصه لفضله

ومن حق الأخ على الأخ: أن يرجو له من الخيرات، والمسامحة وقبول التوبة، ولو فعل من المعاصي الإسلامية ما فعل، كما يرجو ذلك لنفسه

ومن حق الأخ على الأخ: ألَّا ينظر إلى زلَّةٍ سبقت، ولا يكشف له عورة سُترت، وفي الحديث: ((منْ رأى عورةً فسترها... كان كمَنْ أحيا موءودةً من قبرِها))

وقال المشايخ: كل من لم يستر على إخوانه ما يراه منهم من الهفوات... فقد فتح على نفسه باب كشف عورته، بقدر ما أظهر من هفواتهم

وقالوا: إذا رأيتم أحداً من إخوانكم على معصية لم يجاهر بها... فاستروه، فإن تجاهر بها... فوبِّخوه بينكم، وإن لم ينزجر... فوبخوه بين الناس مصلحة له، لا تشفياً فيه؛ فلعله يرعوي وينزجر، وما دام يعصي في قعر داره، ويغلق بابه عليه... فهو لم يتجاهر، إلا إن كان هناك أطفالٌ، يحكون ما يرون؛ فإنهم كالرجال

ومن حق الأخ علي الأخ: ألّا يعيِّره بذنبٍ ولا غيرِه؛ فإن المعايرة تقطع الوُدَّ، أو تكدر صفاءه

ومن كلام الحسن البصري: إذا بلغكم عن أحد زلة، ولم تثبت عند حاكم... فلا تعيروه بها، وكذِّبوا من أشاعها عنه، لا سيما إن كان هو بينكم، ذلك لأن الأصل براءة الساحة، حتّى تقام البينة العادلة عند الحاكم، ثم بعد ثبوت ذلك عنده، فإياكم أن تعيروه أيضاً، فربما عافاه الله وابتلاكم

وفي الحديث: ((من عيَّر أخاه بذنب... لم يمت حتّى يعملَ ذلك الذنب))

ومن كلام سيدي علي وفا: (لا تَعِبْ أخاك بما أصابه من مصائب دنياك؛ فإنّه في ذلك إما مظلوم سينصره الله، أو مذنب عوقب فطهّره الله، ومن الرعونة أن تفتخر بما لا تأمن سلبه، أو تعيِّر أحداً بما لا يستحيل في حقك، وأنت تعلم أن ما جاز على مثلك... جاز عليك

ومن حق الأخ على الأخ: ألَّا ينظر له بعين الاحتقار؛ فقد قال المشايخ: من نظر إلى أخيه بعين احتقار... عوقب بالذل والخزي

وفي الحديث: ((من نظر إلى أخيه نظرة وُدٍّ... غفر الله له))

ومن حق الأخ على الأخ: إذا اطلع على عيب فيه أن يتهم نفسه في ذلك، ويقول: إنما ذلك العيب فيّ؛ لأن المسلم مرآة المسلم، ولا يرى الإنسانُ في المرآة إلا صورة نفسه

وقد صحب رجل أبا إسحاق إبراهيمَ بن أدهم، فلما أراد أن يفارقه... قال له: نبهني على ما فيَّ من العيب، فقال له: يا أخي! إني لم أر لك عيباً؛ لأني لحظتك بعين الوداد، فاستحسنت منك ما رأيت، فسل غيري عن عيبك. وفي هذا المعنى أنشدوا:

وعينُ الرضا عن كلِّ عيبٍ كليلةٌ كما أنَّ عينَ السخطِ تبدي المساويا

ومن حق الأخ على الأخ: أن يرى نفسه دونه على الدوام، وذلك على سبيل اليقين، لا على سبيل الظن والتخمين؛ فقد قالوا: من لم ير نفسه دون أخيه، لم ينتفع بصحبته

ومن كلام الشيخ أبي المواهب الشاذلي: لمَّا علم أهل الله، أن كل نبات لا ينبت ولا يثمر، إلا بجعله تحت الأرض، تَعْلُوه الأرجل... جعلوا نفوسهم أرضاً للكل

ومن كلام سيدي علي وفا: إنما جعل لكم الأرض بساطاً ليعلمَكم التواضع، فتواضعوا تنبسطوا

ومن حق الأخ على الأخ: أن يؤثره على نفسه في كل شيء؛ فقد قالوا: لا يسود أحد على أقرانه إلا إن آثرهم على نفسه، واحتمل أذاهم، ولم يشاركهم في شيء مما استشرفت إليه نفوسهم

ومن حق الأخ على الأخ: أن يخدمه إِذا مرض؛ فقد ذكروا أن الفتوة في خدمة الإخوان

ومن كلام الأستاذ الجنيد - رحمه الله -: ينبغي للإنسان أن يخدم إخوانه، ثم يعتذر إليهم بأنه ما قام بواجب حقِّهم، ويقرلهم بالخيانة على نفسه ولو علم أنه بريء الساحة، ما لم يترتب على ذلك حدٌّ أو تعزير، وإلا... دخل فيمن ظلم نفسه، وذلك حرام

ومن كلام الشيخ أبي المواهب الشاذلي: من تعزز على خدمة إخوانه... أورثه الله ذلاً لا انفكاك له منه أبداً، ومن خدم إخوانه... أُعطي من خالص أعمالهم

ومن حق الأخ على الأخ: أن يحترمه ويوقره، لا سيما إذا استحق ذلك كأن كان من العلماء، أو من حملة القرآن الكريم، أو من عترة رسول الله ﷺ

وفي وصية الإمام النووي: لا تستصغر أحداً؛ فإن العاقبة منطوية، والعبد لا يدري بِمَ يختم له، فإذا رأيت عاصياً... فلا تقدِّم نفسك عليه، فربما كان في علم الله أعلى منك مقاماً وأنت من الفاسقين، ويصير يشفع فيك يوم القيامة، وإذا رأيت صغيراً... فاحكم بأنه خير منك باعتبار أنه أحقر منك ذنوباً، وإذا رأيت من هو أكبر منك سناً... فاحكم بأنه خير منك باعتبار أنه أقدم منك هجرة في الإسلام، وإذا رأيت كافراً... فلا تقطع له بالنار لاحتمال أنه يسلم ويموت مسلماً

ومن حق الأخ على الأخ: أن يثني عليه في غيبته وفي حضوره بطريق الشرع؛ فإن ذلك مما يزيد في صفاء المودة

وقد روى الطبراني وغيره: ((إذا مُدِح المؤمنُ – يعني الكامل – في وجهه... ربا الإيمانُ في قلبِه))؛ أي: لأن المؤمن الكامل إذا مدح... شكر الله على ستر نقائصه وإظهار محاسنه فيزيد إيمانه بذلك، ثم لا يخفى أن ذلك إنما يكون قبل صفاء المودة وصحتها، أما إذا صفت المودة، وصحَّت... فإن الثناء حينئذٍ ليس بجيد، وأنشدوا:

إذا صفتِ المودَّةُ بينَ قومٍ وصحَّ ولاؤُهُمْ سَمُجَ الثَّنَاءُ

ومن حق الأخ على الأخ: أن يكرمه إذا ورد عليه، بأن يتلقاه بالترحيب، وطلاقة الوجه، ويأخذه بالعناق إن كان رجلاً، ويفرش له شيئاً يقيه من التراب

ومن حق الأخ على الأخ: أن يوسِّع له في المجلس إذا رآه، فإن ذلك مما يزيد في تقوية المودة، وفي الحديث: ((إن للمسلمِ حقاً إذا رآه أخوه أن يتزحزحَ لهُ))

ومن حق الأخ على الأخ: ألّا يدعوه باسمه فقط

ومن وصية بعضهم: إذا ناديت أخاك، فعظِّمْه... تثبت مودته، ومن الجفاء للأخ نداؤه الخالي عن الكنية واللقب، ولفظ السيادة، وكذلك أولاده، وأحفاده، غيبةً وحضوراً

ومن حق الأخ على الأخ: أن يعترف له بالفضل، وان يظهر له عدم مكافأته، لا سيما إن كان قد بادأه بهدية؛ لأنه لا يقدر على مكافأة بداءته، كما قال الشيخ محي الدين ابن العربي. وفي الحديث: ((من أودع معروفاً... فلينشره، ومن نشره... فقد شكر، ومن كتمه... فقد كفر، ولا يشكر الله من لا يشكر الناس))

ومن حق الأخ على الأخ: أن يزوره كل قليل من الأيام؛ ففي الحديث ((امش ميلاً عدْ مريضاً، امش ميلين أصلح بين اثنين، امش ثلاثة أميال زر أخاً في الله تعالى))

وفيه أيضا: ((الزائر أخاه في بيته، الآكل من طعامه... أرفع درجة من المطعِم))

وفيه أيضا: ((إذا زار أحدكم أخاه، فألقى له شيئاً يقيه من التراب... وقاه الله عذاب النار))

وفيه أيضا: ((زر في الله؛ فإنه من زار في الله . . . ، شيّعه سبعون ألف ملك))

وحكى اليافعي عن بعض الأولياء أنه قال: رأيت القطب بمكة، على عجلة من ذهب، والملائكة يجرونها في الهواء، بسلاسل من ذهب، فقلت: إلى أين تمضي؟ فقال: إلى أخ من إخواني اشتقت إليه، فقلت له: لو سألت الله أن يسوقه إليك، فقال: وأين ثواب الزيارة يا أخي؟! انتهى

ومن كلام سيدي إبراهيم المتبولي: اسع إلى إخوانك، وإياك أن تنقطع عنهم بحيث يستوحشون فيأتون إلى زيارتك، فإن جميع ما مع الفقير من المدد في هذا الزمان، لا يجيء حق طريقٍ واحدٍ يُمْشَى إليه

وقد كان الإمام الشافعي يزور تلميذه الإمام أحمد بن حنبل كثيراً، ويزوره الآخر كذلك، فقيل للشافعي في ذلك، فأنشد – رضي الله تعالى عنه –:

قالوا يزورُكَ أحمد فتزورُهُ   قلتُ: الفضائلُ لا تفارقُ منزلَهْ

إِن زارني فبفضلِهِ أو زرتُهُ   فلفضلِهِ فالفضلُ في الحالينِ لَهْ

فأجابه الإمام أحمد – رضي الله تعالى عنه –:

إِن زرتنا فبفضلٍ منك تمنحنا   أو نحنُ زرنا فللفضلِ الذي فيكَا

فلا عدمنا كلا الحالينِ منكَ ولا   نالَ الذي يتمنىٰ منكَ شانيكَا

ومن كلام سيدي على الخواص ـ رحمه الله –: الزيارة للإخوان تزيد في الدين، وتركها ينقصه؛ لأنها كتلقيح النخل، وقد قال القوم: إذا قلَّ رأس مالك... فزر إخوانك

قلت: زيارة الإخوان لا تزيد في الدين إلا مع لزوم أدب الزيارة، والله أعلم

ومن حق الأخ على الأخ: أن يصافحه كلَّما لقيه بنية التبرك وامتثال الأمر، وقد روى الطبراني: ((إذا تصافح المسلمان... لم تفَرق أكفُّهما حتى يغفر لهما))

وروى أبو الشيخ: ((إذا التقى المسلمان، وسلَّم أحدهما على صاحبه... كان أحبهما إلى الله أحسنهما بشراً لصاحبه، فإذا تصافحا... أنزل الله عليهما مئة رحمة))

ومن حق الأخ على الأخ: إذا لاقاه، وصافحه أن يصلي ويسلِّم على النبي ﷺ، ويذكّره بذلك، وقد روى أبو يعلى: ((ما من عبدين متحابين، يستقبل أحدهما صاحبه، ويصليان على النبي ﷺ... إلا لم يتفرقا حتى يغفر لهما ذنوبهما، ما تقدم منها وما تأخر))

ومن حق الأخ على الأخ: أن يهاديه كل قليل من الأيام، لا سيما إذا بلغه عنه وقفة، وفى الحديث: ((تهادوا تحابُّوا وتصافحوا يذهب الغلّ عنكم))

ومن حق الأخ على الأخ: أن يرشده إلى ترك البغي على من بغى عليه، وأن ينتصر بالله تعالى؛ إذْ إرشاد الأخ المظلوم إلى الانتصار بالله تعالى والتسليم إليه سبحانه... من أكبر نصرة الأخ

وفي زبور السيد داود عليه السلام: ((يا داودُ! لا تبغي على مَنْ بغى عليك، فمَنْ بغى على من بغى عليه... تخلفت عنه نصرتي))

ومن حق الأخ على الأخ: مساعدته له في التزويج، وقد ذكروا أن الإعانة في ذلك أفضل من إعانة الغزاة والمكاتبين؛ إذ هو أفضل نوافل الخيرات، والأجر يعظم بعظم السبب، فلولا النكاح... ما وُجِد مجاهد ولا عابد لله تعالى

ومن حق الأخ على الأخ: ألَّا يغفل عن عيادته إذا مرض، ولا عن خدمته، لا سيما في الليل، وفي الحديث: ((ما من رجل يعود مريضاً ممسياً... إلا خرج معه سبعون ألف ملك، يستغفرون له حتى يصبح، ومن أتاه مصبحاً... خرخ معه سبعون ألف ملك يستغفرون له حتى يمسي))

وينبغي للعائد ألّا يأكل عند المريض؛ وففي الحديث: ((إذا عاد أحدكم مريضاً... فلا يأكل عنده شيئاً))

ومن حق الأخ على الأخ: أن يرشده إلى الوصية إذا حضرته الوفاة، ولا يتبع الحياء الطبيعي في ذلك، والفائدة في ذلك معلومة

ومن حق الأخ على الأخ: أن يسهر عنده إلى الصباح إذا كان في حالة تفضي إلى الموت، فربما كان الأجل في ذلك الوقت، فيفارقه على وفائه بحقه

ومن حق الأخ على الأخ: أن يصدقه إذا انتسب إلى أحد من الأكابر؛ من أولياء، أو علماء، أو أمراء

ومن وصية الشيخ محي الدين ابن العربي: إذا انتسب أخوك إلى أحد من الأكابر... فاحذر أن تطعن في نسبه ولو في نفسك، فتدخل بين ذلك الشخص وبين الله تعالى، وبين صاحب الفراش، فتقع في إثم كبير، بل ورد: أن الطعن في الأنساب كفر

ومن حق الأخ على الأخ: ألَّا يكفره بذنب ولو لان الناس به؛ إذ لا يخفى قلة ورع الناس اليوم في الكلام، وعسر معرفة جميع الألفاظ التي يكفر بها الإنسان، والتكفير - كما قال شيخ الإسلام السبكي -: أمر هائل، أقل ما فيه أنه أخبر عن إنسان أنه خالد في النار، لا تجري عليه أحكام الإسلام، لا في حياته ولا بعد مماته

ومن حق الأخ على الأخ: ألَّا يبغض ذاته إذا وقع فيما لا ينبغي

ومن كلام سيدي علي الخواص - رحمه الله -: عداوتنا لأفعال مَنْ أمرنا الحق تعالى بعداوته عداوة شرعية، وعداوتنا لذاته عداوة طبيعية، والسعادة في الشرعية لا في الطبيعية، والغالب في الناس بغضهم لذات مَنْ سمعوا عنه أنه وقع في محرم، وأما

إن سمعوا عنه أنه تكلم فيهم بشيء يكرهونه: فإنهم يكرهون أولاده فضلاً عن ذاته، ويحتقرونه زيادةً عن ذلك، وربما يزعم بعضهم أنه مصيب في احتقاره له، وغاب عنه أن من الجهل المحض احتقار عبدٍ اعتنى به الحق تعالى، وأخرجه من العدم إلى الوجود

فاحذر - يا أخي - من ذلك، فإن الحق تعالى ما أمرك أن تحتقر أحداً من خلقه، وإنما أمرك أن تنكر أفعاله المخالفة لشرعه لا غير، فتأمر العاصي وتنهاه وأنت غير محتقر له

وتأمل قوله ﷺ في شجرة الثوم: ((إنها شجرة أكره ريحها)) فما كره ذاتها، وإنما كره ريحها الذي هو بعض صفاتها، فعلم أن عداوتنا للكفار عداوة صفات بدليل أنهم إذا أسلموا وحسن حالهم... حرم علينا عداوتهم

ومن حق الأخ على الأخ: إذا حصل بينه وبينه وقفة... أن يزيد في بثِّ محاسنه أكثر مما كان قبل الوقفة؛ مراعاة للوُدِّ

وقد كان السلف الصالح يمدحون عدوهم كلَّما ذكر اسمه بحضرتهم، بحيث يظن الظانّ أنه من أعظم المحبين لهم، فاقتدِ - يا أخي — بهم، ولا تتوقف في ذكر أخيك بالمعروف أيام غيظك عليه، واحذر من الوقوع في عرضه، فربما وقع الصلح، فيصير ذلك يكدر صفاء المودة، وتذكّرْ ما أكلت عنده من الخبز وما سبق من المعروف، وقلّ من يفعل ذلك

ومن حق الأخ على الأخ: أن يقدِّم حوائجه الضرورية على عباداته المسنونة، ومعلوم أن الخير الذي يتعدى نفعه أفضل من القاصر على فاعله

ومن حق الأخ على الأخ: إذا وقع في حقه بشيء وبلغه... أن يبادر إلى الاستغفار وإلى كشف الرأس، وإطراقه الأرض، والوقوف عند النعال، وإظهار الندم على ما وقع منه في حق أخيه، ويديم ذلك إلى أن يرحمه أخوه، ثم إن لم يرحمه... رجع على نفسه باللوم، واعترف بأنه ظالم، وقلَّ من يفعل ذلك

ومن حق الأخ على الأخ: أن يقبل اعتذاره ولو كان مبطلاً؛ فقد روى الترمذي وغيره: ((من أتاه أخوه منتصلاً من ذنب... فليقبل اعتذاره، محقاً كان أو مبطلاً، فإن لم يفعل... لم يَرِد على الحوض))، وفي معنى ذلك أنشدوا:

اقبلْ معاذيرَ مَنْ يأتيكَ معتذرا ... إن برَّ عندكَ فيما قالَ أو فجرا

فقدْ أطاعكَ من يرضيكَ ظاهرُهُ ... وقد أَجلّكَ مَنْ يعصيكَ مستترا

وأنشدوا:

قيلَ لي: قد أسا إليك فلانٌ ... ومقامُ الفتىٰ على الذلِّ عارُ

قلتُ: قدْ أتىٰ وأحدثَ عُذراً ... دِيَةُ الذنبِ عندنا الِاعتذارُ

وأنشدوا:

إذا اعتذرَ الصديقُ إليكَ يوماً ... فجاوزْ عن مساويهِ الكثيرهْ

فإنَّ الشافعيَ روى حديثاً بإسنادٍ صحيحٍ عن المغيره

عن المختارِ أنَّ اللهَ يمحو بعذرٍ واحدٍ ألفي كبيرهْ

وروى ابن ماجه: ((مَنِ اعتذرَ إليهِ أخوه بمعذرةٍ فلم يقبلْها... كانَ عليه من الخطيئةِ مثلَ صاحبِ مَكْسٍ))

ومن كلام سيدي علي الخواص- رحمه الله -: إذا جاءكم أخوكم معتذراً... فاقبلوه، لاسيما إن طال به الوقوف، فإن لم يجد أحدكم في قلبه رقة لأخيه... فليرجعْ على نفسه باللوم، وليقل لها: يأتيكِ أخوك معتذراً فلا تقبلينه؟! فكم وقعتِ أنتِ في حقه فلم تلتفتي إليه، فأنت إذاً أسوأ منه

وقال بعضهم: الأخ الذي يُحْوِج أخاه أن يعتذر إليه... ليس بأخ صادق ولا من أهل الطريق، فإن أهل الطريق يقيمون للخلق المعاذير قبل أن يعتذروا إليهم

ومن حق الأخ على الأخ: كثرة فرحه له إذا كثرت طاعاته وانقلب الناس إليه بالاعتقاد، ومن لم يكن كذلك... قام به داء الحسد، وفي الحديث: ((الحسد يأكل الحسنات كما تأكل النار الحطب))

ومن وصية سيدي علي وفا: إياك أن تحسد من اصطفاه الله عليك؛ فيمسخك الله كما مسخ إبليس من الصورة الملكية إلى الصورة الشيطانية، لماَّ حسد السيد آدم عليه السلام

وفي مناقب سيدي أحمد البدوي - نفعنا الله ببركاته -: أن صاحب الإيوان بطنتثنا المسمى بوجه القمر، كان ولياً عظيماً فثار عنده حسد حين جاء سيدي

أحمد البدوي إلى طنتثنا، وانقلب الناس إليه بالاعتقاد، فسلب حاله، وانطُفِئ اسمه وذكره، وموضعه الآن في طنتثنا مأوى الكلاب، وانتصر له خطباء طنتثنا، فعملوا له وقتاً، وبنوا لزاويته منارة عظيمة، فجاء سيدي عبد العالِ ورفضها برجله فغارت لوقتنا هذا

ومن حق الأخ على الأخ: إذا أراد سفراً... أن لا يخرج حتى يودعه بالعناق إن كان رجلاً، وبالإشارة إن كان صغيراً، ففي الحديث: ((إذا خرجَ أحدُكم إلى سفرٍ... فليودعْ إخوانَهُ؛ فإنَّ اللهَ جاعلٌ له في دعائِهم البركةَ

ومن حق الأخ على الأخ: إذا رجع من سفر... أن يذهب إليه في منزله، ويسلم عليه ويهنئه بالسلامة، وكذلك ولده، وسائر أعزته إذا رجعوا من سفر، أو شفوا من مرض، فمن حقه أن يذهب إليه أخوه ويهنئه بالسلامة

ومن حق الأخ على الأخ: أن يشاوره في كل أمر مهمٍّ؛ فقد ذكروا أن المشاورة تزيد في صفاء المودة، وفي الحديث: ((من أراد أمراً فشاور فيه امرأ مسلماً... وفقه الله لأرشد أموره))

وكان سيدي علي الخواص يقول: عليكم بمشاورة إخوانكم في كل أمر مهم؛ فإن في الحديث: ((ما خاب من استخار، ولا ندم من استشار))

وأنشدوا:

شاورْ أخاكَ في الخفيِّ المشكلِ   واقبلْ نصيحةَ فاضلٍ متفضلِ

وأنشدوا:

شاورْ أخاكَ إذا نابتْكَ نائبةٌ   يوماً وإن كنتَ من أهلِ المشوراتِ

فالعينُ تلقى كفاحاً ما نأى ودنا   ولا ترى نفسَها إلا بمرآةِ

ومن حق الأخ على الأخ: أن يتفقد عياله وأولاده إذا غاب عنهم

ومن كلامهم: من لم يتفقد عيال أخيه في غيبته... فقد خان الصحبة

ومن حق الأخ على الأخ: أن يشاطره في ماله وغيره

وقال الشيخ أبو المواهب الشاذلي: يجب على الفقير إذا آخى في الله... أن يشاطر أخاه في ماله؛ كما فعلت الأنصار مع المهاجرين حين قدموا عليهم المدينة، وهم فقراء، فكل من ادعى الأخوة في الله... فامتحنْه بهذه الميزان

وقال سيدي أبو مدين التلمساني – نفعنا الله به –: من ميّز بين ثيابه وثياب أخيه في الملك... فما وفّى الصحبة بحق

وقال أيضا: لا تكتمل صحبتك إلا بانشراح صدرك لكل ما أخذه أخوك من مالك، وثيابك وطعامك، ومتى ما وجدت في قلبك انقباضاً من ذلك فأنت منافق في صحبتك

وقال بعضهم: ما تصح الصحبة بين اثنين حتى يقول أحدهما للآخر ((يا أنا))، وليس بأخ من يقول: قصعتي أو ثوبي

ومن حق الأخ على الأخ: أن لا يتكدر منه إذا قال له: أنا أبغضك، ويفتشُ على الصفات التي أبغضه لأجلها، فيزيلها، فإن زال بغضه، وإلّا كرّر التفتيش ثانيا وثالثا

ومن حق الأخ على الأخ: أن يكتم سره؛ إذ السر كالعورة، وقد حُرِّم كشفها،والنظر إليها، والتحدث بها

وفى الحديث: ((من ستر عورة أخيه... ستر الله عورته، ومن كشف عورة أخيه... كشف الله عورته))

وفى وصية الشيخ أبي المواهب الشاذلي: احذر أن تفشي سر أخيك إلى غيره؛ فإن الله ربما مقتك بذلك، فخسرت الدنيا والآخرة

ومن حق الأخ على الأخ: ألّا يُصَدِّقَ مَنْ نمَّ له فيه أبدا

وقد ذكر حجة الإسلام الغزالي: أنه يجب على كل من حملت إليه نميمة ستة أمور:

الأول: ألّا يصدقه، أي النمام

الثاني: أن ينهاه عن ذلك

الثالث: أن يبغضه في الله

الرابع: ألَّا يظن بالمنقول عنه السوء

الخامس: ألَّا يتجسس على تحقق ذلك

السادس: ألَّا يحكي ما نمَّ له به

ومن كلام الشيخ أبي المواهب الشاذلي: إذا نقل إليك أحد كلاما عن صاحب لك... فقل: يا هذا! أنا من صحبة أخي وودِّه على يقين، ومن كلامك على ظنٍّ، ولا يُترك يقينٌ بظنٍّ

ومن كلام الشيخ أفضل الدين: (إذا نَقَل إليكم أحدٌ كلاماً في عِرضكم عن أحد... فازجروه ولو كان من أعزِّ إخوانكم، وقولوا له: إن كنت تعتقد فينا هذا الأمر... فأنت ومن نقلتَ عنه سواء، بل أنت أسوأ حالاً منه؛ لأنه لم يُسمعنا ذلك، وأنت أسمعته لنا، وإن كنت تعتقد أن هذا الأمر باطل في حقنا وبعيد منّا أن نقع في مثله... فما فائدة نقله لنا؟) انتهى

وقد ذكرنا في غير هذه الرسالة: أن من أراد أن يدوم له وُدُّ أصحابه... فليردَّ كلام النمام ببادئ الرأي

ومن حق الأخ على الأخ: أن يذبَّ عن عرضه، لكن مع النية الصالحة والسياسة الحسنة، وفي الحديث: ((منْ ردَّ عن عرضِ أخيهِ... ردَّ اللهُ عن وجهِ النارَ يومَ القيامةِ))

ومن كلام الإمام الشافعي: من علامة الصادق في أخوّة أخيه... أن يقبل علله، ويسد خلله، ويغفر زلَــله

ومن حق الأخ على الأخ: أن يوقظه قبل الوقت ليدخل الوقتُ وهو على أهبة، فلا تفوته السنة الراتبة قبل الفريضة، ولا تكبيرة الإحرام

وكذلك من حقه: أن يوقظه في السحر؛ إذ الشفقة في أمر الدين أولى وأفضل من الشفقة في أمر الدنيا، وينبغي أن يكون ذلك بلطف، فإن النفس ربما تحركت مع الإيقاظ بغلظة

ومن حق الأخ على الأخ: ألّا يداهنه؛ ففي الحديث: ((الدين النصيحة)) وقال القوم: الإخوان بخيرٍ ما تناقشوا، فإذا اصطلحوا هلكوا

ومن الفرق بين المداهنة والمداراة أن المداراة: ما أردتَ به صلاح أخيك، والمداهنة: ما قصدتَ به شيئاً من الحظوظ النفسانية

ومن حق الأخ على الأخ: أن يتهم نفسه بالكبر والنفاق إذا وجد عنده ثقلاً منه، ويسعى في إزالة ذلك من باطنه

وقد صحب شخص أبا بكر الكتاني - وكان على قلبه ثقيلاً - قال: فوهبت له شيئاً بنية أن يزول ثقله عني، فلم يَزُل، فخلوت به يوماً وقلت له: ضع رجلك على خدي فأبى، فقلت له: لا بدَّ من ذلك، ففعل، فزال ما كنت أجده في بطني

ومن حق الأخ على الأخ: أن يقبل نصحه؛ فقد قالوا: من أرشدك إلى ما به تَخْلُص من غضب الحق تعالى... فقد شفع فيك، فإن أطعته وقبلت نصحه... فقد قبلت فيك شفاعته، وإلَّا... فنعوذ بالله من قوم لا تنفعهم شفاعة الشافعين، حيث كانوا عن التذكرة معرضين

ومن حق الأخ على الأخ: أن يعزم على أنه: إن أدخله الله الجنة... لا يدخلها إلا إن دخل أخوه وإن طال الزمان في الحساب، وأن يسمح بمقاسمته في حسناته يوم القيامة

ومن حق الأخ على الأخ: ألَّا يأكل ولا يشرب إذا وقع أخوه في معصية أو محنة حتى يتوب الله عليه، أو يخلصه من تلك المحنة، وقد طوى ابن أدهم حين نزل بأخٍ له بلاءٌ أربعين يوماً، ولم يزل طاوياً حتى ارتفع عنه

ومن حق الأخ على الأخ: أن يرشده إلى تعظيم حرمات الله، والتباعد عن تعدي حدوده، بحيث يصير إذا وقع في أصغر الذنوب... رأى ذلك الصغير من الكبائر

بجامع المخالفة، فلا يزال كذلك حتى يرى الغفلة عن الله لحظة أشد من الزنا وقتل النفس

ثم إذا كمل السالك... رجع إلى أكمل من ذلك، وهو تعظيم تعدي حدود الله على حسب ما وردت في الشرع؛ فإن العبد تابع ما هو مشرع، فيعظِّم الكبيرة على الصغيرة، والصغيرة على المكروه، والمكروه على خلاف الأولى، وما بيَّن الشارع ﷺ مراتب الحدود... إلا ليعلمنا بتفاوتها، فنعظمها بحسب مراتبها

وكذلك القول في قسم المأمورات، فنعظم الواجب أكثر من المندوب، والمندوب أكثر من الأدب، ونندم على كل واحد بحسب تأكيد الشارع عليه، فرجع السالك في حال نهايته إلى صورة بدايته، والقصد مختلف من حيث تفاوت المأمورات والمنهيات في الدرجة، وكانت مساواة الأوامر والنواهي في البداية للسالك من شدة تعظيمه لله تعالى، فاستعظم مأموراته ومنهياته خوفاً وسداً لباب المخالفة، بقطع النظر عن مشاهدة حكمة تفاوتها، كما ورد في الشرع، فثَمَّ مقام رفيع، ومقام أرفع

وعلى ما تقرر يحمل قول الجنيد: (ليس عندي ذنب أعظم من الغفلة عن الله تعالى) فإن الغيبة أعظم من الغفلة، أو أنه رأى أن سبب وقوع العبد في الذنوب الغفلة عن الله تعالى

ومن حق الأخ على الأخ: أن يأمره بستر المقام، إذا تلمَّحَ منه الميلَ إلى الظهور، ومن أحب الخفاء... فهو عبد الخفاء، وكل من خرج إلى الخلق قبل وجود الإذن

الخاص له... فهو مفتون، ومسخَرة للناس، وما خرج الأولياء للخلق إلا بعد أن هُدِّدوا بالسلب إن لم يفعلوا

فالعاقل من ستر مقامه حتى يتولى الله إظهاره بغير مراد منه

ومن حق الأخ على الأخ: أن يتظاهر بعداوة من عاداه بغير حق، أما معاداته بالباطن: فلا تجوز، حتى عدوّ شيخِ الإنسان لا يجوز له معاداته بالباطن، بل يجب عليه مظاهرته بعداوته فقط، كما يجب عليه أن يجتنب مَن غضب عليه شيخُه

ومن حق الأخ على الأخ: أن يقوم له إذا ورد عليه، ولو كره هو ذلك لا سيما في المحافل؛ فقد قالوا: إياك أن تترك القيام لأخيك في المحافل فربما تولَّد من ذلك الحقدُ والضغائن، فتعجز بعد ذلك عن إزالته

ومن حق الأخ على الأخ ألَّا يحدثه بحديث كذب؛ لأن فيه استهانة به، وفي الحديث: ((كبرت خيانة أن تحدث أخاك بحديث هو لك مصدِّق وأنت له به كاذِب))

ومن حق الأخ على الأخ: ألَّا ينساه من الدعاء بالعفو والمغفرة والرحمة كلما وجد وقته صافياً مع ربه، سواء كان ذلك في ليل أو نهار، أو سجودٍ أو غيره

ومن حق الأخ على الأخ: ألّا يحقد عليه، ففي الحديث: ((ثلاثة من كن فيه فإن الله يغفر له ما سوى ذلك: من مات لا يشرك بالله شيئا، ولم يكن ساحراً يتبع السحرة، ولم يحقد على أخيه))

وقال القوم: كل من كان عنده حقد أو مكر أو خديعة أو غش لأحد من الخلق... فهو كذاب في طريق القوم، ولا يجوز ان يكون داعيا إلى الله تعالى

ومن حق الأخ على الأخ: إذا تحدث أن يشخص ببصره إليه حتى يفرغ من حديثه؛ فإن ذلك يزيد في صفاء المودة، كما أن التلاهي عن حديث الأخ، أو قَطْع كلامه قبل إتمامه يورث الجفاء

ومن حق الأخ على الأخ: ألّا يمتحنه؛ فإن الامتحان من جنس كشف العورة، وقد قالوا: إياكم أن تمتحنوا إخوانكم؛ فإن الله لا يمتحن عباده إلا إن علم وفائهم؛ كيلا يخجلهم بإظهار ما كان كاسيا عندهم

وقيل للكُبْرىٰ: ألا تمتحن أصحابك؟ فقال: إذاً نخرجَ كلنا عيوبا

ومن حق الأخ على الأخ: أن يتهيأ للقائه بالحرمة والتعظيم كلّما فارقه، قال الشيخ محي الدين: ولو كان زمن المفارقة يسيرا؛ إحسانا للظن بأن الله نفحه نفحة، أو نظر إليه نظرة من نظراته التي في اليوم والليلة إلى قلوب عباده، فصار بها أعلى مقاما منه، ثم إن كان ذلك الأمر صحيحا... فقد وفّاه حقه، وإن لم يكن صحيحا... فقد

تأدب مع الله تعالى، حيث عامله بما تقتضيه المرتبة الإلهية، من إكرام كلّ وارد على حضرتها، قال: وهذا الأمر قلّ من يتفقد نفسه فيه لاستحكام الغفلة على القلوب

ومن حق الأخ على الأخ: إذا رآه في ما لا ينبغي... أن يعتقد أنه تاب من وقته، وندم في سريرته، وقد كان بعض السلف يقول: إني لاستحي من الله أن أقطع التوبة عن شخص عصى ربه بحضرتي، ثم توارى عني بجدار

وقالوا: من قطع التوبة عن أحد من العصاة... رأى نفسه خيرا منه ضرورةً، وكل من ظنَّ أنه خير من أحد من المسلمين فهو جاهل مخدوع ولو أُعْطِيَ من المكرمات ما أُعطي

ومن حق الأخ على الأخ: أن يحفظ وُدَّه وإن خان هو أو زاغ؛ مراعاة للوُدِّ

قال ابن الخطاب: رأيت ربّ العزة في النوم، فقلت: يا ربِّ! علمني شيئاً آخذه عنك بلا واسطة، فقال: يا ابن الخطاب! من أحسن إلى من أساء إليه... فقد أخلص لله شكرا، ومن أساء إلى من أحسن إليه... فقد بدَّل نعمة الله كفرا، فقلت: يا رب حسبي، فقال: حسبك، انتهى

وهذا الأمر قد صار عزيزا في هذا الزمان، وما بقي من أهله سوى الكلاب، كما هو مذكور في كتاب ((فضل الكلاب على كثير ممن لبس الثياب))

ومن حق الأخ على الأخ: ألَّا يمنّ عليه بما فعله معه من المعروف إذا هو خاصمه ونسي ذلك المعروف، فإنّ ذِكر المعروف في المخاصمة عنوانٌ على عدم الإخلاص فيه، ودليلٌ على خسة الأصل، فإنّ طيّب الأصل لا يمنّ أبدا بما فعله مع أخيه من المعروف، بل يرى الفضل لذلك الأخ الذي أكل عنده مثلاً أو قَبِل منه هدية

وفى الحديث: ((ثلاثة لا ينظر الله إليهم يوم القيامة، ولا يزكيهم، ولهم عذاب أليم: المُسْبِلُ، والمَنّانُ، والمنفقُ سلعته بالحلف الكاذِب))

وقال بعضهم: المنُّ بالمعروف في المخاصمة دُمَّل لا يندمل، أي: لا ينسى، بل يصير يكدِّرُ الصحبة كلما تذكَّره

ومن حق الأخ على الأخ: ألَّا يخاصمه؛ فإن المخاصمة تقطع الوُدّ، وقد قالوا: ما وُجِد أذهبُ للدّين ولا أشغل للقلب من الخصومة، ومن الخصومة يتولد الغضب، والحقد، والخديعة، حتى إنه يكون في الصلاة، وخاطره معلق بالمحاججة، ولا يخفى ما في ذلك

وفي الحديث: ((كفى بك إثما ألَّا تزال مخاصما))

وأنشدوا:

تجنبْ قرينَ السوءِ واصرمْ حبالَهُ ... فإنْ لمْ تجدْ عنه محيصاً فدارِهِ
وأحببْ قرينَ الصدقِ واتركْ مراءَهُ ... تنلْ منه صفوَ الوُدِّ ما لم تمارِهِ

ومن حق الأخ على الأخ: ألَّا يبادر إلى هجره؛ فإن المبادرة إلى مثل ذلك ليست بمحمودة، وخطؤها أكثر من صوابها، وقد ذكرنا في غير هذه الرسالة شروط جواز الهجر

ومن حق الأخ على الأخ: ألَّا يؤاخذه إذا قصر في حقّه مراعاة للوُدِّ، ومن وصية سيدي علي الخواص: اترك حقك لأخيك ما استطعت، وأَقِلْ عثرة أهل المروءات والهيئات من إخوانك، وإياك أن تعتدي على من اعتدى عليك؛ فإن الحق تعالى ما أباح الاعتداء إلا بشرط المثلية، والمثلية متعذرة جداً، وربما زادت، وربما أثرت تلك السيئة في الخصم أكثر مما أثرت فيك، فالمجازاة رخصة للضعفاء

ومن حق الأخ على الأخ: دوام شفقه على أولاده، والقيام بهم بعد موته، قال القوم: من لم يشفق على أولاد أخيه في غيبته، ولم يقم بهم بعد موته... فليس بصادق في أخوّته

ومن حق الأخ على الأخ: ألَّا يقرَّه على بدعة، فإن لم يرجع عنها تركه خوفا على نفسه أن يلحقه شؤمها، وقد كان السلف الصالح يحذرون من مجالسة أهل البدع ويقولون: من كان فيه أدنى بدعة... فاحذروا من مجالسته، ومن تساهل في ذلك... عاد عليه شؤمها ولو بعد حين.

ومن حق الأخ على الأخ: ألَّا يتزوج له زوجة طلَّقها أو مات عنها، ولو أوصاه بذلك، وقال: أنت أحق من الغير

فاعرض - يا أخي - ما في هذا الفصل على نفسك، فإن رايتها متخلقة به... فاشكر الله تعالى، وإلَّا... فعليك بالاستغفار من التقصير في حقوق إخوانك، ليلاً ونهاراً

والحمد لله رب العالمين

الفَصْلُ الثَّالِث

فِي ذكر شيْء مِن آدَابِ القَوم

رَضيَ الله تعالى عنهم

اعلم – وفقني الله وإياك إلى ما يحب – أنّ آداب القوم لا تنحصر؛ لأنها مجموع ما في الكتب الإلهية، والأخبار النبوية، والآثار الصحابية والسلفية، ولكن نذكر لك شيئا من آدابهم؛ تبركا وفتحا للباب، فنقول وبالله التوفيق:

من آداب القوم: أن يفروا – في جميع الشدائد – إلى الله تعالى قبل جميع الخلق؛ لعلمهم على الكشف والشهود أن بيده تبارك تعالى ملكوتَ كل شيء، بخلاف غيرهم فإنهم لا يرجعون إلى الله إلا بعد الوقوف على خلقه

ومن آدابهم: جمع الحواس والقلب حال العمل؛ وقد ورد في بعض الكتب الإلهية: يقول الله تعالى للملائكة الكرام الكاتبين: (اكتبوا عمل عبدي فلان، واكتبوا أين كان قلبه حال العمل؛ ليأخذ ثوابه ممن كان قلبه حاضرا معه)

ومن كلام سيدي علي الخواص: كل عمل لم يحضر العبد فيه مع ربه تعالى ... فهو كالميتة، وهو بالنفاق أشبه، وذلك لأنه يوهم الناس أنه مع الله حال مناجاته، وهو مع الخلق، وقد طالت الطريق على الناس لغفلتهم عن ذلك، فحجبوا بالأعمال عن المعمول له، ولو أنهم لاحظوا المعمول له... لاشتغلوا به عن الأعمال

ومن آدابهم: لا يطلبون بعباداتهم مقاما أو حالا أو تقريبا من الحضرة الإلهية، فقد قالوا: من خدم الله تعالى لطلب مقام... فقد طلب قطيعته، ومن خدمه لطلب ثواب أو خوفا من عقاب... فقد أبدى طمعه وأظهر خسته

وقالوا: مِن أبغضِ الخلقِ إلى الله تعالى مَنْ تملّق إليه في الأسحار بالطاعات؛ يطلب قربه تعالى بذلك

وقالوا: افعلوا ما أمركم به الشرع ان استطعتم، ولكن من حيث مشروعيته والأمر به، لا من حيث علّة أخرى، واتركوا العلل كلها في جميع أعمالكم وأحوالكم، ولا تنظروا إلى ثواب، فمن نظر إلى ثواب في أعماله عاجلا أو آجلا... فقد خرج عن أوصاف العبودية التي لا ثواب لها إلا وجه الحق عز وجل

ومن آدابهم: تفتيش أعضائهم الظاهرة والباطنة صباحاً ومساءً: هل حفظتْ حدودَ الله التي حدها لها أو تعدت؟ وهل قامت بما أُمرت به، من غضِّ البصر، وحفظ اللسان، والأُذُن والقلب، وغير ذلك على وجه الإخلاص أو لم تقم؟ فإن رأوا جارحة من جوارحهم أطاعت... شكروا الله تعالى، ولم يروا نفوسهم أهلا لذلك، وإن رأوها

تلطخت بشيء من المعاصي . . . أخذوا في الاستغفار والندم، ثم يشكرون الله تعالى، إذ لم يقدِّر عليهم أكثر من تلك المعصية، ولم يبتلِ جوارحهم التي عصت حال عصيانها، فإن كل عضو عصى استحق نزول البلاء به حال عصيانه

ومن آدابهم: لا يغفلون عن تفتيش باطنهم؛ فإن الأخلاق الرديّة كامنة في العبد، ومعلوم أن الفقراء إذا ترقوا في المقامات كان وقوعهم في المعاصي الظاهرة معدوما غالبا، فيقع أحدهم بذلك، وينسى تفتيش باطنه، وهو قصور عن درجة أهل العرفان، ومن ظن أن الأخلاق الردية زالت عنه . . . فقد وهم

قال الله تعالى: ﴿ وَمَن يُوقَ شُحَّ نَفْسِهِۦ فَأُولَٰٓئِكَ هُمُ ٱلْمُفْلِحُونَ ﴾ [الحشر: ٩] فلم يقل: ومن يزل شحَّ نفسه، بل أبقى الشحَّ فيها؛ إلا أن العبد يوافي العمل بذلك بعناية الله

ومن كلام الشيخ أفضل الدين: أن الله تعالى قد جعل في طينة الآدميين سائر الأضداد في جميع الأخلاق الحميدة والذميمة، تُشرّق وتُغرّب في ذواتهم، ولكن ما دامت العناية الربانية تحفُّ العبد فجميع الأخلاق الذميمة خامدة متعطلة، فإذا تخلفت عنه العناية... تحركت الأخلاق الذميمة للاستعمال، وخمدت أخلاقه الحسنة

ثم لا يخفى أن طينة الأنبياء عليهم الصلاة والسلام قد طهّرها الله من سائر الرذائل بسابق العناية، فافهم وإياك والغلط

ومن آدابهم: عدم مؤالفتهم للوعد، فلا يعدون أحدا بوعد إلا في النادر؛ لعلمهم أن صدق الوعد لا يكون إلا للأنبياء عليهم الصلاة والسلام لعصمتهم، وأما غيرهم: فربما وعد وأخلف، فيصير فيه خصلة من النفاق

ومن آدابهم: إذا سئل أحدهم عن شيخه... أن يقول: كنت خادمه، أو من المترددين إليه، ولا يقول: كنت صاحبه؛ فإن مقام الصحبة عزيز؛ إذ صاحب الإنسان هو من يشرب من بحره، كما تقدم في أول الرسالة

ومن آدابهم: إذا ذُكِر أحد من أصحابهم في غيبته بحضرتهم... لا يقولون: هو من أصحابنا، أو من أكابر أصحابنا إلا إن كان دونهم بدرجات، فإن كان مساويا لهم أو فوقهم... فيقولون: نحن من أتباعه أو خدّامه

ومن آدابهم: لا يقولون: ذهب الأكابر والصادقون؛ فإنهم ما ذهبوا حقيقة، وإنما هم ككنز صاحب الجدار

وقد يعطي الله من جاء في آخر الزمان ما حجبه عن أهل العصر الأول؛ فإن الله قد أعطى نبيّنا محمدا ﷺ ما لم يعطه الأنبياء قبله، ثم قدّمه عليهم في المدح

ومن كلام صاحب ((الحكم)): بدل ما تقول: أين الأولياء؟ أين الصالحون؟ قل: أين البصيرة؟ هل يصلح للمتلطخ بالعذرة أن يرى بنت السلطان، انتهى

ومثل هذا اللفظ لا يقع إلا ممن لم يكن عنده اعتقاد في أولياء عصره وعلمائه، ولا يخفى ما في ذلك

ومن آدابهم: لا يطلبون ألَّا يكون لهم حاسد؛ فإن الحكم الوجودي اقتضى مقابلة النعم بالحسد، فمن طلب ألَّا يكون له حاسد... فقد طلب أن لا تكون له نعمة

ومن آدابهم: إذا ذكروا ذنوبهم... لا يقولون عليها: لا حول ولا قوة إلا بالله؛ لما في ذلك من رائحة الحجة على الله تعالى، بل يقولون: ﴿رَبَّنَا ظَلَمْنَآ أَنفُسَنَا وَإِن لَّمْ تَغْفِرْ لَنَا وَتَرْحَمْنَا لَنَكُونَنَّ مِنَ الْخَٰسِرِينَ﴾ [الأعراف: ٢٣]، ومع الإفراد: رب ظلمت نفسي فاغفر لي؛ إنك أنت الغفور الرحيم

ومن آدابهم: لا يقولون: نأنس بالله تعالى؛ فإن الإنسان لا يأنس إلا بجنسه، والحق تعالى ليس بينه وبين عباده مجانسة بوجه من الوجوه، فإن رأيت في كلام أحد من القوم أن العبد يأنس بالله تعالى... فاعلم أنه غير محقِّق، ولو حقق... لوجد أُنسه بما مِن الله تعالى، لا بالله تعالى؛ لانتفاء المجانسة

وكذلك كان الجن لا يأنس أحدنا بهم، بل تقوم كل شعرة من الإنسي إذا رأي الجني

وكما لا يصح الأنس بالله تعالى كذلك لا يصح الالتذاذ به تعالى، قال القوم: وهذا الحكم لنا في الدارين، فإن الشارع ﷺ لم يفصح لنا عن سبب اللذة إذا وقعت لنا الرؤية، بل قال: فما أعطوا لذَّةً مثل لذة نظرهم إلى ربهم، وهذه اللذة لا نتعقلها الآن

ومن آدابهم: لا يقولون: نطلب الله؛ إذ الطلب لا يكون إلا لمفقود، والله تعالى موجود ولا يطلب دركه؛ لأنه لا غاية له، وإنما نطلب الطريق إلى معرفة الله تعالى

ومن آدابهم: لا يستعيذون بالله من شيء، وإنما يستعيذون من شره، وكذلك لا يقولون: اللهم أغننا من جميع خلقك، وإنما يقولون: أغننا عن أشرار خلقك

ومن آدابهم: عدم زخرفتهم الكتب التي يرسلونها إلى إخوانهم؛ خوفاً من الكذب

ومن وصية أبي نصر بشرٍ الحافي: إذا كتب أحدكم كتابا إلى أحد... فلا يزخرفه بحسن الألفاظ، فإني كتبت مرة كتابا، فعرض لي كلام إن كتبته... حَسُنَ الكتاب وكان كذبا، وان تركته... سَمُجَ الكتاب وكان صدقا، فعزمت على ذكر الكلام السمج الصدق، فنادى هاتف من جانب البيت: ﴿ يُثَبِّتُ اللّٰهُ الَّذِيْنَ اٰمَنُوْا بِالْقَوْلِ الثَّابِتِ فِى الْحَيٰوةِ الدُّنْيَا وَفِى الْاٰخِرَةِ﴾ [إبراهيم: ٢٧]

ومن آدابهم: كثـرة استغفارهم إذا اعتقدوا فيهم الخلق، وهم في السر على خلاف ذلك

وفي الحديث: ((طوبى لمن وجد في صحيفته استغفارا كثيرا))

وقد حثُّوا على الاعتناء بالاستغفار ليلا ونهارا، سواء تذكر العبد ذنوبا معينة أو لم يتذكر

ومن آدابهم: إذا مدحوا أن يكثروا من الشكر والاستغفار، وأن يقولوا: اللهم أنت أعلم بنا منهم، اللهم اجعلنا خيرا مما يظنون، ولا تؤاخذنا بما يقولون، واغفر لنا ما لا يعلمون

ومن آدابهم: لا يعتمدون على كسبهم؛ فإن الاعتماد على الكسب شرك بالله عزوجل، وقد ذكرنا في غير هذه الرسالة، معرفة طريق الخلاص من هذا الشرك، وأن من خَلُص منه فهو المؤمن الذي يأتيه رزقه من حيث لا يحتسب

ومن آدابهم: عدم نسبة شيء من الأعمال الصالحة إلى نفوسهم إلا بقدر نسبة التكليف فقط

قال القوم: كل عمل اتصل بالعبد شهوده... فهو غير متقبل، فمن شهد له عملاً... فعمله عند نفسه، لا عند ربه، ومن حقَّق النظر... علم أنه لا أثر لمخلوق

في فعل شيء من حيث التكوين، وإنما له الحكم فيه فقط، وغالب الناس لا يفرق بين الحكم والأثر

ومن كلام سيدي علي الخواص: ما دام العبد ينسب الأمور لنفسه ذوقا وإلى الله علما... فهو محجوب، فإذا رفع الحجاب... رأى أفعاله كلها خلق الله تعالى ذوقا دون نفسه، فلا يكمل حال المريد حتى يشهد أفعاله كلها خلقا لله تعالى ذوقا، وأما علمه أنها خلق الله: فلا يكفيه؛ إذ ليس العلم كالذوق

قال: وأكثر المريدين لم يثبت لهم قدم في توحيد أفعالهم لله تعالى، وكذلك يطلبون الجزاء من الله تعالى على ما أجرى على أيديهم من الأعمال الصالحة، وكذلك يطلبون الجزاء من الخلق إذا أجرى الله على يَدِهِم إحسانا لهم، فلولا نسبتهم ذلك إلى أنفسهم... ما طلبوا الجزاء من الله تعالى، ولا من الخلق، وما قال عارف قط: ﴿إِيَّاكَ نَعْبُدُ وَإِيَّاكَ نَسْتَعِينُ﴾ إلا على وجه التلاوة فقط، لا على وجه كونه له شركة في الفعل، تعالى فعل الله عن الشرك، فافهم

ومن آدابهم: التجرد عن العزة والغنى، والتحقق بالذل والفقر، إذا توجهوا إلى الله في أمر دنيوي أو أخروي؛ كيلا يمنعوا عن الإجابة

ومن كلامهم: إذا توجهت إلى الله... فتوجَّه إليه وأنت فقير ذليل، فإن غناك وعزتك - وإن كانا بالله تعالى - يمنعانك الإجابة؛ لأن الغنى والعز صفتان لا يصح لعبد الدخول بهما على الله تعالى أبدا؛ لأن حضرته تعالى لها العزة ذاتية، فلا تقبل عزيزا ولا غنيا

ومن آدابهم: لا يسألون الله شيئا من أمور الدارين إلا مع التفويض وردِّ العلم إليه سبحانه؛ عملا بعموم قوله تعالى: ﴿ وَعَسَىٰٓ أَن تَكۡرَهُوا۟ شَيۡـًٔا وَهُوَ خَيۡرٌ لَّكُمۡۖ وَعَسَىٰٓ أَن تُحِبُّوا۟ شَيۡـًٔا وَهُوَ شَرٌّ لَّكُمۡۗ وَٱللَّهُ يَعۡلَمُ وَأَنتُمۡ لَا تَعۡلَمُونَ ﴾ [البقرة: ٢١٦] فيقول أحدهم في سؤاله: اللهم أعطني كذا وكذا إن كان فيه خير لي، واصرف عني كذا وكذا إن كان فيه شر لي

ومن وصية سيدي عبد القادر الجيلي: احذر أن تسأل الله شيئاً إلا مع التفويض، وأما إذا أعطاك تعالى شيئا من غير سؤال... فذلك مبارك وعاقبته حميدة، وليس عليك فيه حساب إن شاء الله تعالى؛ لكونه جاء من غير استشراف نفس

ومن آدابهم: عدم الاشتغال بالنعمة عن المنعم؛ إذ يقبح بالعبد أن يألف النعمة دون المنعم أو يميل إليها، فإن الميل إلى كل شيء دون الله مذموم، إلا في حقوق الله ومأموراته

وفى وصية سيدي عبد القادر الجيلي: إياك أن تشتغل بما أعطاك الحق سبحانه من المال فيحجبك بذلك عنه، دنيا وأخرى، وربما سلبك ذلك المال عقوبة لك، وإذا اشتغلت بطاعته عن ذلك المال... كان من المال المحمود لا المذموم

ومن آدابهم: محبة العزلة في البداية دون النهاية؛ وذلك لأن المبتدي لضعفه أدنى شيء يشغله عن الله تعالى، ولا هكذا المنتهي؛ لأنه من حين عرف الله تعالى المعرفة المعروفة بين القوم... صار لا يشغله عن الله شاغل، ولا تخلو الخلق عنده من حالين:

إما أن يكون أحدهم أعوجَ فيجب عليه القرب منه حتى يقوِّم عوجه، وإما مستقيما فيستفيد منه العلم والأدب

وإنما لم نقل: لا تخلو الخلق عنده من ثلاثة أحوال، ونعد منها المساوي له من الأقران؛ لقولهم: ليس في الوجود شيئان متساويان من كل الوجوه، فما بقي إلا الزائد أو الناقص، وكذلك القول في الجوع المفرط أوائل دخولهم الطريق مع وجودهم الطعام؛ مجاهدة لنفوسهم، أما حال كمالهم: فلا يجوعون إلا إذا فقدوا الطعام؛ لأنهم مطالبون بإعطاء كل ذي حقّ حقه من جوارحهم، ويؤاخذون بظلمهم لنفوسهم في مرضات الله بعد الكمال، عكس ما كانوا عليه في بداية أمرهم

ومن هنا قيل: جوع الأكابر اضطرار لا اختيار، بخلافهم في بدايتهم، فإنهم يجوعون اختيارا مع وجود الطعام؛ تعذيبا لنفوسهم لتنقاد لهم إذا دعوها لمرضاة الله تعالى؛ لأنها قبل الرياضة تشبه الدابة الحرون

ومن آدابهم: لزوم الرحمة للمسلمين، وفي الحديث: ((الراحمون يرحمهم الرحمٰن تبارك وتعالى))

ومن كلام سيدي علي الخواص: عليك بالرحمة للمسلمين إن أردت أن تُرْحَم، ومن الرحمة لهم أن تحمل همومهم، قال: واعلم أنّ حملنا لهموم إخواننا المسلمين لا ينافي التسليم كما توهمه بعضهم؛ فالعبد يحمل هَمّ إخوانه من حيث كسبهم للذنوب التي استحقوا بها البلاء النازل عليهم، ويسلِّم من حيث التقدير الإلهي الذي سبق به العلم، إذ لا يمكن رد مثل ذلك، فافهم؛ فإنه قد غلط في ذلك جماعة من مشايخ

الجهل زاعمين أنهم مسلّمون لله تعالى، ويخرجون على من يرونه يحمل همّ إخوانه، ويقولون: ما لفلان ومعارضةَ الأقدار، ويتوهّمون أنّ ما هم عليه أكمل، وهو جهل؛ ففي الحديث: ((من لم يحمِلْ همَّ المسلمين... فليس منهم)) وفي لفظ: ((من لم يهتم بأمر المسلمين... فليس منهم))

وقد كان الإمام عمر بن الخطاب - رضي الله عنه -، إذا نزل بالمسلمين بلاء... لا يضحك قط، وكذلك عمر بن عبد العزيز، وسفيان الثوري، وعطاء السلمي، حتى يرتفع ذلك البلاء

قال: ومن مقام القطب: أن يتحمل من البلاء ما لا تطيقه الجبال، فكل بلاء أهل الأرض ينزل عليه أولا، ثم ينتقل منه إلى الإمامين، ثم إلى الأبدال، فلا يزال ينتقل حتى يعم أصحاب الدوائر والمقامات، فإذا فاض بعد ذلك شيء... وزّعَ على عامة المسلمين، فربما وجد أحد ضيقا وقبضا حتى يكاد يهلك، ولا يعرف سبب ذلك؛ فهذا سببه

ومن هنا قالوا: الرحمة خاصة والبلاء عام، وذلك من جملة رحمة الله تعالى بالعصاة، فإنه لو نزل بهم بلاؤهم كله الذي استحقوه بالمعصية... لمحق الله أثرهم، وإنما يوزع على الناس، فيصيب كل واحد قدرا يسيرا لا يكاد يحس به

ومن آدابهم: تحويط المسلمين في المساء والصباح بما ورد من الآيات والأخبار، وتحويط زرعهم من الدودة، وجسورِهم من العصاة، وبحر النيل حتى تتم زيادته في العادة، والفاكهة إذا حصل حر أو برد شديد يرمي الزهرَ

ومن آدابهم: عدم شكواهم إلى الخلق ما يصيبهم [من] بلاء ومحنة وغير ذلك

ومن وصية سيدي عبد القادر الجيلي: احذر أن تشكو ربك وأنت معافى في بدنك، أو لك قدرة على تحمّل ذلك البلاء بالقدرة التي قوّاك تعالى بها، فتقول: ليس عندي قوة ولا قدرة، أو تشكوه إلى خلقه وعندك نعمة ما، أنعم بها عليك، وتقصد بتلك الشكوى الزيادة من خلقه، وأنت متنعم عما له عندك من العافية والنعم، فاحذر من الشكوى لمخلوق جهدَك ولو تقطّع لحمك، فإن أكثر ما ينزل بابن آدم البلاء من جهة شكواه، وكيف يشكو العبد من هو أرحم به من والدته الشفيقة؟!

ومن آدابهم: كثرة شكرهم على النعمة امتثالا للأمر لا طلبا للزيادة

ومن كلامهم: عليك بشكر النعمة؛ فإنَّ مَنْ لم يشكر النعمة... فقد تعرض لزوالها، واحذر أن يكون شكرك لأجلك، بل اجعل شكرك امتثالا لأمر ربك بالشكر، ولهذا قال تعالى: ﴿ أَنِ اشْكُرْ لِيَ ﴾ [لقمان: ١٤]، فافهم

ومن آدابهم: شدة سترهم لمقامهم، فقد قالوا: الكامل من يهضم نفسه حتى يزكّيه ربه

وقالوا: أحسن بذر الحرّاث ما بذره ثم ستره بعد ما بذره، حتى نبت في بطن الأرض، وأقبحه ما نبت فوقها؛ لأنه لا ثبات له

وقالوا: على صاحب الحق ألَّا يهتم بإظهار شأنه اهتماما يحمله على الاستعانة بالخلق، فإنّه إن كان على نور حق فهو يظهر بالله ﴿ وَكَفَىٰ بِاللَّهِ وَلِيًّا وَكَفَىٰ بِاللَّهِ

نَصِيرًا﴾ [النساء: ٤٥] وإن كان على ظلمة باطل، وتسبب في إظهار شأنه وإشاعته فإنه لا يتمتع بذلك — إنْ مُتّع به — إلا قليلا ثم: ﴿وَاللَّهُ أَشَدُّ بَأْسًا وَأَشَدُّ تَنكِيلًا﴾ [النساء: ٨٤]

ومن آدابهم: ترك التدبير، وهو على قسمين: تدبير محمود، وتدبير مذموم

فالمحمود: ما كان فيما يقربك إلى الله تعالى، كالتدبير في براءة الذمم من حقوق العباد، إما وفاء، وإما استحلالا، وفي تصحيح التوبة، وفيما يؤدي إلى قمع الهوى والشيطان

والتدبير المذموم: تدبير الدنيا للدنيا، وهو أن يدبِّر في أسباب جمعها افتخارا بها واستكثارا، وكلما ازداد منها شيئا... ازداد غفلة واغترارا، وأمارة ذلك: أن تشغله عن الموافقة، وتؤديه إلى المخالفة

أما تدبير الدنيا للآخرة: فلا بأس به، كمن يدبِّر المتاجر؛ ليأكل منها حلالا طيبا ويُنْعِم منها على ذوي الفاقة اتصالا، ويصون بها وجهه عن السؤال إجمالا، وأمارات ذلك: عدم الاستكثار والادخار، والإسعاف منها والإيثار

ومن آدابهم: ترك الاختيار مع الله تعالى، فقد ذكروا أن بني إسرائيل لما جعلوا لهم مع الله اختياراً... ضربت عليهم الذِّلة والمسكنة

وقالوا: إياك والفرار من حال أقامك الله فيها؛ فإن الخير فيما اختاره الله لك، وتأمل السيد عيسى - عليه الصلاة والسلام - لما فرّ من بني إسرائيل حين عظّموه كيف عُبِدَ من دون الله تعالى فوقع في حال أشد مما فرّ منه

وقالوا: أصل اختيار العبد إنما هو لظن العبد أنه مخلوق لنفسه، والحق تعالى ما خلق العبد إلا له سبحانه، فلا يعطي عبده إلا ما يصح أن يكون له تعالى

وقالوا: لا تركن إلى شيء، ولا تأمن مكر الله لشيء، ولا لغير شيء، ولا تختر شيئا؛ فإنك لا تدري أتصل إلى ما اخترته أم لا؟ ثم إن وصلت إليه فلا تدري ألك فيه خير أم لا؟ و إن تصل إليه... فاشكر الذي منعك؛ فإنه لم يمنعك عن بخل، وإذا خيّرك الله تعالى في أمر... فاختر عدم الاختيار، ولا تقف مع شيء، ولا تحزن على شيء خرج عنك، فإنه لو كان لك... ما خرج عنك، ولا تفرح بما يحصل لك من أمور الدارين سوى الله تعالى؛ فإنّ ما سواه الله تعالى عدم

وقالوا: لا تختر جلب نعماء، ولا دفع بلوى؛ فإن النعماء واصلة إليك بالقسمة، استجلبتها أو دفعتها، والبلوى حالّة بك ولو دفعتها أو كرهتها، فسلِّم لله في الكل يفعل ما يشاء، فإن جاءتك النعماء... فاشتغل بالذكر والشكر، وإن جاءتك البلوى... فالزم الصبر والموافقة، أو الرضا، والتنعم بها على قدر ما تُعْطى من الحالات، حتى تصل إلى الرفيق الأعلى، وتقام في مقام مَنْ تقدم من الصدِّيقين

ومن آدابهم: أن يرضوا بالدون من كل شيء تحبه النفس من شهوات الدنيا، وأن يثبتوا إذا ضيّق الله عليهم في المعيشة، ثم لا يخفى أن من رضي بالدون من كل شيء

تحبه النفس من شهوات الدنيا، لم يقع بينه وبين أحد منازعة ولا خصومة، واستراح قلبه ودمه من التعب في تحصيل الزائد عن الحاجة، فإن رزق كسرة من الشعير... قنع بها، وشكر الله عليها، وإن رزق حبة... قنع بها، وشكر الله عليها، ثم بعد ذلك إن جاءه أمر زائد... أكثر من الشكر عليه باللسان والبذل

ومن آدابهم: لا يضيفون إليهم شيئا إلا مع الحضور أن ذلك من نعم الله عليهم دون أن يضيفوا ذلك إليهم مع الغفلة وادعاء الملك

ومن آدابهم: لا يقولون لمن قصدهم في حاجة: ارجع وتعال إلينا وقتا آخر، ولا يمنعون سائلا إلا لحكمة، لا لشح وبخل

ومن آدابهم: كل موضع عظّمهم الناس فيه خافوا منه الفتنة... لا يألفونه

ومن آدابهم: قلة التحدث على الأكل؛ لأنهم جالسون حقيقة على مائدة الله، والله ناظر إليهم وإلى آدابهم وإيثارهم لبعضهم بعضا، وشكرهم له عز وجل

وكذلك من آدابهم: لا يأكلون من وسط الإناء؛ عملاً بخبر: ((إن البركة لتبرز في وسط الإناء فكلوا من حافّاته، ولا تأكلوا من وسطه))

ومن آدابهم: إجابة أخيهم التقي إذا دعاهم إلى طعامه

ومن كلام سيدي علي الخواص: إذا دعاك أخوك المؤمن التقي إلى طعامه... فأجبه تسره، ولا تُجب ظالما ولا فاجرا، ولا من يعامل بالربا، ولا من يخصُّ الأغنياء بدعوته دون الفقراء، وإذا أكلت... فلا تتحول حتى ترتفع المائدة؛ فإن ذلك من سنة السلف الصالح، وإذا غسلت يدك... فادعُ بالبركة، واستأذن في الخروج

ومن آدابهم: لا يأكلون وحدهم؛ لما ورد أن شرَّ الناس من أكل وحده

وفي وصية سيدي علي الخواص: لا تأكل وحدك، ولا في ظلمة، ولا تضيع من الطعام شيئاً؛ فإنه ما قدِّم إليك لتأكله، لا لترميه في الأرض، وبادر إلى ما سقط فكلْه؛ فإنه ورد في الخبر: ((أن من أكل ما سقط... صرف الله عنه الجنون والجذام والبرص، وعن ولده وولد ولده إلى رابع أهل بيته))

وليس من آدابهم: صرف وجوههم عن الحاضرين عند الشرب

وقال الشيخ نجم الدين الكبري: إذا شرب أحدكم... فليشرب ووجهه إلى القوم، ولا يصرف وجهه عنهم كما يفعله العوام بقصد الاحترام، وإذا فرغ أحدكم من غسل يده، فليدعُ لمن يصبّ عليه بنحو: طهّرك الله من الذنوب

ومن آدابهم: إذا استبرؤوا... يجعلون يدهم من داخل الثوب، ويخافون من وقوع يدهم اليمنى على فرجهم؛ إكراما للقرآن العظيم وكتب العلم وللسُبحة التي يسبحون عليها

ومن كلام الشيخ أفضل الدين: إني لأستحي أن أدخل الخلاء بثوب وقعت فيه الصلاة، أو أقرأ القرآن وقد تكلمت كلمة قبيحة، وربما أترك القراءة إذا تكلمت كلمة قبيحة زمنا طويلا، حتى أنسى تلك الكلمة، وكذلك أستحي أن أمسك فرجي بيدي اليمنى، قال: وقد بلغنا عن بعض الصحابة أنه لم يمس فرجه بيده اليمنى مذ بايع رسول الله ﷺ إلى أن مات، وبلغني أيضا أن مريدا من مريدي الشيخ نجم الدين الكبري وقعت يده على فرجه في الخلوة، فتعسر عليه الفتح، فلما خرج بعد الفتح قال له الشيخ: قد علمت بوقوع يدك فرجك وأنت في الخلوة، وتوقف الفتح عليك بسبب ذلك يا ولدي، كيف يجلس أحدكم بين يدي الله ويضع يده على فرجه؟ أما علمت أن من كان في الخلوة في حضرة الله تعالى

ومن آدابهم: تقصير ثيابهم، قال الشيخ البصري في قوله تعالى:

﴿ وَثِيَابَكَ فَطَهِّرْ ﴾ [المدثر: ٤]، أي: فقصِّرْ

ومن آدابهم: إذا لبسوا ثوبا جديدا... لا يغفلون عن قول: الحمد لله الذي كساني هذا ورزقنيه من غير حول مني ولا قوة؛ لما روى أبو داود، عن معاذ بن أنس قال: قال رسول الله ﷺ: ((من أكل طعاماً فقال: الحمد لله الذي أطعمني هذا ورزقنيه من غير حول مني ولا قوة... غُفِر له ما تقدم من ذنبه، ومن لبس ثوبا جديدا فقال: الحمد لله الذي كساني هذا ورزقنيه من غير حول مني ولا قوة... غُفِر له ما تقدم من ذنبه وما تأخر))

ومن آدابهم: إكرام أهل الحِرَفِ المشروعة، وتعظيمهم بطريق الشرع؛ لأنهم متخلقون بالأدب مع الله تعالى، ومع الكون، وإن كانوا لا يشعرون بذلك

ومن آدابهم: تعظيم العلماء، وحملة القرآن الكريم، محبة في رسول الله ﷺ، لأنهم حملة الشريعة المطهرة

ومن آدابهم: لا يمرون راكبين على من علّمهم شيئا من القرآن العظيم، ولو صاروا من مشايخ العصر، ولا يمشون أمامه، ولا ينسونه من الهدية والشكر والدعاء، ولا يتزوجون له مطلّقة أو امرأة مات عنها، ولا يتولون له وظيفة عزل عنها، ولو سئلوا فيها؛ لأنه أبو الروح

وقد كان الشيخ شمس الدين الديروطي – صاحب البرج بدمياط - إذا مرّ بفقيه... ينزل عن دابته ويسوقها أمامه ويقبل يده، ثم لا يركب حتى يبعد عنه جدا،أو يتوارى عنه بجدار ونحوه، مع أنه بلغ في العلم الغاية، وشرح ((المنهاج)) وغيره، وفقيهه على حكم فقهاء المكاتب، لم يزد على حفظ القرآن الكريم إلا ما لا بدّ منه، وقلّ من يفعل ذلك في هذا الزمان

ومن آدابهم: لا يجلسون للمشيخة، ولو اجتمعت فيهم شروطها إلا بإذن من الله تعالى، أو من بابه الأعظم ﷺ، أو من شيخ عارف ناصح؛ فإنَّ في الإذن البركة

والسلامة من الآفات في مستقبل الزمان، والمراد بالإذن من الله تعالى: الإلهام الصحيح

ومن آدابهم: لا يزهدون في الدنيا إلا لكونها مبغوضة لله تعالى، لا لعلة أخرى: من راحة بدن، أو تخفيف حساب، وكذلك لا يزهدون فيما في أيدي الناس إلا امتثالا للأمر، وليحبهم الناسُ فيشفعوا فيهم عند ربهم إذا وقعت المؤاخذة على الذنوب، لا لعلة أخرى من إقامة جاه، أو انتشار صيت عندهم

ومن آدابهم: لا يشهدون لهم ملكا في الدارين، ومن هنا صح لهم مقام التجريد في الباطن، فليس لهم علاقة في الدنيا يطلبونها، أو يتأسفون على فواتها، ولو خلع أحدهم ثيابه الظاهرة المعتادة، وجعل على رأسه عرقية فقط، وفي وسطه خرقة تستر عورته فقط، أو خيشة تدفع عنه ألم الحر والبرد فقط... لم يكن عليه في ذلك لوم؛ لمشاكلة ظاهره لباطنه، بخلاف ما إذا لبس هذه اللبسة قبل حصول التجريد بالباطن؛ فإن ظاهره لم يشاكل باطنه، فوقع في صورة المنافق؛ إذ المنافق هو من أظهر خلاف ما أبطن

ومن آدابهم: التباعد عن كل مَنْ يرونه من العلماء لا يعمل بعلمه، مع إحسان الظن به، ومن كلام سيدي علي وفا: علماء السوء أضر على الناس من إبليس؛ لأن إبليس إذا وسوس للمؤمن... عرف المؤمن... أنه عدو مضل مبين، فإن أطاع وسواسه...

عرف أنه قد عصى؛ فيسرع في التوبة من ذنبه، والاستغفار لربه، وعلماء السوء يُلبسون الحق بالباطل، ويورُّون الأحكام على وفق غرضهم وأهويتهم، فمن أطاعهم...ضل سعيه، وهو يحسب أنه يحسن صنعاً، فاجتنبْهم، وكن مع الصادقين؛ فإنك تستفيد منهم العمل بأحكام الدين، بخلاف المتفيهقين؛ فإنك لن تستفيد منهم إلا دعوى العلم، والتكبر على المسلمين

ومن آدابهم: كثرة انقباضهم في نفوسهم إذا رأوا أمرا مخالفا للشرع؛ إيثارا للجناب الإلهي، وشفقة على الفاعل

وليس من آدابهم: أن يقولوا: هذا فعل الله فلا يُنْقبض منه؛ لأنه جهل: ((فقد كان ﷺ يغضب إذا انتهكت حرمات الله عز وجل))

وقد قالوا: ينبغي للمؤمن عينان أو أعين: عين ينظر بها إلى ما في الفعل الإلهي من الحكم البالغة؛ ليسْلَم من الوقوع في الاعتراض على حكيم عليم، وعين ينظر بها إلى مخالفة العبيد لأوامر ربهم، فيغار لله تعالى، فعلم أن إنكار المنكر لا يقدح في مقام التسليم؛ لأن كلّا منهما مأمور به شرعا، فافهم

ومن آدابهم: غض البصر عن فضول النظر، والإسراع في المشي مع السكينة، وإصلاح ذات البين، والتعامي عن عيوب الناس، وسترها ونشر محاسنهم، إلا المبتدعة؛ فإنّ في نشر مساوئهم والتحذير منهم رحمةً للمسلمين، فلا يزيد عذاب المبتدع باتباع الناس له في بدعته، ولا يأثم أحد بسببه

ومن آدابهم: عدم سب الولاة وإن جاروا، لأنهم مسلطون غالبا على الرعية بحسب أعمالهم ونياتهم

ومن آدابهم: عدم الاستنصار لنفوسهم؛ فإن الانتصار للنفس من الأمور التي كلها تعب، ومن سلَّم الأمر لمولاه... نصره من غير عشيرة ولا أهل

ومن كلامهم: إذا انتصر الصوفي لنفسه وأجاب عنها... فهو والتراب سواء

ومن آدابهم: لا يدعون على مَنْ ظلمهم، ولا يطلبون النصر عليه؛ لعلمهم بأن الله تعالى يكره منهم ذلك، وأن طلب النصر على الظالم من الشهوة الخفية

ومن آدابهم: لا يدخلون المساجد بنية النوم والاستراحة،ولا يُخرجون فيها ريحا إلا لعذر، ولا يتحدثون فيها بشيء من أمر الدنيا، ولا يمدّون فيها أرجلهم، ولا يرفعون فيها أصواتهم

ومن آدابهم: لا يقولون ليد النبي ﷺ: يسارا وإنما يقولون: اليمين الأول واليمين الثاني، أو يمين وجهه ويمين خلفه، ولا يذكرون اسمه الشريف إلا مع مصاحبة لفظ السيادة في جميع المواطن، غير تلاوة وأذان، ومعلوم أن تعظيم النبي ﷺ مفروض

على الأمة، وذكر اسمه الشريف بغير لفظ السيادة، منافٍ للتعظيم، وفيه من إساءة الأدب، وقلة الحياء، ما لا يخفى على كل ذي نور

ومن آدابهم: لا يقولون مثلا: الفاتحة للنبي ﷺ، واجعل اللهم ثواب كذا وكذا في صحائف رسول الله ﷺ، فإن أعمال الأمة له أصالة

ومن آدابهم: محبة إخوانهم المسلمين محبة أخوة وإيمان، لا محبة طبع وإحسان

ومن وصية سيدي عبد القادر الجيلي: إذا وجدت في قلبك بغض شخص أو حبه... فاعرض أعماله على الكتاب والسنة، فإن كانت مكروهة فيهما فاكرهه، وإن كانت محبوبة فيهما... فأحببه؛ لئلا تحبه بهواك وتبغضه بهواك، قال الله تعالى ﴿وَلَا تَتَّبِعِ ٱلۡهَوَىٰ فَيُضِلَّكَ عَن سَبِيلِ ٱللَّهِ﴾ [ص: ٢٦]، وقد ذكرنا في غير هذه الرسالة أن حقيقة الحب في الله: ألّا يزيد بالبر ولا ينقص بالجفاء

ومن آدابهم: حفظ الود لمن أكلوا عنده خبزاً، أو ذاقوا عنده ملحا

وذكر سيدي علي الخواص – رحمه الله – أن ذلك كان من أخلاق اللصوص أيام السلطان قايتباي، وحكى من وقائع الشاطر حمور، كبير اللصوص: أنه دخل مرة على تاجر بجوار جامع الغمري بمصر هو وجماعته، حتى وقفوا على رأسه، وأخذوا يفتشون في البيت، فاستيقظ التاجر، فرأى اللصوص واقفين على رأسه، فقال له

حمور: لا تخف على نفسك يا خواجا، فالصبيان إنما يطلبون منك الغداء فقط، فقال: كم أنتم؟ فقال عشرة، فقام وأتى لهم بألف دينار، وزاده من ورائهم أربعمئة دينار، فقال له حمور: شكر الله فضلك يا خواجا، ما كان أملنا فيك هذا كله، فوضع كل واحد نصيبه في جيبه، ورأى واحد منهم حِقّا أبيض يضيء على رفّ بالبيت، فأخذه، وحدثته نفسه - وهو خارج في دهليز البيت - أن يفتحه، وينظر ما فيه، ففتحه، فرأى فيه شيئا ناعما فذاقه فقال: ملح! فسمعه حمور؛ فقال: ردوا ما معكم؛ فإن صاحبكم ذاق ملح هذا الخواجا، ما بقي يرى منا سوءاً مدة حياتنا، فردوا المال كله، فأقسم عليهم الخواجا أن يأخذوا مئة دينار... فأبوا

ومن آدابهم: هجر السارق والخائن، وإخراجهما من بينهم، والفرق بين السارق والخائن: أن الخائن: هو من يسرق ما اؤتمن عليه، والسارق: هو من يسرق ما لا يؤتمن عليه، وقد قالوا: إن الخيانة تذهب البركة من مال الإنسان وعمره، وكذلك القول في السرقة، فما وجدنا قط سارقا إلا والبركة ممحوقة من ماله وعمره

وكذلك من آدابهم: هجر الكذاب، قالت عائشة رضي الله عنها: لم يكن شيء أبغض إلى رسول الله ﷺ من الكذاب، كان يهجر الرجل على الكلمة من الكذب الشهرين والثلاثة

ومن آدابهم: تقديم مَنْ مروءته من حيث نفسه، وميزان ذلك النظر في أمر العبد، فمَن كان إقدامه على الأهوال في دين الله وفى غير دين الله على حد سواء... فذلك

من المروءة النفسانية، ومن كان إقدامه على الأهوال في دين الله فقط... فذلك من المروءة الإيمانية

وكذلك من آدابهم: تقديم الفقيه الصِّرف على الفقيه المتفعل في الطريق؛ لأن الفقيه الصرف سالم من النفاق الذي يقع فيه المتفعل، مع زيادته عليه بالعلوم الشرعية، بل العامي الذي يعبد الله تعالى، ويسأل العلماء عمَّا أشكل عليه في دينه... أحسن حالا من المتفعل في طريق القوم

ومن آدابهم: لا يخرجون لزيارة أحد حتى يتخلقوا بآداب الزيارة، وهي: الشوق إلى المزور، والجزم بفضله وطهارته من المعاصي المعنوية والحسية،وهم بعكس ذلك، والتماس بركة دعائه ولحظه، وتحرير النية بأن يكون الباعث على الزيارة امتثال الأمر لا غير ذلك، وحفظ اللسان من الوقوع في أعراض الناس، وترك ذكر المحاسن، وهذا يشترك فيهما الزائر والمزور، فإن خلت الزيارة من هذه الآداب... فلا نفع بها ولا ثواب، بل هي تكلُّف ونفاق، ثم لا يخفى أنه يجب على الزائر إذا ذكر المزور شيئا من محاسنه أن يعتقد أنه ما ذكر ذلك إلا لغرض شرعي

ومن آدابهم: إعطاء الخبز حقه من الإكرام والتعظيم والتقبيل، ووضعه على العين

ومن كلام سيدي علي الخواص: إياكم أن تضعوا الخبز على الأرض من غير حائل؛ فإن فيه احتقارا لنعمة الله عز وجل

وعن عائشة – رضي الله عنها – قالت: دخل عليَّ رسول الله ﷺ مرة، فرأى كسرة يابسة في جدار وقد علاها الغبار، فأخذها رسول الله ﷺ وقبّلها ووضعها على عينه، ثم قال: ((يا عائشة! أحسني مجاورة نعم الله؛ فإن النعمة قلّما نفرت من أهل بيت فكادت ترجع إليهم))

ومن كلام سيدي أحمد بن الرفاعي: قلة إكرام الخبز كفر بنعمة المنعم، فاجتهدوا في إكرامه ما استطعتم، والتقطوا ما يسقط عند سقوطه، ولا تتركوه إلى آخر الطعام؛ فإن تعظيم نعمة الله من تعظيم الله، وما ابتلي قوم بالغلاء حتى أهانوا الحبَّ لرخصه

وفي بعض الآثار: أن القرص لا يؤكل حتى يتداوله ثلاث مئة وستون مخلوقا أوّلهم ميكائيل، وآخرهم الفرّان

قال: ويكفينا في تعظيم الخبز أن رسول الله ﷺ جعله عديلا لرؤية الله في حديث: ((للصائم فرحتان: فرحة عند إفطاره، وفرحة عند لقاء ربه))

ومن آدابهم: إذا فرغوا من أكل ما قُدّم لهم... يقولون: الحمد لله رب العالمين على كل حال، الحمد لله الذي بنعمته تتم الصالحات، وتعم البركات، ويقرؤون سورة قريش، وسورة الإخلاص

ومن آدابهم: إذا أكلوا عندأحد لم يخرخوا من عنده حتى يشربوا، وقد قالوا: مِن بخل الصوفي أن يأكل ولا يشرب

ومن آدابهم: – إذا أكلوا — مواساةُ مَن حضر ذلك المأكول

ومن كلام سيدي علي الخواص: إذا أكلت طعاما... فأطعم منه مَن حضر إن أردت دوام النعمة عليك، ومَن أكل وعين تنظر إليه، ولم يُطعمها... ابتلاه الله بداء يسمى النفس

ومن آدابهم: تعظيم حقوق الوالدين خوفا من الوقوع في إساءة الأدب معهما، أو في العقوق لهما، وليس للعقوق ضابط في الشرع، إنما هو عام في سائر ما يخالف غرض الوالدين من جميع المباحات، وليس بعد حق الله تعالى وحق رسوله ﷺ أعظم من حق الوالدين

ومن كلام سيدي علي الخواص: من حق والديك عليك: أن تسمع كلامهما، وتقوم لقيامهما، وتمتثل أمرهما، ولا تمشي أمامهما، ولا ترفع صوتك فوق صوتهما، وتخفض جناحك لهما، ولا تمنّ عليهما بالبر لهما، ولا بالقيام بأمرهما، ولا تنظر إليهما شزرا، ولا تغضب في وجههما، ولا تسبقهما إلى أطيب الطعام إذا أكلت معهما بل آثرهما على نفسك، واحرص على تحصيل مرضاتهما

وحق الوالدة ضعفا حق الوالد العرفي، أما والد الدين: فربما كان أجلّ مقاما وحقا من الوالدة، ومن حقهما ألّا تدعوَهما باسمهما؛ فمن دعا أحدا من والديه باسمه... صار عاقّا له

ومن آدابهم: محبتهم لعيالهم محبة شرعية لا محبة الزوجات الطبعيَّة؛ فإن المحبة الطبعية شهوة نفس، ما دام العبد فيها . . . فهو في حجاب عن الله تعالى

واعلم أن الله تعالى حبَّب إلينا النساء بحكم الطبع، ثم أمرنا بمجاهدة النفس حتى تخرج من محبتها الطبعية إلى محبتها الشرعية، وقلَّ من يصبر على مجاهدة نفسه حتى تخرج من ذلك، ومن هنا حذر الأشياخ من تزويج المرأة الحسناء؛ لأن ضررها أكثر من ضرر الشوهاء

ومن كلام سيدي أفضل الدين: من أكثر من مجالسة النساء . . . فسد عقله، وفاته الفضائل، وامتنع الحق تعالى من دخول قلبه، وباض الشيطان فيه وفرّخ

ومن آدابهم: تعظيم كل فقير خامل الذكر مع الاستقامة، أكثر من الفقير المشهور بالكرامات؛ لأن الدنيا ليست بدار نتائج، وإنما هي دار تكليف

ومن آدابهم: لا يصرُّون على ذنب؛ فإن الإصرار من المهلكات، وتصير الصغيرة به كبيرة، وقد حدّ بعض الأشياخ الإصرار بأن يؤخر الشخص التوبة حتى يدخل عليه وقت صلاة أخرى من الخمس

ومن آدابهم: في سوء ظن بأحد أو غيبة ولم يعلم بها صاحبها، أن يقرأ أمّ القرآن وسورة الإخلاص، والمعوذتين، ويهدون ثواب ذلك في صحائف من أساؤوا به الظن، أو اغتابوه

وكيفية الإهداء أن تقول: اللهم صلِّ وسلم على نبيك وحبيبك سيدنا محمد وآله، وأثبني على ما قرأته واجعله في صحائف عبدك فلان

تنبيه:

ينبغي لمن يعلم من نفسه أن عليه للناس حقوقا في المال والعرض، وتعذر رضاهم أن يقرأ مع حضور: سورة الإخلاص اثنتي عشرة مرة، والمعوذتين، كل ليلة، ويهدي ثوابهن في صحائف أولئك الناس، وكيفية الإهداء أن يقول: اللهم صلِّ وسلم على نبيك وحبيبك سيدنا محمد وآله، وأثبني على ما قرأته، واجعله في صحائف من له عليَّ تبعة من عبادك، من مال وعِرض

ومن آدابهم: إذا أراد أحدهم [أن] يتداين... أن يتوجه بقلبه إلى الله تعالى ويقولَ بلسانه: اللهم عليك التداين، فخذ بيدي صدقة من صدقاتك عليّ

ومن آدابهم: محبتهم لعترة رسول الله ﷺ - ولو كانوا على غير قدم الاستقامة-؛ لأنهم جزء منه ﷺ، وللجزء في المودة والإجلال والتوقير نحو ما للكل

وقد قال بعض العلماء: من حقوق الشرفاء علينا - وإن بَعُدوا في النسب - أن نؤثر رضاهم على أهوائنا وشهواتنا، ونعظمهم ونوقرهم، ولا نجلس على سرير وهم على الأرض، لسريان لحم رسول الله ﷺ ودمه فيهم

وكان سيدي علي الخواص - رحمه الله تعالى - يقول: من حق الشرفاء علينا أن نفديهم بأرواحنا، وأن نصطنع الأيدي معهم؛ لمكانهم من رسول الله ﷺ، ومن الأدب ألّا يتزوج أحدنا شريفة إلا إن عرف من نفسه أنه يكون تحت حكمها وإشارتها، ويقدم لها نعلها، ويقوم لها إذا وردت عليه، ولا يقتر عليها في المعيشة إلا إن اختارت ذلك

ومن آدابهم: لا يغفلون عن زيارة أهل البيت

وقد صحح أهل الكشف أن السيدة زينب رضي الله عنها ابنة الإمام علي رضي الله عنه، هي المدفونة بقناطر السباع بلا شك، وأن أختها السيدة رقية رضي الله عنها في المشهد القريب من دار الخليفة أمير المؤمنين بالقرب من جامع ابن طولون ومعها جماعة من أهل البيت، وأن السيدة سكينة رضي الله عنها ابنة السيد الحسين رضي الله عنه في الزاوية التي عند الدرب قريبا من مشهد عمتها ومن دار الخليفة، وأن السيدة نفيسة رضي الله عنها في هذا المكان بلا شك، وأن السيدة عائشة ابنة الإمام جعفر الصادق رضي الله عنهما في المسجد الذي له المنارة القصيرة على يسار من يريد الخروج من الرميلة إلى باب القرافة، وأن رأس السيد الحسين رضي الله عنه في القبر المعروف بالمشهد قريبا من خان الخليلي بلا شك، وضعها طلائع بن رُزّيك نائب مصر في هذاالموضع في كيس أخضر من حرير أخضر على كرسي من خشب الأبنوس، وفرش تحتها المسك والطيب، ومشى معها هو و عسكره لما جاءت من بلاد العجم حفاة، من ناحية قطية إلى مصر، وأن السيد محمدا الأنور عم السيدة نفيسة رضي الله عنه في المشهد القريب من جامع ابن طولون مما يلي دار الخليفة في

الزاوية التي هناك ينزل إليها بدرج، وأن أخاه السيد الحسن والد السيدة نفيسة في التربة المشهورة القريبة من جامع عمرو، وأن رأس الإمام زين العابدين، وأن رأس السيد زيد في القبة التي بين الأثر قريبا من مجراة القلعة، وأن رأس السيد إبراهيم بن السيد زيد في المسجد الخارج من ناحية المطرية مما يلي الخانقة، وهو الذي اختفى من أجله الإمام مالك

هذا ما حضرني في هذا الوقت من المدفونين في مصر من أهل البيت، فعليك – يا أخي – بزيارتهم وقَدّمها على زيارة كل ولي في مصر، عكس ما عليه العامة، فقلّ أن ترى أحدا منهم يعتني بزيارة أحد ممن ذُكِر كاعتنائه بزيارة بعض المجاذيب، وهذا من جملة الجهل

ومن آدابهم: لا يميلون إلى شيء من أحوالهم

ومن كلام سيدي إبراهيم المتبولي: أكثر ما يخاف المؤمن ميل نفسه إلى أعماله الصالحة على وجه اعتقاد الإخلاص فيها، ولو كشفا وذوقا

ومن كلام سيدي علي الخواص: لا تفرحوا بما تُعْطَونه من الكرامات والأحوال والعلوم والمعارف حتى يكشف لكم الغطاء، هل هي بطريق الاستحقاق لكم أو بطريق الوعد؟ فإن العطايا التي بطريق الوعد لا ينبغي لعاقل أن يفرح بها إلا إن كانت قطعية، وما معكم شيء إلا بطريق الوعد وحسن الظن فقط

ومن آدابهم: يشهدون الكمال في صاحبهم والنقص في أنفسهم، ومن شهد ذل... كره العزلة عن الناس إلا لغرض شرعي آخر، كأن يخشى أن يحصل لهم منه شيء يتضرَّرون به

ومن آدابهم: يشهدون على الدوام أن الله تعالى أرحم بهم منهم، وكذلك لا يقع منهم قنوط من رحمة الله تعالى في وقت من الأوقات

ومن آدابهم: يتحفظون من التعصب في محبتهم لأحد من الصحابة - رضي الله تعالى عنهم -، أو لأولادهم إذ الواجب على كل أحد أن يحب أصحاب رسول الله ﷺ تبعا لحب رسول الله ﷺ، ويحب أولادهم كذلك، ويقدم أولاد السيدة فاطمة - رضي الله عنها - على أولاد سائر الصحابة

وذكر الشيخ عبد الغفار القوصي أنه كان له صاحب من أكابر العلماء، فمات فرآه بعد موته، فسأله عن دين الإسلام، فتلجلج في الجواب، قال: فقلت له: أما هو حق؟ فقال: نعم؛ هو حق؛ فنظرت إلى وجهه فإذا هو أسود كالزفت، وكان رجلا أبيض، فقلت له: إن كان دين الإسلام حقا فما سواد وجهك؟ فقال بخفض صوت: كنت أقدم بعض الصحابة على بعض بالهوى والعصبية

ومن آدابهم: يعتنون بإفادة كل جليس معهم وإن لم يكن معتنيا بالفائدة، وكان بعضهم لا يجلس أحد معه إلا ذكر هو وإياه مجلس ذكر، ثم يصرفه بعد ذلك، ويقول: من لم يصلح لاستفادة العلوم... يصلح لذكر الله

ومن آدابهم: لا يزورون أحدا ولا يأكلون من طعامه إلا إن علموا أنه كثير التوقيف عما بأيدي أهل زمانه، ذو حرص على خميرة العجين

ومن آدابهم: لا يبادرون إلى إجابة من طلب أن يكون مريدا تحت إشارتهم وتربيتهم، وقد قالوا في الزمن السابق: إنْ صحّ للشيخ في عمره كله مريد واحد صادق... فهو أعز من الكبريت الأحمر

وصفات المريد الصادق على وجه الاختصار أربعة:

الأولى: صدقه في محبة الشيخ

الثانية: امتثال أمره

الثالثة: ترك الاعتراض عليه

الرابعة: سلب الاختيار معه

فكل مريد جمع هذه الأربع... فقد صحت قاسميته، وصار كالحرّاق الناشف إلى الزناد، ومن طلب المريدين أخذ العهد عليه وحرّاقه مبلول، فلا تعلق فيه شرارة الزناد، بل كل شرارة وقعت عليه طفئت

ومن آدابهم: يتهمون نفوسهم في المواظبة على الخير ومجالس الذكر، فقلّ من يواظب على خير ويجده الناس عليه، ويسلم من الآفات

ومن شأن النفس إذا ألفت التعظيم لأجل عبادتها أن يشق عليها تركها؛ لا لأجل مجالسة الحق تعالى فيها، فليمتحن السالك نفسه إن رأى عندها استحياء إذا ترك إظهار تلك العبادة، فليعلم أنها كلها رياء، ويجب عليه التوبة والاستغفار، وإن رآها ليس عندها استحياء... فليشكر الله تعالى الذي نجاه، ثم لا يأمن

وقد وقع لبعض السلف أنه صلى الصلوات الخمس في الصف الأول، فتخلف يوما فوجد في نفسه خجلا، فأعاد تلك الصلوات كلها، وقال: إنما كانت مواظبتي رياء وسمعة

ومن كلام سيدي علي الخواص - رحمة الله عليه -: كل من وجد في نفسه خجلا إذا ترك إظهار ورده في القرآن الكريم أو الصوم أو الزهد أو الصمت... فأعماله كلها رياء وسمعة، لا يجد في صحيفته منها شيئا يوم القيامة

ومن كلام سيدي علي المرصفي: لا يليق بفقير أن يجمع الناس على مجلس ذكر إلا إن كان قد خرج عن حب الرئاسة، وإلا أهلك نفسَه، وقد أدركت الفقراء وما يتجرأ أحد أن يجلس مع جماعة في مجلس ذكر إلا بعد موت شيخه، أو إذنِه له، بعد أن شهد له الكمال

ومن آدابهم: لا يستلذ أحدهم بما يحصل له من صورة الخشوع والرعدة، وضم الأكتاف، وإطراق الرأس إلى الأرض، ولا يسامح نفسه في ذلك إلا إن كان مغلوباً

وقد رأى الإمام عمر بن الخطاب – رضي الله عنه – رجلا يصلي وقد ضم كتفيه، فضربه، وقال له: ليس الخشوع هكذا، إنما الخشوع في القلب، انتهى

ففرَّ – يا أخي – من الوقوع في مثل ذلك، وإن رأيت أحدا فعل ذلك، فاحمله على أنه مغلوب

ومن آدابهم: يغضبون باطنا على كل من ادعى عندهم دعاوى كاذبة، ويباسطونه ظاهرا ثم يُعلمونه سرا بكذبه إن رأوا نفسه تحتمل مثل ذلك، وفي هذا الأدب جمع بين الغيرة لله والنصح لذلك العبد، وقلّ من يجمع بين هذين الشيئين

ومن آدابهم: طلب كل ما يحتاجون إليه من باب الله تعالى دون باب أحد من عبيده، ولا ينظرون إلى باب غيره إلا من حيث كون الخلق كالقناة التي تجري فيها الماء لا غير، فالفضل لمن أجرى الماء في القناة، لا للقناة

ومن كلام سيدي عبد القادر الجيلي: تعامَ – يا أخي – عن الجهات حال طلبك حاجة من ربك... يفتحْ لك باب فضله، وإلا... فلا يفتح لك باب فضله؛ لأنه تعالى غيور

ومن لم يصل إلى ذلك فمن لازمه الاعتماد على الأسباب والوقوف معها، وعدم شكر الوسائط امتثالا للأمر، وذلك شرك

وإياك أن تحذف واسطة رسول الله ﷺ في كل حاجة طلبتها؛ فإن ذلك من سوء الأدب معه ﷺ، وتكون إذ ذاك مبتدعا لا متبعا، فافهم

ومن آدابهم: إذا كانوا يقرؤون القرآن الكريم أو الحديث الشريف، وأرادوا أن يكلموا إنسانا في حاجة... فلا يكلمونه حتى يستأذنوا الله تعالى ورسوله ﷺ بقلبهم ولسانهم أن يكلموا ذلك الإنسان، ثم إن غفلوا عن الاستئذان وكلّموا أحدا... استغفروا الله تعالى حتى يلقي الله في قلوبهم أنه قبِل استغفارهم

وقد وقع للشيخ أفضل الدين أنه كلّم إنسانا وهو يقرأ في الحديث قبل أن يستأذن النبي ﷺ، فاستغفر الله تعالى سبعين مرة

ومن آدابهم: لا يشتغلون حال الأذان بشيء أدبا مع الله تعالى

وقد حكى بعضهم عن امرأة من الباغيات، أنها رئيت في هيئة حسنة لما توفيت، فقيل لها: كيف ذلك؟ فقالت: أذن المؤذن مرة وكنا فيما لا ينبغي من رفع الصوت، فأمرت رفقتي بالسكوت حتى فرغ المؤذن، فغفر الله لنا بذلك

ومن آدابهم: إذا وجعتهم أرجلهم من القرفصة لا يمدونها حتى يستأذنوا الله تعالى، وكذلك الحكم في مدِّها نحو المدينة الشريفة، أو نحو ولي من الأولياء، لا يمدونها حتى يستأذنوا النبي ﷺ أو ذلك الولي، كل ذلك لشهودهم أنهم بين يدي

الله تعالى وبين يدي رسوله ﷺ على الدوام، شعروا بذلك أو لم يشعروا، وإن لم يكن ذلك كشفا كان إيمانا

وقد وقع لأبي إسحاق إبراهيم بن أدهم: أنه مد رجله حين وجعته من القرفصة قبل أن يستأذن؛ فعوتب في ذلك، فلم يمدَّ رجله بعد ذلك إلى أن مات

وكذلك وقع لأبي محمد الجريري: أنه مد رجله قبل أن يستأذن، فعوتب في ذلك فلم يمد رجله إلى أن مات

ومن آدابهم: مواظبتهم على الاستغفار ثلاثا، وعلى قراءة القرآن، وآية الكرسي، وآخر سورة الكهف، وقل يأيها الكافرون، وقل هو الله أحد، والمعوذتين عند النوم، وعلى التسبيح ثلاثا وثلاثين، والتحميد ثلاثا وثلاثين، والتكبير أربعا وثلاثين، لخبر أبي داود والترمذي: ((خصلتان لا يحصيهما عبد إلا دخل الجنة وهما يسير، ومن يعمل بهما قليل، يسبح الله دبر كل صلاة عشرا، ويحمده عشرا، ويكبره عشرا، فتلك مائة وخمسون باللسان، وألف وخمس مائة في الميزان، وإذا أوى إلى فراشه... يسبح ثلاثا وثلاثين، ويحمد ثلاثا وثلاثين، ويكبر أربعا وثلاثين، فتلك مائة باللسان، وألف في الميزان، وأيكم يعمل في يومه وليلته ألفين وخمس مئة سيئة؟ قيل: يا رسول الله! كيف لا يحصيهما؟ فقال: يأتي أحدكم الشيطان وهو في صلاته فيقول: اذكر كذا، اذكر كذا، أو يأتيه عند منامه فينوِّمه))

ومن آدابهم: شدة كراهتهم النوم على حدث أكبر أو حدث أصغر

ومن كلام سيدي علي الخواص - رحمه الله -: إياك أن تنام على حدث ظاهر أو باطن من محبة الدنيا و شهواتها؛ فربما أخذ الله تعالى روحك تلك الليلة، فتلقى الله تعالى وهو عليك غضبان، بحسب قبح ذلك الذنب الذي نمت عليه

وفي الحديث: ((يحشر المرء على دين خليله، فلينظر أحدكم من يخالل))، وفي الحديث أيضا: ((إن الله منذ خلق الدنيا لم ينظر إليها)) أي نظر رضا عنها، وعن محبتها وإلا... فهو تعالى ينظر إليها نظر تدبير، ولولا ذلك... لذهبت في علم الله تعالى، ولم يبقَ لها وجود، فافهم

فمن نام على محبة الدنيا، ومات في تلك الليلة... حشر مع مبغوض لله تعالى، لم ينظر إليه منذ خلقه، فهذا الأمر قلَّ من ينتبه له في هذا الزمان حتى يتوب منه، بل غالب الناس لا يعد محبة الدنيا ذنبا

وقد كان مالك بن دينار يجمع أصحابه ويقول لهم: تعالوا نستغفر من الذنب الذي أغفله الناس، وهو حب الدنيا

ومن آدابهم: العمل على تصفية صدورهم من الغشِّ؛ ليصلحوا لدخول الحضرة الإلهية التي هي أشرف وأفضل من الجنة، فإن دخولها محرَّم على مَنْ في قلبه غشٌّ لأحد من الخلق

وفي الحديث عن أنس بن مالك - رضي الله عنه - قال: قال رسول الله ﷺ ((يا بني! إن قدرت أن تصبح وتمسي وليس في قلبك غش لأحد... فافعل، ثم قال: يا

بني! وذلك من سنتي، ومن أحيا سنتي فقد أحياني، ومن أحياني... كان معي في الجنة))

وقال الشيوخ: مقاساة الجوع والصبرُ عليه سهل، ومعالجة الأخلاق والتنقي من سفسافها صعب شديد

والمراد بالغش: الغل والحقد والبغض والحسد وسوء الظن، ولا يقدر على تصفية صدره من هذه المذمومات إلا من زهد في الدنيا وفى الرئاسة؛ فإن منبع ذلك من حب الدنيا ومن حب الرئاسة، ومن هنا ظهر فضل الصوفية وكمال شرفهم على غيرهم لزهدهم في الدنيا، وفي محبة الرفعة عند أهلها، ولاستمساكهم من التقوى بأوثق العرى، فعلم أن من زهد في الدنيا واستمسك بالتقوى.... صارت نفسه مأمونة الغائلة من الغل والحقد والبغض والحسد وسائر المذمومات، فهذا حال الصوفي

وقال بعضهم: مجمع حال الصوفية أمران، هما وصف الصوفية، وإليهما الإشارة بقوله تعالى: ﴿ اَللّٰهُ يَجۡتَبِىٓ اِلَيۡهِ مَنۡ يَّشَآءُ وَيَهۡدِىٓ اِلَيۡهِ مَنۡ يُّنِيۡبُ ﴾ [الشورى:١٣]، فقوم من الصوفية خُصُّوا بالاجتباء الصِّرف، وقوم منهم خُصُّوا بالهداية بشرط مقدمة الإنابة، فالاجتباء المحض غير معلَّل بكسب العبد، وهذا حال المحجوب المراد، يناديه الحق سبحانه بمنَحه ومواهبه من غير سابقة كسب منه، يسبق كشفُه اجتهادَه

وأما أهل الهداية الذين شرط الحق سبحانه وتعالى لهم الإنابة: فقال تعالى: ﴿وَيَهۡدِىٓ اِلَيۡهِ مَنۡ يُّنِيۡبُ ﴾ [الشورى:١٣] فقد طولِبوا بالاجتهاد، وقال تعالى: ﴿وَالَّذِيۡنَ جَاهَدُوۡا فِيۡنَا لَنَهۡدِيَنَّهُمۡ سُبُلَنَا ﴾ [العنكبوت:٦٩] يُدرِّجهم الله في مدارج الكسب بأنواع الرياضات والمجاهدات، وسهر الدياجر وظمأ الهواجر، يتقلبون في

رمضاء الإرادة، ويخرجون عن كل مألوف وعادة، وهي الإنابة التي شرطها الحق سبحانه لهم، وجعل الهداية معروفة بها، وهذه الهداية أيضا هداية خاصة؛ لأنها هداية إليه سبحانه غير الهداية العامة، التي هي التهدِّي إلى أمره ونهيه، بمقتضى المعرفة الأولية، وهذا حال المحب السالك الذي سبق اجتهاده كشفَه، وهذا أثمر وأكمل من الأول

ومن آدابهم: يفتتحون قيام الليل بركعتين خفيفتين، يقرؤون في الأولى بعد الفاتحة بآية: ﴿ وَلَوْ اَنَّهُمْ اِذْ ظَّلَمُوٓا اَنْفُسَهُمْ جَآءُوْكَ فَاسْتَغْفَرُوا اللّٰهَ وَاسْتَغْفَرَ لَـهُمُ الرَّسُوْلُ لَوَجَدُوا اللّٰهَ تَوَّابًا رَّحِيْمًا ﴾ [النساء: ٦٤]

وفي الركعة الثانية: ﴿ وَ مَنْ يَّعْمَلْ سُوٓءًا اَوْ يَظْلِمْ نَفْسَهُ ثُمَّ يَسْتَغْفِرِ اللّٰهَ يَجِدِ اللّٰهَ غَفُوْرًا رَّحِيْمًا ﴾ [النساء: ١١٠]

وقد حُبِّب لي أن أقول بقلبي ولساني بعد السلام:(يا سيدي! يا رسول الله! استغفر لي ربك، صلى الله عليك وسلم،(ثلاث مرات أو أكثر،(اللهم عملتُ سوءا وظلمت نفسي، فاغفر لي صدقة من صدقاتك عليَّ يا أرحم الراحمين)، ثلاث مرات وأكثر

واعلم أن الفقراء يكرهون النوم في الثلث الأخير من الليل أشد من كراهتهم للمعاصي الظاهرة، وقد مكث ابن المؤذن بناحية منية أبي عبد الله أربعين سنة، لا يضع جنبه الأرض بالليل، فكان سيدي محمد السروي يقول: هنيئا لابن المؤذن، لم يدع مددا ينزل من السماء في الليل إلا وله فيه نصيب.

ومن آدابهم: كثرة ثنائهم على الله تعالى إذا نزل بهم ما يسوؤهم عادة؛ لعلمهم بأن تقديراته تعالى على عباده عين الحكمة لا بالحكمة، لأنها لو كانت بالحكمة... لكانت أفعاله تعالى معلولة تحت حكم الحكمة، ومن هنا كان لا يجوز السخط على شيء من أفعاله أبدا، ومن سخط... فهو جاهل، ولو كشف للعبد عن ما أعد الله له في نظير صبره على البلايا في الجسد أو المال أو الولد... لكان هو يسأل الله تعالى في نزول ذلك به، وأيضا: فإن كل واقع في الوجود بالإرادة الإلهية، وسبق علم لا يصح تغييره، والرضا به واجب

ومن آدابهم: لا يتداوون من مرض إلا إن اشتد، بحيث يشغلهم بالالتفات إليه عن كمال الحضور مع الله تعالى، وما دام أحدهم يتيسر له الحضور النسبي في عبادته... فلايتداوى

ثم لا بد مع التداوي بشرطه من مراعاة نية التداوي، وذلك بأنْ تداوى قياما بواجب حق أَمةِ الله تعالى؛ إذ الحق تعالى هو المالك للجسم، والعارف إنما يتداوى لأجل كون ذاته أَمَةَ الله تعالى لا لنفسه هو، ففرقٌ بين مَن تداوى قياما بواجب حق ربه وبين من تداوى قياما بحق واجب نفسه، ﴿ وَمَا يَعْقِلُهَآ اِلَّا الْعٰلِمُوْنَ ﴾ [العنكبوت:٤٣]، ونظير ذلك محبتهم العفو من قبل الحق سبحانه وتعالى فلولا علمهم بمحبته تعالى له... ما طلبوه منه، فافهم

ومن آدابهم: شدة كراهتهم لمناجاة الحق تعالى إذا تلطخ ثوبه أو بدنه بنجاسة ولو من حصول مرض؛ تعظيما لمناجاة الحق تعالى، لا سيما إن حصل لأحدهم إدرار بول ومشي بطن، فمَن ناجى الله تعالى في حال تقذّر بدنه أو ثوبه... فهو خارج عن أدب الأكابر

ومن هنا اتخذ الأكابر السجادات النفيسة في الصلاة؛ تعظيما لحضرة خطاب الحق تعالى، وخوفا أن يدوس أحد برجله في محل تخيلوا فيه وجود قرب الحق تعالى لا لعلة أخرى من علل النفوس

ومن آدابهم: إذا استشارهم أحد في الأخذ عن أحد من مشايخ الزمان... أن ينصحوه ولا يغشوه، فيقولون له: إن أردت الطريق... فعليك بفلان وإياك والاجتماع بفلان، لكن يكون ذلك القول سرا؛ لئلا يتولد من ذلك مفسدة، ويكون بحق، وإلا... كان غشا لعباد الله، وطريق الحق في ذلك أن يكون ذلك الشيخ ناقصا لا قَدم له في الطريق، وأن ذلك المريد لا نصيب له عند ذلك الشيخ

وكان سيدي علي الخواص لا يذكر أحدا بسوء، ومع ذلك فكان يقول لأصحابه كثيرا: إياكم والاجتماع بالشيخ الفلاني؛ فإنه جلس بنفسه من غير إذن شيخ، فيصرح باسمه ولا يكني عنه؛ نصحا للمسلمين، وكان يقول: من لم يجد في عصره شيخا صادقا ناصحا يربيه... فحسبه محبة الله تعالى ومحبة رسول الله ﷺ، وحسن الاعتقاد، والرضا بالإقامة في الأسباب بنية نفع العباد، ونفع نفسه

وإذا اجتمعتم بأحد من مشايخ هذا العصر الذين جلسوا بأنفسهم، وزلَّ بكم القدم... فإياكم ونسبته إلى القطبية، ولا تزيدوا على وصفه بسيدي فلان، وإياكم بعد الاجتماع عليه أن تقبضوا وجوهكم عن إخوانكم وتقرمطوا آنافكم وتطأطئوا رقابكم، بل كونوا كما كنتم قبل اجتماعكم عليه، ومن فعل ذلك مع إخوانه... حصل بينه وبينهم ما لا خير فيه من التقاطع والتدابر والتباغض، ويصيرون كأنهم في دين وهو في دين، وما نهى الأشياخ المريد أول توبته عن مخالطة إخوان السوء... إلا خوفا عليه أن يرجع إلى فعل ما كان تاب منه بمخالطتهم

ومن آدابهم: يندمون إذا أتوا شيئا من المنهيات، أكثر ما يندمون إذا فاتهم شيءٌ من المأمورات

وقد قالو: مقام الصدِّيقية أكمل وأرفع من مقام الشهادة، والصديقية في اصطلاحهم: اسم لترك المناهي، والشهادة: اسم لالتزام الأوامر

ومن آدابهم: لا يشتغلون بالرياضة والخلوة طلبا لحصول الولاية

وكان سيدي علي الخواص يقول: حكم هؤلاء الأشياخ الذين يأخذون العهد على المريدين بالجوع والرياضة ليصيروا أولياء، حكم من أراد أن يجعل شجرة أم غيلان تطرح عنبا، أو شجر الجميز يصير تفاحا، وذلك لا يصح له أبدا

واختلى شخص، وأكثر من الذكر،وبالغ في الجوع طلبا للولاية، فذهب إليه وقال له: يا مبارك الحال! اخرخ من الخلوة، وما قُسِم لك... لا بدَّ من حصوله،

والولاية الخاصة لا تنال بعمل، وليس لها طريق ظاهر تطلب منه، إنما هي أخذة تأخذ العبد على أي حالة كان، فتقلب عينه وليا خالصا في أسرع من لمح البصر، وهي مرتبة مخصوصة لأقوام مخصوصين، على عدد مخصوص، لكن العدد بالمراتب لا بالأشخاص؛ فقد يكون في المرتبة الواحدة شخصان أو أربعة أو أكثر، وقد يكون في المرتبتين واحد، وقد يكون الرجلان بمنزلة الرجل الواحد

وأما الولاية العامة: فقد تنال بعمل كما أشار إلى ذلك قوله تعالى: ((ولا يزال عبدي يتقرب إليَّ بالنوافل حتى أحبه))

فما حصلت محبة الحق تعالى لهذا العبد إلا بعد تَفعُّل، وذلك معلول عند الخواص، محمود عند غيرهم؛ لعدم من يرشدهم إلى تحقيق الأمر في طريق الخواص

فاخرج - يا أخي - من الخلوة، وتب إلى الله تعالى، واطلب بأعمالك تحصيل مقام الصديقية والشهادة

لا تَحصُّل مقام الولاية، فأبى، فمات بعد يومين

ومن كلام سيدي أفضل الدين: المتأهلون في أيام الفترات أحسن حالا من هؤلاء الذين يدخلون الخلوة في هذا الزمان؛ فإن هؤلاء اشترطوا في التخلي شروطا لم يشترطها المتأهلون من الجوع المفرط، وعدم الكلام، وعدم النوم، وغير ذلك، مما أضعفت أبدانهم، وكثرت به تخيلاتهم، وفسدت به عقائدهم، حين ظهر لهم ما ظهر من النور والظلمة، ومن الصور الحسنة والمهولة من كلاب وحيّات وغيرها، مما هو كامن في طبع الإنسان؛ فإن جسده هو النسخة الجامعة لما في العالم العلوي والسفلي

ثم لا يخفى أن ما ذكرناه من ذمِّ الخلوة إنما هو في حق من يطلب بخلوته أمرا دنيويا، أما من يطلب بها صفاء المعاملة مع الله تعالى في المأمورات الشرعية... فهذا لا بأس به

ومن آدابهم: رؤية نفوسهم في كل مجلس جلسوا فيه مع المسلمين - لا سيما الفقراء - أنهم أكثرهم ذنوبا

وقد حُبّب إليّ أن أقول في كل مجلس جلست فيه مع المسلمين: (اللهم إني اعترفت بين يديك بأني أكثر هؤلاء ذنوبا وأقلهم حياء وأسوؤهم أدبا، فبحق أسمائهم الظاهرة اغفر لي)

ومن آدابهم: إذا أرادوا [أن] يأمروا أحدا بخير أن يحرِّروا نيتهم؛ فربما كان في ذلك علة تقدح في الإخلاص، فليمتحن مدعي الإخلاص نفسه، بما لو تفرقت جماعته إلى شخص من أقرانه، فإن حصل عنده تأثير... فأمره ودعاؤه لحظ نفسه لا امتثالا لأمر الله تعالى

ولذلك كان لا يتصدر للدعاء إلى الله تعالى في كل عصر سبق إلا أكابر الأولياء الذين خرجوا من حظوظ النفوس، وأما أمثالنا... فإن تَصدّر ربما أهلك نفسه وأتباعه

ومن آدابهم: رد كل ما يأتيهم من مال الولاة؛ لأنه مخلوط بالحرام والشبهات

ومن آدابهم: لا يأكلون للمفتقد طعاما

ومن كلام سيدي إبراهيم المتبولي: لا ينبغي لفقير أن يأكل من طعام أحد إلا إن كان بحيث لو أخبره بجميع زلاته السابقة التي عملها بينه وبين الله تعالى لم يتغير اعتقاده عليه، وإلا... حرُم عليه الأكل

ومن آدابهم: إذا أكلوا عند أحد أو شربوا... أن يقولوا: (اللهم إن كان ما أكلناه عند عبدك أو شربناه حلالا... فوسّع عليه واجزه خيرا، وإن كان حراما أو شبهة... فاغفر لنا وله، وأرضِ عنا أصحاب التبعات يوم القيامة صدقة من صدقاتك علينا، يا أرحم الراحمين)

ومن آدابهم: إذا أرادوا الدخول في عمل من الأعمال الصالحة... يقولون بقلبهم ولسانهم: (نعمل ذلك أو نقول ذلك امتثالا لأمرك يا مولانا ومولى كل موجود وأنت خالقه)، ولهذه الكلمة تأثير عظيم، فإذا فرغوا منه... حمدوا الله إذْ أهَّلهم لذلك، واستغفروا الله من تقصيرهم فيه ثلاث مرات

وقد حُبّب لي أن أقول: (استغفر الله العظيم من تقصيري في كل عبادة عدد أنفاسي)

وآداب القوم كثيرة كما تقدم، وفي هذا القدر كفاية

والحمد لله رب العالمين

خاتمة

فِيْ آداب الذكر المتفق عليها

اعلم - وفقني الله وإياك إلى دوام ذكره - أن آداب الذكر إذا كان باللسان ستة وعشرون أدبا، منها ما هو سابق على الذكر، ومنها ما هو حال الذكر، ومنها ما هو بعد الفراغ منه

فالسابق خمسة:

الأول: التوبة النصوح: وهي أن يتوب من كل ما لا يعنيه من قول أو فعل أو إرادة، وفي كلامهم: ((منِ ادعى التوبة، ومال إلى شيء من شهوات الدنيا المباحة... فهو كاذب))

الثاني: الغسل أو الوضوء

الثالث: تطييب ثيابه وفمه

الرابع: تحرير النية، وهو أن يكون الباعث له على الذكر امتثال الأمر، لا غير ذلك

الخامس: مصاحبة التعظيم للمذكور

وأما التي حال الذكر فستة عشر:

الأول: الجلوس على مكان طاهر، كالجلوس في تشهد الصلاة

الثاني: وضع الراحتين على الفخذين

الثالث: استقبال القبلة إن كان يذكر وحده، وإن كانوا جماعة تحلّقوا

الرابع: تطييب مجلس الذكر

الخامس والسادس: دوام الإخلاص والصدق

السابع: أن يكون المأكل والملبس حلالا

الثامن: أن يكون الموضع مظلما

التاسع: تغميض العينين من الذكر

العاشر: استحضار معنى الذكر

الحادي عشر: ألّا يشرك معه غيره

الثاني عشر: نفي كل موجود من القلب سوى المذكور

الثالث عشر: أن يكون جهرا

الرابع عشر: أن يكون بقوة تامة

الخامس عشر: أن يخيل شخص شيخه بين عينيه

السادس عشر: اجتناب اللحن

وأما التي بعد الفراغ من الذكر فخمسة:

الأول: ذم النفس لحظة

الثاني: ألّا يشرب حتى يمضي عليه درجتان أو ثلاث

الثالث: أن يسكت سكتة طويلة

الرابع: ترقب وارد الذكر

الخامس: الشكر على التيسير، والاستغفار من التقصير

فهذه آداب الذكر المتفق عليها

وأما غير المتفق عليها... فكثيرة، أوصلوها إلى مأة أدب، ولم أر في مشايخ هذا الزمان شيخا يعرف للذكر عشرة آداب

تنبيه:

أفضل صيغ الذكر هو إدارة كلمة الإخلاص؛ فإن لها أثرا عظيما لا يوجد في غيرها من سائر الأذكار

تنبيه آخر:

جعل بعضهم للسكتة المتقدمة ثلاثة آداب:

أحدها: استحضار العبد أنه بين يدي الله، وأنه مُطّلِع عليه

ثانيها: جمع الحواس بحيث لا تتحرك منه شعرة، كحال الهرة عند اصطياد الفأر

ثالثها: نفي الخواطر كلها، وإجراء معنى الذكر على القلب

تنبيه آخر:

قد علم أن الصواب في حق الذاكر إذا سكت وسمع قوّالا ينشد كلام القوم... ألّا يتحرك، ولا يتلفظ أو يمدح النبي ﷺ، وأن يصلي سرا لا جهرا

وهذا آخر الرسالة التي اقتضتها الباطلة، ولعمري - مع صغر حجمها - إنها لكثيرة الفوائد، لا يرغب عنها إلا عدو أو حاسد، احتوت على ما لم تحتوه الكتب الكبار، تستحق أن تسمى برسالة الأنوار، أخبارها وجيزة، آدابها غريبة عزيزة

أسأل الله تعالى أن ينفع بها من كتبها أو قرأها أو سمعها، وأن يجزي خيرا مِن اطّلع على هفوة فأصلحها، وأن يصلي ويسلم على مولانا وسيدنا محمد الكريم الأمين ﷺ ، وعلى سائر الأنبياء والمرسلين، وعلى آلهم وصحبهم أجمعين، عدد ذكر الذاكرين، وسهو الغافلين، وصلى الله على سيدنا محمد، وعلى آله وصحبه وسلم تسليما كثيرا إلى يوم الدين

تمت بحمد الله وعونه وحسن توفيقه

والحمد لله رب العالمين

Glossary

A

'abd	slave; servant, esp. of Allāh ﷻ
abdāl (see badl)	
adab (pl. ādāb)	etiquette, incl. morals, manners, conduct and general behaviour; punctilio with regards to legal acts
adhān	call to congregational ritual prayer
Ahl al-Bayt	Household of the Prophet Muḥammad ﷺ, and by extension, his ﷺ descendants
Ahl al-'Irfān	People of Divine Gnosis; revelatory knowledge of Allāh ﷻ and the created world given to the ṣūfī
Anṣār	the Helpers, the original inhabitants of Madīnah who welcomed the Muslims from Makkah to live with them when the latter were persecuted
'ārif	spiritual gnostic of Allāh ﷻ
athar (pl. āthār)	non-prophetic report

B

badl (pl. abdāl)	substitute; a gnostic in constant contemplation of Allāh ﷻ

C

D

dhākir	one who makes *dhikr*
dhawq	tasting; direct experience of knowledge
dhikr (pl. adhkār)	reminder; remembrance, esp. of Allāh ﷻ and making mention of Him ﷻ
dīn	religion, esp. Islām; a complete code of life; loan that must be repaid, i.e. repayment of

	the favours that Allāh ﷻ has provided us with obedience and complete submission to Him ﷻ

E

F

faqīr (pl. fuqarā')	poor, needy; in the context of this book and topic, he is one who is independent of needs from people and only dependent on Allāh ﷻ
futuwwah	spiritual chivalry

G

Ghawth	Succourer; Head of the *awliyā'*

H

ḥadd	limits set by Allāh ﷻ, the transgression of which incurs a penalty strictly prescribed by Allāh ﷻ
ḥadīth	report or tradition of Prophet Muḥammad ﷺ
ḥudūd (see ḥadd)	
Ḥujjat al-Islām	meaning 'Proof of Islām', a title given to Imām Muḥammad al-Ghazālī (450AH/1058CE - 505AH/1111CE) for his steadfastness and authoritative stance on the true teachings of Islām
al-ḥukm al-wujūdī	entification into existence

I

ikhlāṣ	sincerity; being pure of any form of negativity in any aspect
imām	guide; one whose example is to be emulated
īmān	faith; belief in the tenets of Islām
i'tikāf	religious seclusion in a masjid often observed by Muslims during the last ten days of Ramaḍān

J

jinn	spirits; created beings made of fire and living parallel lives to humans yet invisible to them

jadhb	to be immersed in something, esp. in the love for Allāh ﷻ

K

kashf	disclosure of true realities and secrets where proof is not required
khabar (pl. akhbār)	report, tradition, narration, esp. from someone other than the Prophet Muḥammad ﷺ
khalṭah	association, mixing in with other people
khalwah	solitude
khānqah	a ṣūfī lodge
khilāf al-awlā	unorthodox, against customary or conventional legal practises
khushū‘	submissiveness; humbleness to Allāh ﷻ
Kirāman Kātibīn	Honourable Scribes, they are two angels appointed to write down a person's good and bad acts and omissions

L

M

majdhūb	one who is madly attracted to Allāh ﷻ
makrūh	disliked, legally repugnant that one ought to avoid it
mandūb	an optional act for which reward is anticipated
maqām (pl. maqāmāt)	station, esp. a spiritual standing with Allāh ﷻ
mawaddah	cordiality; close and friendly relationship
Mīzān	Divine Weighing-Scales that will be established on the Day of Judgement to weigh the deeds of people
mu'adhdhin	caller of *adhān*
Mubtadi‘ah	Heretics who have innovated and inserted into Islām what is not of it, esp. harmful beliefs and acts
Muhājirs	the Migrants, those who migrated from Makkah to Madīnah to escape persecution

munājāt	intimate discourse
murāqabah	the ṣūfī being aware of the presence of Allāh ﷻ and accompanied with self-scrutiny of his thoughts and actions
murīd	seeker, disciple, esp. of a spiritual guide

N

najīb (pl. nujabā')	noble; leader in faith who bears the burdens of others esp. those who are less active
naqīb (pl. nuqabā')	chief among the spiritual hierarchy who knows what is hidden inside the minds of others
nujabā' (see najīb)	
nuqabā' (see naqīb)	

O

P

Q

qawwāl	devotional singer
qiblah	direction for ritual prayer; spiritual focal point
Quṭb	Spiritual Pole; Axis of spiritual hierarchy
Quṭbiyyah	Spiritual Polarity

R

riyāḍah	disciplining the self; training and inculcating good character

S

sālik	traveller to Allāh ﷻ
shahādah	testimony, bearing witness; martyrdom
sharīf	someone of nobility, esp. a descendant of the Prophet Muḥammad ﷺ
shaykh	teacher, instructor, master, esp. in spirituality and traditional sciences
shirk	associating partners with Allāh ﷻ; polytheism

shukr — gratitude, esp. to Allāh ﷻ by submitting to His ﷻ will and expressing devotion to His ﷻ commands

ṣiddīq — someone who is utmost honest in all aspects of his life – outward as well as inward

ṣīddīqiyyah — the station of utmost honesty and sincerity with Allāh ﷻ in all aspects of one's life

T

taṣawwuf — Islāmic behaviourism; disciplining oneself to achieve proximity with Allāh ﷻ

tashahhud — the optional prayer offered in the latter portion of the night, esp. when one awakes after sleeping for a while

U

Ummah — Community, esp. of a Prophet ﷺ

'uzlah — reclusion, avoiding the company of people

V

W

wājib — incumbent; an act whose prescription is proven by inconclusive and non-definite evidences

walī (pl. awliyā') — saint; close friend of Allāh ﷻ

wilāyah — sainthood; close friendship with Allāh ﷻ

X

Y

Z

zāwiyah — a place where the spiritual teacher holds his classes

Bibliography

Qur'ān

Abū Dāwūd, Sulaymān ibn al-Ash'ath ibn Isḥāq al-Azdī (202AH/817CE - 275AH/889CE). *as-Sunan.* Riyādh. Dārussalām. 3rd Edition. 1421AH/2000CE.

Al-Bukhārī, Abū 'Abdullāh Muḥammad ibn Ismā 'īl ibn Ibrāhīm ibn al-Mughīrah ibn Bardizbah (194AH/809CE - 256AH/869CE). *al-Jāmi' aṣ-Ṣaḥīḥ.* Riyādh. Dārussalām. 3rd Edition. 1421AH/2000CE.

An-Nasā'ī, Abū 'Abdurraḥmān Aḥmad ibn Shu'ayb ibn 'Alī ibn Sinān (215AH/829CE - 303AH/915CE). *as-Sunan aṣ-Ṣughrā.* Riyādh. Dārussalām. 3rd Edition. 1421AH/2000CE.

At-Tirmidhī, Abū 'Īsā Muḥammad ibn 'Īsā ibn Sawrah ibn Mūsā as-Sulamī (200AH/824CE - 279AH/892CE). *al-Jāmi' al-Mukhtaṣar.* Riyādh. Dārussalām. 3rd Edition. 1421AH/2000CE.

Encyclopaedia of Religion and Ethics - online version, digitized by the Internet Archive in 2011 with funding from Boston Public Library. Vol. XI. Ed. James Hastings, Charles Scribner's Sons, Topic: Ash-Sha'rānī, p.448-450. (http://www.mocavo.com/Encyclopaedia-of-Religion-and-Ethics-Volume-11/817844/472).

Ibn Mājah, Abū 'Abdullāh Muḥammad ibn Yazīd (209AH/824CE - 273AH/887CE). *as-Sunan.* Riyādh. Dārussalām. 3rd Edition. 1421AH/2000CE.

Lane, Edward William (1801 - 1876CE). *Arabic-English Lexicon (online version).* London. Williams and Norgate. 1863CE.

Muslim, Abu'l-Ḥusayn Muslim ibn al-Ḥajjāj ibn Muslim al-Qushayrī an-Naysābūrī (206AH/821CE - 261AH/875CE). *al-Musnad aṣ-Ṣaḥīḥ.* Riyādh. Dārussalām. 3rd Edition. 1421AH/2000CE.

Ash-Sha'rānī, 'Abdulwahhāb, Introduction to *Risālat al-Anwār fī Ādāb aṣ-Ṣuḥbah 'inda'l-Akhyār.* Damascus, Syria. Maktabah Abū Ayyūb al-Anṣārī. 1428AH/2007CE.

Ash-Sha'rānī, 'Abdulwahhāb ibn Aḥmad, *Ādāb aṣ-Ṣuḥbah*. Damascus, Syria. Dar al-Farabi. 1429AH/2008CE.

Ash-Sha'rānī, 'Abdulwahhāb ibn Aḥmad, *al-Mīzān al-Kubrā ash-Sha'rāniyyah*. Lebanon. Dar Al-Kotob Al-Ilmiyah. 2009CE.

Winter, Michael. *Society and Religion in Early Ottoman Egypt: Studies in the Writings of 'Abd al-Wahhab al-Sha'rani*, New Brunswick (USA) and London (UK). Transaction Publishers. 2009CE.

About the Translator

Muḥammad Ṭāhir Maḥmood Kiānī, son the saintly Ḥājī Muḥammad Tāj 'Alī Kiānī (1356AH/1938CE – 1415AH/1995CE), is a graduate in Law and Islāmic Law. He teaches classical Arabic grammar and Islāmic Sciences, writes and lectures on various topics, as well as translating from Urdu and classical Arabic into English. His most notable translations are *Mukhtaṣār al-Qudūrī – A manual of Islāmic Law According to the Ḥanafī School*, *Al-Fawz al-Kabīr – The Great Victory on Qur'ānic Hermeneutics* and *Qaṣīdat Aṭyab an-Nagham fī Madḥ Sayyid al-'Arab wa'l-'Ajam* ﷺ *– The Sweetest Melody*, *Al-Khaṣā'iṣ aṣ-Ṣughrā – A Summary of the Unique Particulars of the Beloved Prophet Muḥammad* ﷺ.

Notes

صَلُّوا على الحَبِيب ﷺ

Crowned & Renowned

Made in the USA
Coppell, TX
11 January 2023

10944059R00143